1. Talbooth.
2. Cross
3 St. Laurence Church.
4 Post Office
5 Museum.
6. Town Hall
7. Forres House
8 Nelson's Tower
9 Grant Park. (Sunken garden, bowling green, putting green,
10 Sueno's Stone   (childrens play area etc.
11 Witches Stone
12 Police Station

FORRES: A ROYAL BURGH

ALFRED HOUGHTON FORBES, J.P.

Provost 1965 - 1975

FORRES
A Royal Burgh

1150-1975

by

ALFRED HOUGHTON FORBES

MORAY & NAIRN COUNTY LIBRARY
1975

Published by
Moray & Nairn County Library
Cooper Park, Elgin, Moray

Printed by
Macdonald Printers (Edinburgh) Limited
Edgefield Road, Loanhead Midlothian

THE AUTHOR'S FOREWORD

THE INSPIRATION of this work, if anything so discursive can be thought of as having a single source, came from Councillor Charles K. White. The occasion was the announcement of the decisions of the Wheatley Committee, whereby Forres was to be absorbed by a new Moray District, becoming simply an electoral ward.

The comprehensive and invaluable *Annals of Forres* compiled by the late Dr Douglas was published in 1933 and Councillor White proposed that the history of the burgh should be brought up to date, whereupon Honorary Treasurer Norman Redman suggested that I as provost should undertake this. I agreed, although my sole qualification was that my term of service in the Council almost coincided with the period, having been first elected in 1935. I have omitted any references in the chronicle to the years from 1900 to 1933, as these are adequately described in Robert Douglas' *Annals.*

As the work proceeded I felt that a mere recital of the decisions of the Council during that period would be dull indeed and that some social aspects should be included, of both the past and the present. Scottish history is much neglected and I therefore added a chronicle of events which might help to build a more balanced picture of burghal life in the centuries.

The burghal system made the town dwellers a very homogeneous society, so that what happened in Kelso, Edinburgh or Tain was as likely as not repeated in Forres and other burghs.

But it is the work of an amateur, with no reference to reliable authority, being much dependent on a formerly retentive memory. But memory is as likely to recall the interesting if doubtful as it is to remember the factual but dull.

I am grateful for the advice given by Mr Archibald Macdonald, LL.B., M.B.E., and Dr Douglas J. Murray, Honorary Treasurer; and for the help of Mrs Sellars who put her wide experience in publishing and her skill at typing at my service.

But my gratitude goes fully to Mr Frederick J. Guthrie, B.A., A.L.A., Chief Librarian to the Joint County Council of Moray and Nairn, who read, revised, advised and saw these pages through the long process of getting into print. I hope he feels that it was worth all his time and work.

INTRODUCTION

ANYONE WHO KNOWS Provost Forbes knows that he is a lively personality, a "character," a man who despite his years is bubbling over with nervous energy. The personality of the Provost shines through much of what is written here; the wit, and not infrequent scepticism, are characteristic of this man known and admired by a great many Forresians and Moray people.

Mr Forbes is quick to state that he "is no scholar" but readers of this book will acknowledge that although it bears few scholarly pretensions it nevertheless shows a depth of learning which only a lively and enquiring mind such as his can acquire over a long number of years in his native town.

Many of the items in the chronicle may be considered unimportant or trivial but life itself consists of series of minor events. Historians of much earlier periods would be delighted to have such information, the tiny pieces of the jigsaw which, when put together, form our social history. Here also is a mine of information, with rich seams of "unwitting testimony," for the student of local government prior to its reorganisation. The chronicle is most revealing of social attitudes, exemplified by the issue of shoes with three-inch soles to poor children, and the provision of council houses.

I have no doubt that local people will find this book wholly absorbing; I hope that it will also have a much wider appeal.

F. J. GUTHRIE.

CONTENTS

FORRES HIGH STREET

THE EARLIEST DAYS

THE FIRST PEOPLE to arrive in this part of Scotland left their traces at Kingsteps, near Nairn. The time is taken as 5000 B.C. and they would have been few in number. A thousand years later it is estimated that the total population in Scotland was under one hundred souls. Without agriculture the population can scarcely increase. The population of the large continent of Australia never exceeded 200,000 until it was a home for Europeans. It required more than 300 square miles to supply enough food for one person.

It is likely that Forres would also be a scene of human activity at this early date, and a probable site of a settlement even if only for a short time, such as when the salmon ran plentifully. Only at the Waterford crossing can the River Findhorn be forded at most times. When impassable from heavy rains the only alternative to waiting patiently for the water level to fall was to travel many miles upstream where it narrowed enough for it to be jumped, or shallow enough to be waded.

The river in its early course 2800 feet up in the hills had carved deeply through the glacial drifts of the uplands, and in its middle course ran even deeper through the gneiss and granite before it burst through the softer red sandstone to reach the sea. Its flow was swift until it reached Relugas, and then was placid in its lower reaches.

In addition to the distance to be traversed upstream, the land was bleak and inhospitable, and for centuries without inhabitants. Only when the population had occupied all the good land in the eighteenth century did anyone try to wrest a living from the harsh and acid soil. The paler green patches and the occasional rowan tree show where this effort was made, to be finally abandoned in the nineteenth century. While the arrival of the great flocks of sheep and the later introduction of game birds have been given credit or blame for the depopulation of the Highlands, the process started much earlier.

One can only speculate where these people came from and by what means. They are not thought to be Proto-Celts, and may have been akin to the Basque races, for they are known to have used a kind of agglutinative language, similar to that used by the Basques today, between 1600 B.C. and A.D. 600 which is almost historic times. The Greeks thought they were a tribe of the Iberi, which had at one

11

time lived in Eastern Europe and had, like so many other people later, moved westwards. Another theory was that they were a branch of the fair-haired Berbers. Still another was that they had come from the lost continent of Atlantis. If they were of the Basque people, the route from north Spain to Cornwall and thence up the west coast of Britain to the Great Glen would be a natural one. It was used by the Phoenicians, or by their agents in Cornwall, to get copper at Bona at the east end of Loch Ness to be used with the Cornish tin to make bronze. Copper was also mined at Tomintoul at a very early date and perhaps elsewhere.

During the Pleistocene period, the geological epoch before man, there were many changes in the levels of the land and the sea, especially in Scotland. At different times the sea had been 100 feet, 50 feet and 25 feet higher than at present. It had also sunk at one time to a level about 300 feet lower, so that much of the North Sea could be crossed dry footed. The trees and peat found below the bottom of the Moray Firth are dated from this time, as are the same materials found twenty and thirty feet below the surface of the ridge on which Forres stands.

The River Findhorn had flowed east for many miles, and as the land slowly sunk, or the sea rose, a great loch was formed, later shrinking to form the Loch of Spynie, which in historic times extended from near Lossiemouth to a point between Cardenhill and Roseisle. Later the river changed course, reaching the sea nearer Forres, leaving the old course deep and dry. The sands which followed the disappearance of the glaciers later filled this channel, which is well known to geologists as the "Fault of Spynie." When the Findhorn breaks its banks at flood time it appears to the observer as if it is trying desperately to regain its old course to the east.

Once settled, the Forres area supported a relatively large number of people if we judge by the relics they left behind. The arrow heads found in the Culbin Sands alone equal at least the number found in the rest of Scotland. Last century the Scottish Society of Antiquaries began a collection for their museum and were surprised by the numbers they were offered. Within a year they had been offered collections with as many as 1200 flint arrow heads as well as flint knives, scrapers and grain rubbers (the precursors of the stone querns), discs, rings, jet earrings, necklaces, bronze pins and needles, brooches and finger rings. Many of the bronze items were enamelled, and there were tweezers differing little from those made today.

Other articles found near the town include a cinerary urn, a bronze mounting resembling the ornamental handle on a modern coffin and some pieces of glass. As iron rusts the only articles in this metal to survive are some fish hooks, part of a sword and a peculiarly formed horseshoe. In the Culbin Sands there are traces of iron working, the slag from a bloomery and the waste materials of a forge. The bloomery would have smelted the nodules of iron found in peat, and the forge would have worked the resulting metal into shape.

Some articles of gold have been found, the best preserved a lunula, a neckband made of two crescents, the ends meeting in knobs. Some articles of lead have also been found and it is known that this metal was mined near the site of Lossiemouth.

This does not tell us much about our ancestors except that they did have such skills, and there was enough food to allow men to specialise in the arts and crafts. It does not allow any dates to be fixed, as we know only that the Stone Age lasted longer in Scotland than elsewhere and there is little trace of a Bronze Age. That Age could have been curtailed or made unnecessary by the utilisation of the bog iron, no tin being found in Scotland.

The Califer Hill is taken to be the first site of a permanent settlement. The sea may have been higher and nearer, or the lower ground too wet to produce crops. The graves at Templestones, south-west of Blervie Castle, date from the Stone Age, as does the fort on Cluny Hill. This fort was clearly visible two centuries ago when George Chalmers, the historian, commissioned Robert McWilliam, surveyor, to send him a report on it. The shape was between round and oval, enclosing an area of 6 acres, 3 roods and 25 falls Scots. On the southern side there is a small fort 12 feet square. These outlines were retraced in 1972 by a class from Forres Academy with their teacher, Mr Ron Philp.

The Findhorn had flowed past Cassieford on its way to Loch Spynie, and this ford would be under the observation of the hill fort.

The construction of such a fort and other works such as the Clava Cairns beside the River Nairn shows that a considerable number of people must have been engaged and that some authority existed to organise and carry out such large projects. Such people had long passed the subsistence stage of agriculture and had a surplus of food to allow many members to devote their time and energy to such labours.

There must have been external enemies also, probably arriving by sea; the estuary with its sloping beaches was ideal for the type of vessel used. Professor Childe thought that the builders of the Clava Cairns were colonists from across the Firth, from Sutherland, and others could have come from further afield, for he also says, "It must be concluded, despite all seeming improbabilities, that there were adventurous voyagers from France and Portugal who landed and settled on the western and northern coasts of Scotland."

The first mention of the country was by a Greek sailor, Pythias, from the Greek colony at Massilia, the present-day Marseilles, who sailed around these islands in 336 B.C. He learned from the natives that the country was called "Ynys Prettanoi," which in the course of time became Brettanoi and finally Britain. The meaning, he said, was "Beautiful island."

Wave after wave of peoples spread out from the original birthplace of the human race, and those moving westwards reached Britain, where they remained until America was discovered. Anthropologists agree that many different tribes and races arrived, as shown by the skull shapes and bones, so that we are a very mixed type indeed.

Pythias, like all explorers, would have been searching for some land or people, and this may have been the Hyperboreans, "the people beyond the North wind." Such a people were being discussed in Greece a century or more before Pythias' time. Herodotus wrote about them in 450 A.D. and another but less well-known Greek, Hecateus, dealt more fully with the subject.

This people were favourites of Apollo, the Sun God, and dwelt beyond the north wind, enjoying perpetual youth, unbroken peace, and a continuing spring. Two maidens, Opes and Arge, had arrived in Greece seeking the isle of Delos, the birthplace of Apollo and sacred to him. They were followed shortly afterwards by another two maidens, Hyperorche and Laodice, as well as by five young men, the "Perpheres" or bearers of gifts for the god.

These messengers never returned to their native land, but the Hyperboreans continued to send gifts wrapped in wheat straw, handed on from tribe to tribe from the far distance of their origin. These parcels did arrive. As the Greeks' knowledge of geography extended, this mythical country moved further away until it was finally attributed to some favoured part of Scotland where wheat could be grown. The Moray Firth coast met this requirement, and it is known that in that early time the weather was more favourable than at present, as is shown by the higher tree line. This tradition lasted in

14

Europe for many centuries, and last century Draper mentions it in his *Intellectual Development of Europe* with a sentence: "In the North there was a delicious country of the Hyperboreans, beyond the reach of winter." We will come upon Apollo further in these pages.

THE ROMANS

ONLY WHEN THE Romans came to Britain have we anything definite about Scotland. The Roman Navy had sailed all round Britain, and continued in these waters for nearly four centuries. Agricola invaded Scotland in 82 A.D. but was ordered to withdraw by Rome once news had reached there. His expedition was reported by Tacitus who accompanied him, but his references are vague and there has been no agreement as to how far north he reached. Some believe that he reached the Moray Firth, and that Roman soldiers occupied a fort at Burghead for a number of years before being withdrawn to the south. As the Roman armies were supplied as much as possible by sea, Burghead would seem to be a natural place for a port of call.

Most historians accept that Agricola came little farther north than Perthshire, but one of the most authoritative writers does not accept this. G. S. Crawford in his *Topography of Roman Scotland* says: "In any case I cannot believe that the Romans stopped at Glenalmond. They must surely have reached the Moray Firth, which is the logical objective when once the area north of the Grampians has been entered." Mr Crawford surveyed every trace of the Romans on the ground and from the air. It may be a case again of old traditions being correct.

Some Roman remains have been found around Forres, but they could be the results of encounters with the Romans further to the south. Mr R. Brodie of Brodie, F.R.S., recorded that when the streets of Forres were being repaired in 1797 he was given a number of coins and medallions in a soft metal of the reign of Emperor Diocletian (A.D. 245-313) found during the work. These he sent to the Antiquarian Society of Edinburgh. A number of weapons and other articles were found at Nairn around the same time. Later a hoard of Roman coins was found in the region of Fort Augustus, but no one has suggested that the Roman armies were ever there. But this route through the Great Glen had been used by the traders from Cornwall in their search for a supply of copper for Phoenicia.

For long it was held that the Romans had reached Forres, which was an overnight stop on their occasional march south through the hills to the Dee. The Latin name for the fortress at Burghead was "Castra Alata," and in Greek "Ptoroton," both meaning the Winged

16

Fortress. It was claimed that this, along with Varis, was shown on the maps of Ptolemy, although there are no such maps now in existence showing this, but it is likely that the navigators in British waters would make entries on their charts which were drawn in Rome or Alexandria, just as present-day sailors make such additions to their charts. The maps that survive are from these two cities.

Claudius Ptolemy (c. A.D. 65-138) was a Greek geographer living in Alexandria in Egypt, and he based his maps of the world on those of an earlier map maker, Marinus of Tyre. Marinus probably got his information from the Phoenician traders who sailed regularly to Cornwall for tin and other imports. In Cornwall also they got copper, required for making bronze. This copper was assembled at Bona, at the east end of Loch Ness, and conveyed by boat and porterage to the coast of Loch Linnhe, probably by the natives, but perhaps at times by either the Phoenicians or the men of Cornwall.

Ptolemy invented meridians of longitude and latitude, placing the centre of longitude on the island of Rhodes. His distances were too low, greatly reducing the circumference of the earth. He wrote in his native Greek and the later translations into Latin and Italian do not always agree with the original. As the maps wore out they were copied, and during the many centuries they were renewed many errors inevitably were repeated and exaggerated, and existing copies differ in many details.

The first English translation was made only this century by Dr Edward L. Stevenson, and published in 1932 by the New York Central Library through the interest of the chief librarian, Mr John Fraser Black, a Scot and compiler of the *Surnames of Scotland*. Only 250 volumes were printed with 27 maps. This translation was made from a compilation printed in Italy in 1460. This was 32 years before Columbus sailed to discover America, and it is of interest to note that his fellow Genoan, one Toscanelli, showed Columbus these maps, which showed that India and Cathay could be reached by sailing west. The maps, of course, did not show the Americas, but a medium-sized ocean between Europe and Asia. The distance on the chart agreed closely with the distance sailed by Columbus and convinced him that he had reached India.

The first map in the atlas is of these islands, Insula Britannica, Hibernia and Albion, the latter still used as a poetic name for Scotland. The shapes are recognisable but the orientation is wrong. From the border Scotland lies at right angles to England, so that the

Moray coast and that of north Caithness face east while the west coast and the Hebrides face north. The early navigators had no compass, and they were trained in the Mediterranean Sea where the sun sets always in the west. Sailing in these northern waters in the summer, as they did, the sun would set much more to the north, and in the Pentland Firth almost due north. They had no means of correcting this error, which was perpetuated in each new copy made.

The Orkneys are clearly delineated, as are Duncansby Head, the Ila river (the Ullie or Helmsdale), the cliffs of Cromarty and the Estuarium Varar (the Beauly and Moray Firths). Varar continues today as the Farrar of Strathfarrar, and historians surmise that the name Varis was a misreading of Varar. Next is the River Loxa, obviously the Findhorn, its origin being shown well inland among wooded mountains. Then follows the Spey, named the Tuessis, shown much shorter than the Loxa, and then comes the Deva (the Deveron) and the Itena, easily recognised as the Ythan river.

There is no trace of the Lossie, but another ancient map of Scotland shows a river with three tributaries flowing east, entering the sea near Lossiemouth. Some geologists hold that the present course of the Lossie between Dallas and the sea is a comparatively new channel, as its frequent changes would indicate. The stream running through Rafford to the Mosset was much later referred to as the Lochty, and may have been a former channel of the Lossie, its flow reversed during some earth changes. In some Romance languages the letter "X" was pronounced as "Sh" and sometimes as the Scots "Ch." The resemblance between Loxa and Lossie is too close to be coincidental, and when the river changed its course it took the name with it, leaving our Findhorn to get a new name from the western invaders from Erin or Eire.

If Forres did exist as Varis that name would have been a Pictish one, and not Gaelic as claimed by the "Gaidheal."

Returning to Ptolemy's map, the western sea is the "Oceanus Hyperborium," the ocean beyond the north wind. The Pentland, more correctly Pictland, Firth is entered as the "Oceanus Duecaledonium" and the North Sea is the "Oceanus Germanicum."

The Roman name for Scotland—Caledonia—meant the wooded country, and if the prefix "due" has its ordinary meaning, Duecaledonium would be the ocean of the two Caledonias, thus confirming the tradition that there were two Pictish kingdoms, North and South, united into one in A.D. 873.

18

The belief that the Romans had reached and settled in Burghead for some 80 years was reinforced in 1757 when an Englishman, Charles Bertram, published in Copenhagen a work that purported to be travels of a thirteenth-century monk, a Richard of Cirencester. This monk, a Welshman who served in Westminster, followed the tracks of the Romans, describing minutely the various forts and detailing the *iters* or daily marches of the legions. According to the book he had used the maps of Ptolemy.

The route followed was from Hadrian's Wall to Burghead, where the Roman navy was able to send supply ships to maintain the garrison there. According to Richard, the Romans, like all good soldiers, had an alternative escape route to the south if the main route was blocked by inimical troops. This was by way of Forres, a distance given as ten miles, thence south until the Knock of Braemoray was passed, when the road or path turned east to where a small bridge crosses the little burn that runs down from Carn Ban na Caorach, where half a century ago could be seen the meagre remains of the abandoned township of Ourack, the Anglicised name for the hill of Caorach, thence by Achnagallin until the Spey was reached at the ford near Cromdale. This was given as 18 miles from Forres, and is much shorter than the present road. Allowing for the change in the length of the Scottish mile, the figures given are very nearly correct. This road has been opened since the track of the railway was abandoned.

From the Spey another *iter* of 29 miles took the soldiers to "Tamea" which cannot now be identified. On the third day they proceeded by Strathavon and what is now the Lecht road, reaching the Dee where the Clunie Water joins it on the south side. Thereafter the road led them to Glenshee to the great Roman fortress at Inchtuthel on the Tay. This road from Forres was known in the sixteenth and seventeenth centuries as the "Roman road to Tuessis," and is shown in an early map in the possession of Forres Town Council.

On the normal route from the south the same detail is given. From Aberdeen the route led to Inverurie, Foggy Lone (Aberchirder), Deskford, Cullen and the Spey, where the ford at the Bog of Gicht was crossed. Another day's *iter* brought them to Burghead.

Richard gave the site of the battle of Mons Graupius (A.D. 84) as being the Knock Hill just north of Foggy Lone. This history has been totally rejected by most modern historians and Richard has been dismissed as a mythical figure. He lived between 1335 and 1401, and

19

in 1391 he received a licence to visit Rome. He wrote at least one book which still exists, *Speculum Historiale de Gestis Regum Angliae, 447-1066.* This was edited in two volumes in 1869 by Prof. J. E. B. Mayor of Cambridge. It is thus likely that Richard had an earlier source relating to the period before A.D. 447 from which he obtained his information.

AFTER THE ROMANS

IF IT IS accepted that the Romans did not come to Forres, no authentic historical reference is made to the town for many centuries. The *Annals of Forres* say that according to Bocthius in 535 A.D. a King's Chancellor of the name of Toncet seized the goods of some Forres merchants and hanged the owners to get rid of any evidence. But the supposed author of this piece of history, Ancius Manlius Severimus Boethius, was executed by the Roman emperor in A.D. 524. Only 45 at his death, he is judged the greatest scholar Rome ever produced, writing mostly on music, philosophy and arithmetic. Later writers claimed his name as authority for their own writings. The rulers of ancient Rome looked on philosophers much as present-day governments look on sociologists, as dangers to themselves and to the state, hence the legal murder of Boethius. Toncet then is a figure of fiction.

For the years between the withdrawal of the Romans and the arrival of St Columba from Ireland in 563 there are few references to Scotland, or at least to North-East Scotland. What is known about Scotland and Ireland is culled from the meagre records of other countries.

Apart from a few stones with Ogam inscriptions, no writing before the seventh century is known, and this applies to much of Western Europe also. When writing came with Christianity there was little to write upon. The only material was parchment and vellum made from the skins of animals. The making of this required much labour and skill. Paper was not known until several centuries later, although it had been made in China much earlier.

The spread of the knowledge and use of paper gives an indication of the long time taken for new ideas and inventions to be received. In A.D. 751 the Chinese advanced into the Mongolian Empire and laid siege to the great city of Samarkand, which had been captured by the Moslems. They were driven back, but some were taken prisoner. These had been papermakers and taught their skills to their captors. The Arabs carried this craft to their other dominions, including Spain by way of Morocco. It took 438 years for this knowledge to reach France where the first paper was made in 1189. Dutch traders brought paper into Britain. This paper was made from linen and as much linen was produced in Scotland, paper making was soon introduced. So important was this trade that the export of lint was prohibited, and the printing industry became important in the country, remaining so to this day. The earliest written paper found in England dates from 1309.

Writing was an invention of religions and almost everywhere the first scribes and historians were the priests, who thus became the first bankers and financiers. Ecumenical and centralised churches like those of Rome and the Eastern Orthodox religions were the only institutions with the facilities for handling and transferring money, thus becoming the first lawyers. This applied to Scotland also. All writing was at first done in Latin in Europe, the local tongues having never been reduced to writing.

Like the rest of barbarian Europe, Scotland had a non-literate tradition with time-honoured and socially approved modes for the conservation and transmission of law, genealogy, song, myth and story in the vernacular. So great was memory used and developed that a writer in the past has said that the Scots "lived in the cathedrals of their minds." When Christianity brought literacy, this ancestral memory from the pagan period continued with the lower classes, especially the traditions and beliefs of witchcraft. These traditions became the subject of repressive legislation from Rome.

THE STORY OF THE STONES

PROBABLY THE OLDEST STONE in the Forres district is that one in Victoria Road known as the Witches' Stone. A plate attached says that it commemorates the burning of witches on Cluny Hill, and marks the spot where the barrel with one of the bodies halted after being rolled down the Cluny Hill. This is a false tradition, as the stone stood there for many centuries before much notice was taken of witchcraft in Scotland. The persecution was a temporary phenomenon here, lasting only from 1563 when the practice of witch-craft was made a capital offence until 1736, when an embarrassed Parliament quietly repealed the Act, but in Scotland only. We will deal with this when we reach 1663.

In most villages and towns in the north of Scotland there was a large stone at the north-east corner, so placed that it caught the first rays of the morning sun on certain days. Here the sun deity was worshipped and offerings made of fresh milk, thus ensuring the fertility of crops, animals and women. The stone at Nairn disappeared some years ago when road improvements were made, as they have gone from most places. According to local belief, to pass the stone at Forres without spitting on it brings bad luck, and many carry out this little ceremony without realising its significance. In an age when drinking utensils were few or unknown, a small quantity of food or water would be passed to a child or invalid by mouth. Earlier this century the ironing women in the hand laundry at the foot of the Burnbrae sprayed the sheets and clothes with water or thin starch by mouth, when using the old style heating irons. In this way the worshippers would make their libations of milk on the stone.

The sun god had a hundred names in Europe, the best known being Apollo, but in Celtic mythology he was the Gregualach and the stone was the Clach na Gregualach. There are two similar but smaller stones still in the town, both built into houses, one at 60 High Street and the other at the north end of North Street, at No. 27.

The proprietor of Drumduan, when building Bronte Cottage, ordered the mason to build the "witches' stone" into the foundation of the new building as a protection from the evil eye or other ills, but public protest made him change his mind, and put it back to its

23

original position with an iron clasp to hold together the two portions into which it had been broken.

Inverness still has its stone, now the Clach na Cuddin, "the stone of the water luggies." These were the wooden pails which the women used for carrying water from the Ness to their homes. All would pause at the stone, and perhaps spit also, but as a social meeting place its importance and use changed. They would rest their pails on the stone whilst they exchanged gossip.

The well was always an important place, and parents of daughters "going into service" in the big houses before the introduction of piped water would ask the prospective employer if their daughter could be "the lassie that goes to the well." Domestic staff had little time free and this was often the only chance for young men and women in service to meet.

Another local stone is that in the grounds of Brodie Castle. This also is incorrectly called the Rodney stone. It had been used to pave the aisle of the old Parish Church of Dyke, and only when that church was demolished was its significance realised. The villagers had the belief that Captain Hardy was born in Dyke, and by extension they put this stone to the credit of Admiral Rodney. But Sir Thomas Masterman Hardy, Captain, R.N., was born in Dorsetshire in 1769 and died in 1839 as Admiral and First Sea Lord.

How long the Sueno Stone has stood is unknown, and many theories have been put forward but none of them have been proved, and are now unlikely to be. One not previously put forward and no more or less improbable than those, is that it may have been contemporary with the Romans in Scotland.

Readers of Roman history will know the pillars, arches and sculptures erected by Roman generals to celebrate their victories. These were the works of the best artists available, the detail in many being almost photographic. The captive kings, chiefs, soldiers and women with their personal details, including hair styles, are reproduced faithfully and minutely. Those to be found in the province of Dacia, now part of Rumania, come specially to mind.

During the time of the Empire the greater proportion of the Roman army was often recruited in occupied territories, only the cavalry, which was the elite, being composed of Romans. Scots would have been recruited when the Romans held the country as far north as Inchtuthel in Perthshire. It would be surprising if the adventurous and martial young Scots from further north did not enrol for service as volunteers, and would undoubtedly distinguish themselves. On completion of their service they would return home skilled in the arts of war.

It is not improbable that they used these skills on their return and one very successful commander may have thought of copying the Romans and have a stone erected to celebrate some victory. Only amateur sculptors would be available, and the drawer of the cartoon would have had little practice in that art, lacking paper or parchment. Perhaps wood was used or smooth sand. There is a theme in the work on Sueno's stone, but all of it has the hallmark of the amateur.

There are some Ogham stones in the Forres district, but there are only 22 of these engraved boulders in all Scotland.

The giant stone at Gateside of Alves, north of the road leading to Pluscarden, had a tradition that lasted many hundreds of years. Until recently there was a tiny hamlet there, and the children used to dance around the stone, nine times "widdershins" or anti-clockwise. If this was done it was thought that a knight in armour holding a gleaming sword would appear, although there is no record of this actually coming about. At the turn of the century, on the basis of this old tale, a party from the Scottish Antiquarian Society excavated the site and found the skeleton of an Iron Age man with some relics.

There are other graves in the area, a number being in the Divie valley, marked on the Ordnance Survey map as of the Stone Age.

FEUDALISM

THE RESIDENTS of the 66 Scottish burghs entitled to use "royal" have been proud of the name, although most have been vague as to what was involved. They knew that they had privileges of some kind in the past, remnants of which still survived.

The frequency of the use of the word "feu" connected them with the feudal system, of which chivalry was the offshoot. But so specifically Scottish is the word "feu" that some English dictionaries do not include it, though "feudal" and "feudalism" are listed. It came from old French and meant the holding of land in return for a fee or rent, the "feu-duty."

Feudalism meant holding land in return for military service to an overlord further up the social and economic scale. The famous Blackstone laid down the maxim: "The fundamental maxim of all feudal tenure is this; that all lands were originally granted out by the Sovereign, and are therefore holden of the Crown."

After the fall of the Roman Empire in the sixth century, Europe fell into chaos until the ninth century when the new feudal system began. Ambitious men set out to carve great estates from the prevailing anarchy, and this they did by force of arms, gathering round themselves bands of men as ambitious and ruthless as themselves. They were promised lands, wealth and honours for their aid and arms. Traditions of loyalty, service and hierarchy were developed and built into the new system, and this percolated through the stratified society where each man had his place, from which it became difficult to rise.

Vesey Norman in his *The Medieval Soldier* writes that "the military system of most of Western Europe during the twelfth and thirteenth centuries was feudal." That is, it was based on the holding of land in return for military service given to an overlord. The holder of the land was supported by agricultural labour and food from the peasants, in return for defending them against raiders, for defending the realm in time of war and for administering justice to them in his courts.

France was the true cradle of feudalism, where the principle "no land without a lord; no lord without a fief" was established. In Scot-

26

land, because of the very special circumstances that existed there, this became "no lord without land; no man without a lord."

Many of the French terms were carried to Scotland, undergoing a sea change in the voyage. In France a bailie was a kinsman appointed by the king to administer the estates inherited by a minor or an unmarried daughter until the son became of age or the daughter married. During the term of his office the bailie was invested with the fief. In Scotland the bailies were four councillors appointed to look after the interests of the crown, and each responsible for the governance of a quarter of the burgh.

Germany was different also; there the dukes accepted their titles from the king, but claimed that the lands belonged to their tribe and not to the crown. This claim to the land may be the origin of the Teutonic obsession with the purity of blood, race and descent.

In Normandy the feudal system was more stratified than elsewhere, each stratum holding fiercely to its rights and privileges, an attitude carried from Scandinavia. Of the 5000 knights who accompanied Duke William to invade England in 1066, only half were Normans. The Duke, soon to be king, could not persuade his tenants to join him; they were not obliged to serve outside his realm in Normandy, and did not see why they should enlarge his estate and still remain in the class into which they were born.

The Duke had to recruit 200 great lords from all over Europe, and these were brave and violent men unused to restraint, and he had great difficulty in controlling them after the Conquest. They were not bound to him by birth and tradition as were the people he had to leave behind. The severity of his rule was aimed as much at these unruly lords as it was at the cowed and defeated Anglo-Saxon subjects.

Despite this, England was a more easily ruled country than Scotland, where rebellion and insurrection seemed to be inborn traits of the natives, especially in the North and West, where the Anglo-Saxons were thinly spread. Scotland was slow to emerge from the Middle Ages and because of a succession of infant sovereigns and contested regencies rarely had a period of firm and strong rule. The sixteenth century still bore the rude manners of a former age, despite a veneer of French urbanity. The country's institutions were rudimentary, its Parliament a feudal assembly where personal aims came before the interest of the nation. The powers of the king were limited by the powers and ambition of some noble families. The first General

Assembly of the Protestant Church in 1560 was the first truly representative body, fresh and vigorous

Early in the development of feudalism in England and on the Continent the new towns grew up under the protection of the great abbeys and castles. These were "burgs"—fortified places, in France "bourges" and bringing a new word "bourgeois" to describe the non-military, non-religious, practical, materially-minded society produced by the system. In England the name became borough, and in Scotland, because of the Norse influence it became "borg" and finally "burgh." In Scandinavia "borg" is pronounced something like "bir-ye."

The great difference between the burghs of Scotland and those elsewhere was that in Scotland the burgesses selected their own rulers, at least for the first three and a half centuries. This was something unique.

Scotland was forged into a nation from at least four different cultures, customs and languages: the Gaelic Scots from Ireland; the Saxons and other Teutons; the very first arrivals, the Picts, and the Welsh or Britons from the Stewartry. It took a long time to form a recognisable nation, if not a united people. On this union was superimposed a ruling class recruited from soldiers of fortune and adventurers of all kinds from Normandy, Aquitaine, Burgundy, the Low Countries, and the German states. Some came from Scandinavia and the Lazlos came from Hungary to found the family or clan of Leslies. The flow from England was as constant as today, and all were welcomed by the kings. The first Brus to arrive in Scotland was given 200,000 acres of land in Ayrshire, the first step to founding a dynasty of kings.

Names now considered truly Scots came at this time, several scores of them: Baliol, Bisset, Berkeley or Barclay, Comyn in its many forms, Colville, Douglas, Dunbar who was from a line of Northumberland princes, Fraser and Gordon, all through the alphabet to Sinclair, Stuart and Sommerville. Their vassals and followers often took their names, but few won them by marriage for they wed only from their own class.

In England a generation ago, a footman applying for a post with a name like Henry Plantagenet, or a maidservant Elizabeth Tudor, would be considered an impudent fraud using such false names. But Robert Bruce and Mary Stuart are to be found in every Scots town.

Most of these knightly names came in the reign of David I (1124-

1153), himself the Duke of Northumberland and married to a Saxon princess. Both were educated in England and had spent many years at the English court, and were experienced in the administration of England. These new lords had little loyalty to the idea of Scotland as a nation, for many also held land in England, Wales, Ireland and on the Continent. They recognised the King as their feudal superior and called him King of the Scots, as recognition of the fact that he ruled the people while they owned the land. Almost all thought themselves as equals and as rivals, rather than as the obedient vassals they were in England and elsewhere. They held jurisdictions which soon became hereditary, and the fines and forfeitures they imposed became an important source of income. In court their vassals and friends had preferential treatment, and they used the law to further the interests of their families and connections. They had the drive and energy of their kind and demanded the comforts and luxuries due to their status. As a result Scotland began to move from its previous sub-sistence economy and started to increase the supply of the goods demanded, either for direct consumption or for export to get the currency for the import of foreign goods. Commerce came into being, and if a system other than that of royal burghs had been introduced, the production of goods at home would not have been so manacled and restricted as it became, to the detriment of the people as a whole.

Moray had, in the centuries since the union of the Picts and the Scots, produced a succession of claimants to the throne or to parts of the country, very often with good claims because of the old style of inheritance. The kings realised that they required dependent allies as well as a secure source of income, as necessary then as now for the proper government of a country.

King Alexander saw that the most likely place to look for this support was in the towns, and he bound them more closely by making them his own royal burghs. He made six of these—Edinburgh, Strevelin or Stirling, Perth, Aberdeen, Roxburgh and Berwick. Forfar and Elgin may have been recognised in some way in 1057, but no records exist

As other royal burghs were erected four of the original six—Edinburgh, Stirling, Perth and Aberdeen—were formed into "The Court of the Four Burghs." Problems arising in the new burghs were dealt with by this court, which in 1497 became the Convention of Royal Burghs, with enhanced powers and authority. It was formed "to see to the welfare . . . of the merchants and the common profit of the burghs." It dealt with all things burghal, conferred with the king, dealt with commerce and often interfered in foreign affairs.

After the Reformation, the General Assembly of the Church of Scotland took much the same independent line in church affairs and dabbled in foreign policy when it affected the church. The Scottish Parliament had little to do apart from raising money, and also handed much of its work to the "Lords of the Articles," who governed without reference to Parliament.

When the Scots Parliament was united to the English by Cromwell and again in 1707 more permanently, its absence was scarcely noticed by the great majority of the Scots people. Originally containing only Lords and Bishops, it was increased by the merchants of the royal burghs. In 1496 the king brought in burgesses as members of Parliament in the hope that they would form a body like the knights from the shires in the English Parliament, and which would form a counter-force to the barons and prelates who until then made up Parliament. This attempt failed, for the merchants were as narrow and selfish in their views as the two other "Estaits." All Three Estates met together until the Union.

The Burgh members met either in Stirling or Edinburgh. They used their position to enact legislation in their own interests, which was often vindictive to the craft guilds. They blocked the election of craftsmen to Parliament and when in 1496 it was enacted that retiring councils appointed their successors each year, they made sure that few if any craftsmen were among the new members.

THE FOUNDATION OF THE ROYAL BURGH

BY THE YEAR 1150 Forres had been for some time a town with a castle and a church, both made of wood, and both burned more than once. It was under the nominal superiority of the Earl of Moray. The superior would get either a rent in kind, eggs, poultry or butter, or alternatively so many work days from the tenant on his own lands at the sowing and the harvest.

At this time the fief was vacant, not yet having become an hereditary estate, and its disposal was wholly in the king's hands. There was no formal body to attend to the affairs of the town, and the requirements would be minimal. As in all permanent settlements some form of council arose spontaneously to deal with the problems that arise in any society.

In May the king stayed for some days at the Castle of Spynie and on the 19th May granted a charter to the Abbey of Kinloss. That for the burgh would be presented on that day or soon after, for the abbots and priors were the instruments of his government. David I was noted for the personal attention he gave to the details of his work. We know that he perambulated the lands given to the Abbey, and doubtless looked also at the lands to be given to the burgh.

Tradition indicates the point on Califer Hill, at the boundary of the lands of Burgie at Castlehill croft where, seated on his horse, he pointed south to the distant river where Downduff is, and then to the sea to the north, saying that all the land between this line to the east and the river to the west was the Common Good land of Forres.

Kinloss Abbey certainly received a charter, probably written by the monks—for almost all writing was the work of churchmen, the only scholars. The charter was often referred to and quoted by the monks in later years. It is unlikely that the town received a written charter. The custom was to have one read, which belonged to some other burgh, not necessarily a Scottish one, the words being changed to suit—as the lawyers say, *mutatis mutandis.* The charter of one of the boroughs in Northumberland could have served as a model. In other cases, in England and in Scotland, the charter of a town in France or Belgium was often used.

The contents of the charter had to be memorised, as had so much else at that time, and as problems arose from the fallibility of human memory, or because of changing circumstances, recourse had to be made to the Court of the Four Burghs which later became the Convention of Royal Burghs. It was many years before paper came into general use, and longer still before writing became a common skill.

Full details of the charter are to be found in the *Annals* and need not be repeated here. What was said at this ceremony is not known, but the duties and the privileges of the new burgesses would be laid down. The town had to be planned for the future, as the few small wooden huts and houses would be huddled beside the church and castle.

The plan of Forres was typical of small burghs and has been used as an example in at least two works: in Chalmers' *Caledonia* and Professor Mackenzie's *The Scottish Burghs*. The plan shows Forres much as it is today, but not of course so much built up. The King's Hie Gait was flanked by the North Back and South Back Streets. Tolbooth Street and the Kirk Vennel, now Gordon Street, are also on this map. The Kirk Vennell crossed the Mosset at the Lea ford and the road continued to Waterford. Crossing the river, the traveller would go by way of Moy, Loanhead and Lochloy to Nairn. This continued to be the main road until such time as a bridge was built over the Findhorn. About 100 yards south of Loanhead a milestone can be seen in the heather saying "Nairn 11 miles." This was the road used by the armies on the way to Culloden, and the hollow west of Loanhead is still known as "The Soldier's Hollow," where the troops camped for a night.

Neither Tolbooth Street nor the Kirk Vennel were set off at right angles from the High Street, and as the feus were marked off in a local measure, the rigg, of approximately 18½ feet, each feu ran parallel to the roads. This meant that no room on the High Street was exactly square. This did not matter much in simpler and more primitive days. But this century when Mr A. M. W. Cormack, dentist and later a bailie, married and took house at 58 High Street difficulties arose. His wife, a Glasgow girl, ordered fitted carpets to be made in that city, having obtained the sizes of the rooms. When they arrived they did not fit, being some inches short at two corners, while they projected up the wall at the other two. Immediate recourse was made to a solicitor, who fortunately was the Town Clerk, and he suggested that the angles be measured as well as the lengths.

Each feu, which ran from the Hie Gait to the back streets had to be built upon within two years, the feuar to take residence there and do his business from that address. The period or "kirset" varied from town to town, although two years was the most common term. When Dingwall was erected into a royal burgh in 1227 the kirset was set at ten years because of the disturbed state of the country and district. The feu duty was for the use of the ground upon which a house was built, and was retained for ever by the superior who, in the case of a royal burgh, was the king. If a house became derelict or was abandoned it reverted to the crown.

The narrow feus meant that the houses had to be erected with the gable to the street and the door opening from the lane or close. This was also good for defence and privacy. The remainder of the ground was to be used for the cow which almost all households had, and for a horse and poultry. Earlier this century milk was still being sold from the back street entrances in Orchard Road. A byre or shelter was usually built for the animals. The close protected the cattle from the frequent thieves from the higher lands. It was not uncommon in rural areas for the cattle and the family to enter their houses by the same single door which could be more easily defended against robbers.

To ensure that the feuars did not encroach on the land of their neighbours, stone markers were placed on the boundaries, and these were regularly examined by two officials chosen annually. These were the "linemasters," an honorary post still filled. The last holders were Dean of Guild Dr J. M. Brewster and Mr James M. Smith, master joiner. One of the last marker stones which had been in position for over 824 years was removed when making the Leys Car Park.

Each burgess had to "watch and ward" and had to have enough weapons to be able to do so. Periodically these had to be shown to the king; later the Royal Chancellor made this inspection and finally it was carried out by the bailies.

The land surrounding the town was also divided in riggs of 18½ feet wide, running for considerable distances. Between each rigg the land was left uncultivated, and the weeds which grew there were considered to be a valuable reserve of fodder in the winter time. A burgess could have more than one rigg, but these did not adjoin. To ensure that all had a share of the good and the poorer riggs, the cultivator had to change each year, the riggs being allotted by lot. There was thus no incentive to manure ground which was to be left the following year.

Even the best land soon was exhausted and so many riggs had then to lie fallow for a year or more. The yields of grain were low, a threefold return being accepted as normal. In the eighteenth century improved methods of agriculture were introduced, and the riggs were combined into larger areas, which could be leased for periods rarely exceeding seven years.

The grain had to be sent to the water-powered mills of the superior. The king held the Mills of Forres, although they were at an early date given to the Priory of Pluscarden. The miller took so many fistfuls or "locks" from each sack of meal, and the traditional size of the miller's "thumb" was a common subject of complaint. The town having, like the barons, the rights of "pit and gallows," employed a hangman who was also paid by so many locks of meal. He preferred to be known as the locksman rather than by his correct designation. His wife had to bring up any orphan child, even although the children's plight resulted from her husband's work.

King James II enacted that the nearest relative was responsible for any person unable to support him or herself, a tradition that lasted into modern times.

A town cross was essential, for here all public announcements had to be made. and here all goods brought into town by anyone but a merchant of a royal burgh had to be exposed for sale. The town merchants had first choice, and did not pay petty customs. Any goods unwanted by them were sold to the public, the vendor handing over the petty customs to the town's officer. Goods from a foreign country had to pay "great customs" which went to the king. At ports there was another official, the "custumar" who collected this import tax.

Some form of shelter was needed for the collector of petty customs or tolls, and this hut evolved into the Tolbooth which became also the prison and the council chambers. The council was elected from all burgesses and numbered 17 from an early date. It was a large number for a small town, but the merchants were often absent buying and selling in a Scotland now open to them free of any taxes. The council had to include enough to permit a sufficient number being available for emergency meetings.

Four councillors were elected bailies, each responsible for the proper order of a quarter of the burgh. Money was coming into general use, for David I, who introduced this form of royal burghs, promoted commerce and trade so much that he had to bring in a silver coinage. Until this time only copper coins were in use. A treasurer was elected and at some point a Dean of Guild.

Merchant guilds and craft guilds preceded town councils on the Continent and may have done so here. The craftsmen combined for

34

protection and as welfare bodies with religious connections. The chairman was the Deacon or Dean, a title taken from the church where the deacon kept the money and gave aid to the needy and sick members of the guild. It was accepted that the Dean took precedence after the provost.

At first the king visited his royal burgh regularly, to collect his revenues, to issue laws and judge the serious cases of crime. Such visits were important dates in the calendar. Accompanied by his retinue, he lodged in the castle, and grazings had to be reserved or "hained" for the horses. This word "haining" was originally a well-watered meadow, but in course of time took the meaning of this special use.

As the country developed, with more royal burghs and many more duties to attend to, the king was replaced by his chamberlain. His circuit or "eyr" was as important and perhaps more ceremonious than that of his master. Even the chamberlain had to give up this task and one of the four bailies was appointed to look after the king's money and other interests, such as the multures, which were the "prepositura." In the course of time the royal burgh collectively had to provide a fifth and later a sixth of the income of the Crown, the Convention of Royal Burghs fixing the amount to be paid by each burgh.

The bailie responsible, the prepositus, soon outranked the other three and with his title converted to provost became the chief member of the Council. Not all burghs had a provost; Linlithgow and Lanark did not have provosts until 1540 and 1541. As late as 1708 there were nine burghs without one, and Selkirk "had always forborn to choose another provost because they were brought into a great deal of debt by their former provost Haining." It is uncertain whether this was a name, or meant that the provost had reserved or hained the money to himself.

In course of time many rules and regulations came into being. The burgess had to maintain certain arms and could be called upon to use them on the king's behalf. He could be tried only in his burgh court, and had many other privileges and duties. A traveller had a right to graze his horse in any royal burgh as long as it did not eat the crops. Royal permission was required before a bailie or a sergeant could open a brewhouse or a bakery. The barm used for fermenting bread and ale was the same, and such a right given without restriction could undermine the integrity of these two who were made responsible for the maintenance of the law. So dangerous was the occupation of constables that two had to be conscripted every six months. The burgess had to accept the obligations of "scottyn, lottyn, wakyn and wardyn," the first two being the hallowed words for taxation, and the second two for police duties. In Forres these last were formal only. Burgess silver had to be paid on entry of one's name on the burgess roll, and when paper became available a ticket was issued. This was a valuable document, a combination of passport and trading licence.

Before being able to settle in another royal burgh a burgess had to obtain a certificate, the "testification." Without one, entry would be refused. The worst punishment a resident of a royal burgh could receive was expulsion from the burgh without it, becoming almost an outlaw, for the landward dwellers did not like the residents of royal burghs, whom they considered as exploiters of a monopoly.

The fees for the issue of these tickets became an important source of revenue for the burghs, and the ceremony of admission as a freeman of a burgh became more elaborate, justifying a higher charge, culminating in the ceremony of "Granting the Freedom of the Burgh." When this became purely honorary after 1833 the silver casket, the illuminated parchment and the feast with its many toasts, became "de rigeur."

At the beginning of the nineteenth century the fee in Forres was six guineas, a considerable sum, but the freedom was a valuable asset to politicians seeking election to Parliament or entrepreneurs with interests in various parts of the country. The granting of these freedoms was also used by burghs to curry favour or reward benefactors.

Elgin had a long list of freemen, the first entry in 1541 referring to an Alexander Malcolm. The last entry there was in 1797 when Alexander Smith was made a freeman "in regard he was amongst the first tradesmen who came forward as a volunteer." This would be for defence against the French who were expected to invade Britain.

Aberdeen had very high fees, which varied according to the means and position of the aspirant, and strangers were charged more than known men. The City Guilds were very wealthy and no brother once enrolled would be allowed to suffer financial hardship.

THE PEOPLE — THEIR ORIGINS AND
LIVING CONDITIONS

HAVING DEALT WITH the establishment of the Royal burgh we can now speculate about the people, for there are no firm facts. After the first year the majority of the residents were newcomers, for the whole purpose of erecting a new burgh was to draw settlers with new skills and aims. Angles, Saxons, Flemings and Scandinavians would arrive, the Flemings being in the majority.

One of the earliest in Moray was the Fleming Berowald Freskin who became wealthy in the first generation and was given the lands of Innes. He was the founder of several noble families, the Earls of Douglas and of Moray among others. Falconer, Winchester or Winster, are other early names from the south.

The language spoken is not known, probably Pictish in its earliest days, with a good admixture of Norse. Many Moray words still in use are pure Norse, and now better understood along the shores of the Hardanger Fjord than those of the Moray Firth. Stob, carl, speer, gyang, cnock, snee, blae, bikk, forbye, sweigh, hoose, braw, sma, brent were in daily use before the advent of films or radio.

The town's name is most likely Pictish. There are many names with the prefix "for" which is said to be connected with water, especially where it shallows: "ais" is Pictish for a hill. Names with this prefix include Forfar, Forsinard, Fortingall, Forteviot, and Fortrose, all before the introduction of Gaelic. Between Pitneisk on the Findhorn and Pitlochry on the Tay, and Pittenweem on the Firth of Forth there are still 74 placenames with the prefix "pit," a farm or hamlet in the Pictish language.

The new burghs were advertised through the churches, the sole means of communication, a continuing relic of the great Roman Empire, when all roads led to Rome and all communication was taken over by the Church of Rome.

While life in the burghs was hard it was better than in most rural areas for ordinary people. Only there was law and order maintained, for a commercial community needs both. Outside the burghs the land-owners made the law, as they had the power of pit and gallows. The fines imposed on offenders was part of their income, and they could also seize the goods of any one appearing before them. There was no

37

appeal except directly and personally to the king, who often received little better treatment from his barons.

The royal burghs would soon have been swamped by an influx of people, but entry was strictly controlled. Those welcomed were men with a little capital and thus able to enrol as burgesses. This gave them all the privileges given in the charter once they had agreed to pay the annual "burgage" and erect a suitable house of a value fixed by the burgh council. This had to be done within the "kirset." In Forres this was two years.

As many merchants peddled their goods outside the burgh it was often inconvenient to act as police or defenders, and such persons could pay an annual fee which went to pay some other resident to take up duty when required. This was the "burgh maills," and a few pounds are still collected by the burgh chamberlain, although it is unlikely that those paying consider it anything more than some strange feudal imposition.

The Forres merchants travelled and sold their goods in Ross-shire, Sutherland, Caithness and even Orkney. As the merchants prospered they allowed some immigrants to build up a work force. Their businesses took all of their time and they could not cultivate their long narrow feus behind their houses on High Street—"the King's Hie Gait"—and they built houses for let thus forming the closes which are a feature of Forres. Misbehaviour by such cottars could be rewarded by expulsion from the town without "testification" certifying that they were of good character. This was a severe penalty almost akin to death by starvation.

Flyting (criticising) the magistrates or immoral conduct were sufficiently serious to earn this punishment. Those unfortunate enough to meet this fate would probably become paupers condemned to wander throughout the country, begging. The barons might accept them if they were useful as supporters or had any desirable skill, but normally they had more followers than they could care for. Begging was also a punishable offence; able-bodied beggars could be whipped, branded, mutilated, treated as slaves and ultimately the burgh bailies could impose the sentence of hanging.

Each household had to grow and produce much of its food, and all were entitled to a share of the town's lands, and of the grazing for their cows, sheep and horses.

The houses were small, usually of two apartments. As the merchants prospered they would add a storey, using the ground floor solely as their business premises, and later a third or fourth storey would be added. More than one existing building on High Street shews traces of this process, with dormer windows being added in the present century.

The buildings were, until the seventeenth century, wholly of wood, with a thatch of turf, heather, or bracken. Straw could not be used for roofing as it was needed to maintain their animals through the winter. Fire was a constant hazard, and the curfew or "couvre-feu" was sounded by the town drummer along the street each evening. Most fires were of peat, and were smothered with ashes so that by removing the ashes in the morning and blowing on the red embers heat could quickly be obtained. This fuel is difficult to get started. The original forests which gave the country its name had gone except in the more remote parts of the Highlands, having been used for fuel and building. Timber was imported from the Baltic at an early date, and grain, wool and hides exported to pay for the timber.

The drum again sounded in the morning, usually at 5 a.m. When a bell was fitted to the town clock in the Tolbooth in 1589 the correct time was available to all, but the bell was at a later date used to sound the curfew and also the morning call. Until a warning siren was installed in 1939 this bell was used to sound the "tocsin" to call out the fire brigade. This was operated by a spring-loaded hammer which gave a very rapid beat, and could be set off from the High Street near the Tolbooth door.

When the British army withdrew from Dunkirk, the danger of invasion by the Germans grew and the bell was silenced to be retained as a warning of invasion. It was sounded in September 1940 as in most of the country. When the war ended the bell ringing did not restart, and its chimes are now only heard to call the people to church on Sundays.

Until the reign of David I, who granted a charter to Forres, the Scots coinage was wholly of copper, the penny being the largest coin. With the introduction of royal burghs by this king, commerce increased so much that a silver coinage was brought into use, and Forres had a mint for some time. But trade increased more quickly than the supply of coins, and as paper was scarce and very expensive the merchants made tokens of wood to be used in buying and selling. This practice continued in North-East Scotland into the early nineteenth century.

The chief purchase, then as now, was food; the staple was oatmeal which formed the main food of the poorer people. This grain if not balanced by vegetables and other foods brings on skin disorders, and the records of the Dispensary for the Poor set up around 1820 shows that skin trouble was the chief complaint. When a widow or invalid had to rely on the charity of the council, the relief was usually a boll of meal. In time of famine also, the council would purchase oats and sometimes wheat from abroad for distribution. The recipient had to arrange for this to be milled at the Mills of Forres.

The death rate was high and life expectancy low, but the birth rate was very high also. Many women had a child each year, of which few survived for long. But there was always an increase in the population with not enough employment, so that emigration was constant, and thousands of young men served and died as mercenaries in Continental armies.

The chief crop grown was a form of barley known as bere or bear. It had three rows of seed compared to the four rows of barley itself. It gave a better return than oats, three seeds being harvested for each one sown. There was not much margin for bad years. It was used in broths and stews and for brewing ale, the only beverage apart from milk, much of which was needed for suckling the calves.

Barley mills were invented later than oat and wheat mills, and until such time as they became common the barley was treated at home by placing the grain in a slightly hollowed stone slab and beating with a "knocking stone" to remove the husk or "awn." It was used parched or singed first. The result was termed "knockit bere."

A variety known as grey oats was also grown. It did not give such a good return as bere, but it would grow in poorer soil and had a tough stem which held the grain in gales or storms. Wheat was grown but mostly by the monks at Kinloss, who held much of the best land and also had a daily allowance of white flour for bread and a measure of barley daily for ale. Much of this they could sell to the wealthier people. Rye was confined to the acid and peaty uplands, but peas and beans were grown locally for both humans and beasts.

Good land such as that around Forres has been farmed for over four thousand years and by the seventeenth century the plough had developed from a crooked stick to an enormous unwieldy instrument needing six men and as many oxen. This meant that the feuars had to co-operate for both sowing and harvest. The horses were little more than ponies about eleven hands high.

When armour came into use by the barons and knights, more

powerful breeds of horses had to be imported, culminating in the giant and handsome Clydesdales. Forres was founded in the midst of peatlands and as the peat was consumed the good land was developed, and gave amongst the highest yields per acre in Europe.

Forres was thus fortunate and was always considered by its fellow burghs to be a fairly rich little town, and inclined to be independent in its ways with the government and the Convention of Royal Burghs.

With the first industry in the shape of flax treating and the making of linen in the late eighteenth century, most workers were for some part of the year at least engaged in the fields and woods. There they were able to get many of the supplements which added flavour and some nourishment to their restricted diets. It is known that there are 320 varieties of wild foods in Britain, 130 of these being found everywhere, and in addition there are more than 3000 different forms of fungi, only 24 of which are dangerously poisonous. But not many fungi were eaten in this area. Only during the last two hundred years have vegetables been freely grown. Until that time kail alone was grown in fields and gardens. The common cornfield weed, "fat hen," was sometimes grown in gardens for convenience, but most was collected in the fields. It is on occasion still cooked as a vegetable.

Among the herbs and plants most commonly added to stews and broths were dandelion, still a common vegetable in Japan, both leaves and roots being used. The roots of wild parsnip, water lily and marshmallow were eaten, and the bitter vetch provided small peas, and the cooked roots resembled chestnuts in taste. The root of this plant was a subsistence food in the Western Isles during famines, and it was also used at all times to flavour whisky.

While the flowers of the sea holly are now picked for home decoration, the six foot long roots were formerly eaten, and when sugar became more easily obtainable after the sixteenth century, they were boiled and candied. One of the most common of flowers, the Star of Bethlehem, supplied a form of onion for boiling, while the tuber of the purple orchis was highly prized as it had more nutritive value than any other plant product, one ounce being enough to sustain a man for a day. Water cress, wood sorrel, hawthorn, beech, wild rose, buds, sow thistle, chicory, yarrow, rose bay, shepherd's purse, charlock and goosegrass could all be added to the pot for nourishment and flavour. Sir John Sinclair tells that the poor in time of famine in Caithness would ask permission to gather nettles. Nettles were allowed to flourish in the St Laurence kirkyard for human consumption.

41

Much of this knowledge is now forgotten although Forres children still dig up earthnuts among the trees at the river side near Greshop House, holding them in their hands so that the warmth brings out the full flavour of the ginger. They are still called locally "ginger tatties."

THE FINAL CHAPTER

ON 15TH MAY 1974 the royal burghs came, to all intents, to the end of their lives. For a year the town councils would continue in being while the duties and properties were taken over by the regions and districts which were to take their place. The very oldest burghs had lasted nine hundred years, and Forres had been one for 824 years. To have survived so long proved that the system had merits, although it had its share of faults.

During the Parliamentary debates on the Reform Bill of 1833, a law lord had said: "The Scottish burghal system is the longest lived political and economic system ever invented," and we must agree when we consider that the longest lasting national constitution is that of the United States of America, soon to celebrate its two centuries of existence.

As the royal burghs grew and developed, and the majority did grow, they evolved an ethos and philosophy in a special bourgeois way. The nobility and the clergy, living mostly outside the burghs, constituted a homogeneous class sharing the same "esprit de corps," conscious of their mutual solidarity. The burgesses were different, living in segregated communities where the spirit of class was replaced by a local spirit and patriotism.

Each burgh was a little separate world, but there was a limit to its exclusiveness and self protection. Each did its utmost to favour its own trade at the expense of the others, and bitter complaints were continuously made to the Convention of Royal Burghs about wrongs, real or imagined, done to them. They combined for mutual aid when pressed, but were not above trying to gain an advantage even then. All this is understandable in commercial society, especially in a poor small country where life was hard for most.

Despite the narrowness of their views and aims they had much to their credit. They created urban administration without the help of models, and had to invent everything—financial systems, burgh schools, new laws, water supplies, market places, police forces, medical services, orphanages, law enforcement, social aid, firefighting and defence against external enemies.

In the burghs the citizen was producer and consumer and the regulations intervened in both respects. The consumer was protected

43

from high prices, the producer from competition; high prices, shoddy goods, false weights, all were covered. There were no trade unions, no proletariat, but there were privileges and exclusiveness. No manufacturer could expand his business nor practice a new theory of the division of labour as described by Adam Smith in his revolutionary book *The Wealth of Nations*. The principles he expounded could not be put into practice within a royal burgh and as a consequence new industries and new methods had to be developed outside the burgh boundaries, and new and large towns grew up, in the end taking away the trade of the royal burghs.

The burghal system had one inherent fault; it hampered the development of industry, the purpose of its original introduction. The craftsman was manacled to his skill and could sell only to a customer what had been ordered or bespoken. Anything else that he had made had to be offered to a merchant for sale, and he could not take any work outside his own craft. The merchant felt superior to the craftsman and working with one's hand debarred a man from joining the merchant guild. The baker, the tailor, or the saddle-maker could not enter the "high" society of the burgh. An apprentice had to pay a large fee to get his certificate and had to undergo a severe test of his skill. The number of workmen and apprentices was limited, and their prices were fixed by the merchant guild.

If the apprentice married the daughter of his master he could enter the craft guild at a lower fee; this was known as "entering by the near hand." But the number of marriageable daughters was limited, and on completion of his apprenticeship, if unable to fill a local vacancy, he had to travel to find one. This travelling earned him the title of journeyman of his trade.

James Watt, the inventor of the steam engine, was not a time-served mechanic and could not get any one to take an interest in his invention. The university of Glasgow employed him as an instrument maker outside the rules of the burgh. Despite this he had to go to England before he could take any steps to develop the engine.

Only one other country, India, held back the craftsman. There it was done by the caste system which bound him to his class and trade; in Scotland it was done by the burghal system.

In the thirteenth and fourteenth century urban life in Scotland flowered, but having reached its full development, it began to decay. No transfusion of new ideas was allowed, and from the sixteenth century the new towns with the new industries soon surpassed them.

Leadership and influence lay with the wealthier merchants, who were often arrogant and overbearing. There were always some who prospered beyond the others even in a restricted society; some gave their fortunes to found hospitals and other institutions. Within the burgh there was civil liberty and equality, but social and political equality were absent. In time some became plutocratic, oligarchic and allied themselves with the landed gentry, marrying into that class, and combining to exploit the burghs and the residents, robbing them of the lands of the Common Good. In Aberdeenshire the old song "Aiberdeen and Twal Mile Roon" recalled the time when that area was part of the city Common Good, but all this land had been disposed of by 1833. Since then the city has bought it back for building purposes.

In Forres the Grants controlled the town for most of the eighteenth century, the first provost of the name becoming Earl of Seafield, and the two following Earls were also provosts.

Despite its despoilation through the centuries, Forres survived and retained a considerable Common Good. The income from this meant that the residents did not have to pay rates until the middle of the nineteenth century, when the Burgh was forced by law to levy rates which had to be paid by owners and occupiers, in proportions laid down by the state.

To sum up: the burgesses of Scotland were a privileged class constantly guarding their rights and status, especially their freedom from any rule but their own. Dwelling in a feudal country they were not part of the feudal system, being even freer than the clergy. Their allegiance was to the king only, and they did not have to make homage to him as every other class had. Apart from the nobles they were the only ones allowed to bear arms and they restricted the use of these arms to the defence of the king when in their neighbourhood, and to enforce the peace in their own burghs. They rarely used them for any other purpose, and the burghs were more often than not immune from the turmoil and fighting which seemed endemic in most districts. Most burghs had walls of turf or dry stone dykes, which were more effective in keeping in enemies than keeping them out.

Interested in their own affairs and living as much as possible within the burgh boundaries, either at home or abroad, they were easily differentiated from the mass of the population of the country. In close contact with each other and shaped by the same aims, they were surprisingly homogeneous. These aims were to live and thrive by trade while the rest of the land was occupied in subsistence agriculture.

Trade and commerce made them literate and numerate, and they benefited from their constant comings and goings across the North Sea. In the small burghs few were wealthy enough to be an upper class until the sixteenth century at the earliest, but later the expansion of foreign trade changed this, so that the merchants held themselves apart from the shopkeepers and tradesmen, consorting with and in many cases joining the local gentry then appearing.

Most burgesses were employers of labour, household servants and field workers, for it was still necessary to produce much of the food consumed. They were receptive to new ideas from the Continent and the new heresies had their first recruits in the burghs, where Protestantism had its strength. The Catholic religion did not approve of the accumulation of wealth, while the Protestant ethic supported the practice of thrift and abstention. Every action was aimed at their self-advancement; they formed nothing that was not of direct benefit to their order and interests.

CHRONICLE

363 B.C. This is taken to be the date of the voyage of the Greek Pythias from Massilia (Marseilles). He travelled round Britain and even further north. He landed in Britain and "travelled all over it on foot." An astronomer, he was the first to fix latitudes and reported Tarbat Ness as being situated on 58 degrees, with a long summer day of 18 hours. He noted changes as he moved north: fermented liquor was made from corn and honey; corn was threshed in barns and not in the open as in the Mediterranean lands; and various grains disappeared as one moved north. He reported the native name as "Prettanoi," meaning beautiful land.

No further mention is found of Britain for two centuries, and his report was treated as fiction.

EARLY A.D. Scotland was said to be made up of six Pictish kingdoms, Moray being one extending to the Dornoch Firth in the north, to the west end of the Great Glen, and bounded on the south by the Mounth. This was the range of peaks stretching from Ben Nevis to the sea at Stonehaven. Fife was most likely another of these kingdoms, as the Scots made few incursions there.

82 A.D. The Roman general Agricola invaded Scotland, fighting a battle at Mons Graupius. This site is unknown and the name corrupted to "Grampius."

180 A.D. The first Scots invited from Ireland to fight as mercenary soldiers. They were given "sword lands," on which they settled. Their name "Scotti" is said to mean invaders, but an alternative is that this was the name for their weapon, the short sword. The Saxons on invading England got their name because of their battle axes or "saexes."

368 A.D. A number of Scots went as mercenaries into England to support a native revolt there against Roman rule. This uprising was so serious that the Emperor Theodosius had to come from Italy to suppress it, hence the reference to the events. From this time the Scots began to move eastwards in Scotland, pressing the Picts before them into the north and east, until both races were united by Kenneth Macalpine.

432   This is recorded as the date of the death of St Ninian, who after conversion to Christianity had gone to Rome, returning to convert South Scotland. He introduced parishes, a unit which did not change radically until 1975, remaining until then as a base for church government and later in local government.

475   This is taken as the date of the end of the Roman Empire in western Europe. Following the breakdown of rule from Rome, anarchy and chaos prevailed, the people reverting to subsistence agriculture, the towns having to be abandoned. From this chaos arose gradually burghal development.

563   St Columba came to Scotland from Ireland, settling in Iona. He visited the Pictish King Brud at Inverness, accompanied by two Pictish monks, St Comgal and St Coinneach (Kenneth) as interpreters. The Pictish tongue was still in general use in eastern Scotland.

717   The Pictish king, Nechtan, expelled from the north the monks based on Iona. Roman church monks moved up from Northumbria to fill the vacuum, but there were not enough of them, and the Culdee church sent priests from Ireland. This Culdee church pre-dominated in Scotland until the churches were reformed by King David I and his Queen, Margaret.

780-1070   The period of the "Norse Expansion." Gwynn Jones in his book *The Vikings* gives many details of the happenings in Scotland where they settled in large numbers along the coast, Nairn being for long a Norse stronghold.

843   Kenneth Macalpine united the Picts and Scots into one nation, which continued free and independent until 1707.

880   The Orkneyinga Saga tells how Earl Sigurd of Orkney defeated Maolbrige, the Mormaer of Moray, and cut off his head to let it hang from the pommel of his saddle while he rode home to the north. The head had a jagged tooth which chafed and broke the skin on Sigurd's knee and infected it so that the Earl died of blood poisoning. He was buried by the banks of a river, the Ekkialbakka. Dr Skene gives this river as the Findhorn.
    The site of battle was probably near Forres as Darnaway was the home and stronghold of the Mormaer, but it would take a day or two for the infection to have fatal results. Sigurd had the lands of Sutherland and Caithness, several days' ride from Moray. The

river is most likely the Oykell, for "bekka" is Norwegian for a stream, and Ekkial very much resembles Oykell.

885   Two factions fought a fierce internecine battle at Hafrsfjord, and very many of the defeated side fled to Scotland, where they settled, and then used the country as a base for raids to attack and pillage their former homeland.

Earl Sigurd, already mentioned, was a brother of Rognvald who had been given the Orkneys by the Norwegian King Harald "Harfragi," the "Fairhaired," who ruled there and also occupied the Hebrides. This Rognvald was notorious for his attacks on Scotland. We also know from the Icelandic Landnambook, "the Book of Settlement," that some of the settlers on that island came from Caithness and were Christians, although of a most perfunctory kind. This expansion was kindled by the overpopulation of Norway, and drove them to the sea, sailing as far as Byzantium and Archangel. According to some scholars, they may have circumnavigated Greenland and settled in Nova Scotia for three years around 1006.

They were traders and dealt in glass, fish, hides, salt, wine, glue, horses, cattle, polar bears, falcons, walrus ivory, seal oil, honey, wax, malt, silks, woollens, amber, nuts, soapstone, ornaments, dishes, lamps, millstones, weapons and silver.

It is likely that they were the start of the tradition of exporting and importing in the North and East of Scotland, with the Baltic and Northern Europe, which continues to this day.

953   The title of Mormaer of Moray appears for the first time. The holder of this office was a powerful and important figure. The king could take away the title and lands but could not appoint a successor without discussing it with the people. This mormaer was Cellach, who had rebelled and was slain by Malcolm I. "Mor" was great and "maer" was from Norse, and is the same word as mayor.

961   The Vikings had long held the Northern Isles and Caithness and Sutherland and now crossed the shores of the Moray Firth. They landed in force at Cullen Bay and advanced inland to fight the "Battle of the Bauds," where the Scots King Indulf was killed.

965   His successor, Duff, was killed "on the classic ground of Forres." Forres has elsewhere in early days been described as a fatal place for kings.

1000   About this time is found the first example of writing in Scotland. This was in the "Book of Deer," a record kept by the

Abbey of Deer in Aberdeenshire, one of the earliest church establishments. The entries extend to about 1150 and refer to the grants of land and other privileges. It was written in Latin, but in the margins and spaces a writer, with a cramped Roman style, inserted many notes in Irish Gaelic. The writer would be an Irish monk because Scots Gaelic had no orthography until three centuries later.

The Advocates' Library in Edinburgh contains most of the MSS of the year 1400 to 1600, and with one exception all are in Irish Gaelic. The exception is in the Gaelic of the west of Scotland, with a phonetic spelling which makes interpretation difficult. It is thought to belong to a date between 1512 and 1526.

1000   The Norsemen had been settling along the shores of the Moray Firth for a century and a half, but the Picts were now beginning to turn them out.

1006   A mention of Scotland is made in Greenland at this time, and may have referred to Moray. Thorfinn Karlesefni, a son-in-law of Eric the Red (who had reached America earlier), took three ships and 160 persons including some women with the intention of setting up a colony in the new land. When the ships reached their destination two Scots, Heke and his wife Hoka, were sent ashore to explore and report. Unlike sailors, they were used to travelling on land, hence the reason for being chosen. They are described as wearing a large piece of material wrapped round their bodies, and drawn between their legs, and tucked in at the waists. This was the philamor of the Scots. They brought back a good report, and also some grapes and wild wheat. It is possible that the two Scots had been "displaced" from Moray and were looking for a new place to settle.

1014   The Vikings were driven from Burghead. This was their last remaining colony on the south side of the firth, but many settlers remained elsewhere and were in time absorbed. Nairn had been a wholly Norse town, and many remained to be absorbed by the local residents. This happened along much of the Moray coast as well as in the Western Isles. There the place names show that the Gaels lived inland, and the Norse on the sea shores. Names such as Mac Railt in Argyll, formed from the Gaelic Mac and the Norse Harald, indicate the intermarriage between the two races.

1020   The Mormaer of Moray, Finlaec, was murdered by his nephew somewhere in Moray, probably at Darnaway. This was

50

the home of the various landowners of Moray. The province for which he was responsible was larger than the present county. To the north it extended well into Ross-shire and to the west to the end of Loch Lochy. It touched Loch Ericht in Perthshire, and a pendicle went almost to Turriff, though most of this boundary was further west nearer the Spey.

1032   Another Mormaer of Moray, Gillacomgan, was burned to death with fifty of his men probably by Macbeth (properly MacHeth). In this year Macbeth was welcoming immigrants from England, and giving them grants of land. The historian calls them Normans, although the Norman Conquest of England was still 34 years in the future. Ambitious knights were looking hungrily across the Channel for estates and power.

1039   The Battle of Torfness where Earl Thorfinn defeated King Duncan. The actual site of this affair was three miles away from Burghead near Duffus, and was known also as the "Battle of the Langstane." (The "langstane" was moved to Altyre in 1820 when the Laird of Altyre inherited Gordonstoun estate on condition that he took the name of Gordon. He did this for a number of years, being termed Sir William Cumming Gordon, but later changed to the present day Gordon Cumming. The stone still stands in the "field of the long stone").

1039-1056   Macbeth reigned during these years. He had married Gruoch, widow of the Mormaer of Moray, Gillacomgan. Gillacomgan's son, Lulach, became the stepson of Macbeth, and succeeded as king after Macbeth was slain at Lumphanan in 1056. Lulach was king for only four and a half months before he was slain by Malcolm III who had also killed Macbeth. The descendants of Lulach had a double claim to the throne and for two centuries the family spawned a number of claimants, the cause of much of the bloody strife in Moray.

1074   At the instigation of Queen Margaret, Bishop Fothald called a church council to correct the irregularities which had crept into the Scots Church, especially the proper keeping of Lent. Such irregularities originated in the Culdee church which was still strong in the North East, its centre being Monymusk. The principal prolocutor at the council was Queen Margaret, an Anglo-Saxon princess whose family had fled with so many others to Scotland after the Norman Conquest. She spoke only English and the king,

51

who had been for some time exiled in England, acted as interpreter. English soon became the language of the Scottish court, and so of the country. Thus English was spoken in Scotland four hundred years before it was the speech of the English court. Norman-French was used until the time of Henry VIII.

1075   Bergen in Norway was founded and grew rapidly in importance, being one of the chief ports of the "Hanse" or association of trading towns around the North Sea and the Baltic. Aberdeen was one of the chief towns and acted as agents for the royal burghs of the North East including Forres. Lubeck, Hamburg and Novgorod, the chief city in Russia, were other main centres. The number of towns enrolled was between 70 and 77. The close connection between these ports and burghs lasted many centuries after the Hanse disappeared. Forres had trade with Russia at these times. There was trade between Norway and Scotland much earlier than this.

There was little trade across the English Channel, England being self-sufficient in most things and very insular.

1087   Another Mormaer of Moray, Malsnectai, died in the Abbey of Deer where he had taken refuge from his enemies. He had become a devout Christian and had given much of the Moray land to the Abbey. One tale says he was slain although now a monk. This was two years after the death of Macbeth, and he may have been killed for giving the estate to the church. He would have held the lands for his lifetime only, but perhaps wished to save his life by giving his land and becoming a priest.

1097   Malcolm Canmore died this year. He had done much to advance Scotland. He introduced surnames, making Scotland the second country to do so. He altered the title of mormaer to earl, applied feudal law to the clans, and welcomed English and Saxon refugees, giving them lands and privileges. After his death the Gaelic-speaking population began to expel these foreigners, but with little success. He granted charters of various kinds, but only verbally, and many of these verbal charters lasted until the eighteenth century. Tain seems to have been one of the towns, getting some privileges and a promise of royal protection.

1105   The Annals of the Irish monastery of Innisfallin record the arrival of a camel from King Edgar of Scotland (1097-1106) as a present for Murcherlach O'Brien, King of Limerick. There would still be many blood ties between the Irish at home and those who had over the centuries settled in Scoltand. The camel was probably brought back from the Crusades by a Scot. This shows how the royal burghs, which had a monopoly of foreign trade, must have had excellent communications with other countries.

1107   The bishopric of Moray was set up in this year with the bishop's seat in Elgin. The bishop was the principal instrument of the royal power in the province, and made Elgin very important. The king would have recognised Elgin in some way, probably by a verbal charter, for it was now the "king's toun." The burgh charter is dated 1224, but this may have been granted to regularise the status of the town. Alexander I reigned from 1078 to 1124 and was followed by his brother, David I, who handed over some charters. It is probable that Forres did not have the charter later claimed to have been "burned or destroyed." The existing charter of Forres of 1494 would have been made up at the request of the burgh.

1115   The Church of the Culdees was absorbed into the Roman Catholic church at the behest of Alexander I.

1120   Alexander stamped out a rebellion in Moray with such severity that he was called "the Fierce." He then set up salt works on the coast, and gave permission for oak trees to be taken from the royal forests at Darnaway and Longmorn for fuel for the salt pans. He imposed a tax or "can" on the salt, and this became an important item of revenue. Salt was the only means of preserving food at a time when the shortage of winter fodder entailed the slaughter of all animals except those required for breeding.

1125   David I (1124-1153), in a charter to the Priory of Urquhart, referred to "my burgh of Elgin." Jedburgh had been erected this year and is taken as the first of David's burghs. He practically invented the system, although Alexander I had given rights to certain towns, including Aberdeen, Edinburgh, Perth and Stirling. These four towns developed into the Court of the Four Burghs, the precursor of the Convention of Royal Burghs. Roxburgh and Berwick were also made royal burghs but Roxburgh was later razed to the ground and Berwick was incorporated into England in 1302 by Edward I. At this time it is said to have been a greater port than London, and this may have been Edward's reason for seizing it.

There is no trace of any documents for these burghs, but Stirling is thought to have been erected in 1119 and Edinburgh in 1124. The eighteenth-century historian, George Chalmers, spent many years examining the documents in the Paper Office in Edinburgh, later to become the Register Office. He concluded that David I had made Elgin a royal burgh in his reign.

1130   Another Mormaer of Moray, Oengus, was slain at Strath-cathro. More than 4000 of his men were said to have been killed with him, but victors are always liable to exaggerate their successes. Oengus would have the new title of earl, but the old title may still have been in use.

1150   Forres was made a royal burgh and full details are given in the chapter dealing with the burgh's foundation.

1156   Another of Moray's many rebellions broke out. The rebel claimant to the throne was bought off with the earldom and lands of Ross, which was still the northern part of the Province of Moray.

1174   Another rebellion which was suppressed with such ferocity that it was called the "Massacre" of Moray. After these rebellions the prisoners were often shipped across the firth to Ross and Sutherland. There they took the name of Murray, still common there, whereas it is rare in Moray.

1180   King William the Lion (1165-1214) confirmed most of the charters of the burghs "north of the Mounth," saying "charter burgesses . . . to hold what they had in his grandfather's time." The Mounth was a line drawn from the peak of Ben Nevis through other peaks, Ben Alder, Ben Dearg and Lochnagar, at that time named Lochinvar. It continued to the sea just south of the Dee. This line was originally drawn in 970 to separate North Pictland from South Pictland. All streams rising between this boundary and the Great Glen either flow into the Glen or the North Sea, none flowing southwards. It was replaced in time as a political boundary of the Highlands by a line from Dumbarton (Fort of the Britons) touching castles through Perthshire and the Mearns to Dunottar Castle. Here it swung inland again to Braemar, and then through Kildrummie, Rhynie, Rothes, Dallas and Rafford, finally reaching the River Findhorn near Mundole, the river being the boundary to the sea.

This Highland line was often forgotten, but always revived when the Highlands needed special attention. It was the southern limit for General Wade when he built the military roads. It was also the line for Thomas Telford for his work, and also for the special work of the Church of Scotland for the erection of churches and missions. It was used by the Highlands and Islands Medical Service, and again by the Government when setting up the Highlands and Islands Development Board in 1965. In 1929 Nairn had been removed from the Highlands and combined with Moray to form the Joint Council of Moray and Nairn, an unhappy marriage from the beginning. Under the 1974 reorganisation of local government, Nairnshire was returned to the Highland Region.

1197   Hugh Freskin, son of the earliest known family in Moray, distinguished himself by suppressing a rebellion by the Earl of Caithness and was given that Earl's lands, but with the title of Earl of Sutherland. The first Freskin was a Flemish merchant, who bought or got the lands of Innes. The family also in the course of time held the Earldom of Moray and also of Douglas.

We note here that the Scottish peerage was feudal in origin but no personal dignity was attached to the ownership of land as in England. The only Scottish dukedom was Rothesay, and there was no marquisate or viscounty. At the Union of the Crowns in 1603 there were only 87 titles and of these James VI had created 63.

1212, 1215, 1229   Rebellions in Moray in each of these years.

1228   A Highland rebel, Gilescope MacScolane, invaded the province setting fire to Inverness and several wooden castles before being dealt with.

1230   This is taken as the date of the pacification of Moray.

1233   Pluscarden Priory has an entry in its records referring to the "mills and castle of Forres" which they had received from the crown. There is a reference also to the "bailiwick of Forres." The town did not yet have a provost.

1249   A large ship was launched at Inverness built for a French owner, Hugh de Chattelas, Comte de St Paul and Blois. The ship was named after him. There were still many fine stands of timber in the north and there would be skilled and most likely cheap labour. The size of the ship would be relative, for Scotland never succeeded in building a good merchant marine. In 1607 a speaker in the English Parliament said that shipping in Scotland was *ad misericordiam*.

Alexander II died this year, and we learn something of Forres from his records. The land of Wester Lawrenceton was given by the town to the crown in exchange for the right to hold a fair of St Laurence. This was how this saint became the patron.

Another document speaks of the lands of Blervie, and the *rune Pictorum*, the cairn of the Picts, which is at Templestones, lying between Burgie and Ulern, the former name of Blervie. Blervie has different spellings, the meaning being "rough ground."

Templestones was known then as Auchindathin, another Gaelic name. Other names on the document are "Tobercrunkel," now the Deer's Well, and "Toberafeyne," which was mentioned as early as 1121. The two names are Gaelic but the monkish scribe would have spelt the words phonetically. The first was "the well with one mouth" and the other was "the well of the fingal or fair stranger."

An even earlier charter of Malcolm IV (1153-1165) speaks of the Kilbuyack road where it diverged from the existing route and took high ground south of the Knock of Alves. It will be noticed that the names on the high ground are Gaelic while those in the Laich are not.

1263   The Sheriff of Forres paid £7 13s for the freight of 540 cattle to Leith. Most movement for any distance was by sea, and there was a considerable trade between Findhorn and the Forth.

1264   The Sheriff, William Wiseman, was also Provost of Elgin, and spent £10 on building a new wall outside the King's Chamber in Forres Castle. He was also the keeper of the castle and would hold the king's share of revenue until such time as it was collected by the king or his chamberlain.

He also disbursed ten shillings for the carriage of 10 hogsheads of wine from a ship at Findhorn to Forres, and he also paid out 16s 10d for two men who spent 14 weeks looking for hawks. These would be caught and trained for the sport of the king and court. He also replaced a mew for the king, this being a cage where hawks were kept when moulting.

It is noted later that two hogsheads of the wine were sold for 103 shillings and threepence.

1270   The Chapel of Laurence was built by Alexander III for the soul of his wife, Margaret. This king was fond of the district and spent much time hunting in the royal forests, one being at Longmorn.

1280   The king's daughter was to marry the King of Norway and a large dowry was required. The burghs had to pay a good part of this tocher and a special stent was made on all the burgesses. This is the first mention of this special collection of money.

1291   A charter to the Abbey of Dunfermline speaks of coal being produced there. Later coal was given at the doors of churches to the poor. In Forres peat would have been given.

1292   The church revenues in Scotland, as in other countries, had to a great extent to be remitted to Rome. Finance was mostly handled by Italian bankers, and two of these are named at this time. One was Roczard of Lucca, an Italian, and another was Nicholas de Colle, who might have been French. Lucca was the financial centre of western Europe, and a mint had been set up there in the ninth century. Whether either handled the money affairs of the king is not known, but this year a quit claim was issued relieving the king and queen of debts they were due to the people of Forres. The town would most likely have received some privilege in exchange for cancelling this bill.

1298   King Edward I of England wrote a letter to Pope Boniface that held the seeds of the wars between Scotland and England for the next three centuries. It was not an honest letter for he did not give the full story. Alexander I of Scotland, like his predecessors, was a holder of lands in England with English titles. David I had been Earl of Hereford, and also held much land in Northumberland and was addressed there as "Prince." Robert Bruce was also an English noble as was John Balliol. All holders of such land had to make regular homage to the King of England, which they did.

In this year Alexander III went to England to perform this duty. The ceremony was an important one with a fixed ritual, and would be well rehearsed. Edward wrote to the Pope: "Alexander III, King of Scots, our cousin, did homage to Henry, our father, for the Kingdom of Scotland, and afterwards to us."

According to the Scots records, what Alexander actually said was, "I become your man for the land I hold of you in the Kingdom of England for which I owe homage: reserving my Kingdom." The Bishop of Norwich officiated and here said that he should also give this right to King Edward. Alexander replied: "None has the right save God alone; nor do I hold save God alone."

The Pope accepted Edward's letter as true and correct, and the church gave its recognition of the Kings of England holding the superiority of the Kingdom of Scotland, and as such the feudal masters of the Scots rulers.

Edward destroyed the castle of Nairn, this being the second one built there. The first had been built very near the sea and was destroyed by the action of the waves. It had been captured by the Vikings in the reign of Malcolm I (944-53) and may have been of some age at that time. The town of Nairn was occupied by the Vikings for some time.

Sir Reginald de Chen, probably the founder of the Cheyne family, was keeper of Forres castle and submitted to Edward by letter, saying he was also sheriff of Forres and Elgin. He appealed that action be taken against the Bishop of St Andrews and John Comeyn of Badenoch, who had entered the province with their men, although it was "a province which had always been under the immediate government of the king," and had laid waste the land and villages.

He mentions these lands and villages—Darnaway, Drakies, Dyke, Brodie, Kyntessac, Altyre and Balnaferry, as well as the prepositura of the castle of Ulern (Blervie). This castle must have belonged to the king at that time. Another place mentioned is Byn, and this may have been the old name for Culbin, or perhaps Bins Ness.

Among the officers in the castle was a balistarius who was in charge of the crossbows, catapults and other weapons. The weapon of the ordinary soldier was a pike, and sergeants had halberds similar to those still owned by the town and used on ceremonial occasions.

There was also a janitor or keeper of the gate, and if a trespass or wrong was done against a burgess he had the right to stand before the gate and demand that justice be done.

The castellan or governor could not interfere in civil affairs, but at Easter, Whitsun or Christmas he could demand of a burgess pigs, geese and poultry for the king's use, payment having to be made in silver money. The upper classes celebrated these festivals with great style and pomp.

1300 Beaver skins were being exported from Inverness. These animals were very plentiful in the region of Loch Ness, but were later exterminated by over-hunting.

There was a "population explosion" all over Europe about

this time. The reason is not known, but perhaps the newly emerging nations had enough security and peace to allow the land to be cultivated properly. Good food would help to increase the population, but within a generation or so the new ground taken into cultivation was soon exhausted under the system of cultivation, bringing famine and disease, culminating in the plague. The Black Death in 1348-9 carried off one-third of the population in England, and Scotland would not have fared much better.

The resultant scarcity of labour put the peasants temporarily in a strong position, and vassalage was weakened, the workers demanding money wages and the freedom to move to any work. More money had to be minted resulting in the introduction of inflation which since that date has continued overall at a rate of three per cent per annum. Up to the time of David I copper coins had sufficed in Scotland, but with the rise of royal burghs commerce had increased and during his reign silver coins had to be issued. Forres had a mint for this purpose at one time, the official being the *argentier*.

1303   Edward returned again to Kinloss, staying in the Abbey for three weeks, and one night in Lochindorb Castle on his return journey. From Elgin he sent a great many letters. The Roman Church had inherited from the Roman Empire a wonderful system of roads and communications, with post houses at regular intervals in all the countries under Roman rule, and all roads leading to Rome.

As mentioned earlier, the Pope used Italian financiers to collect and remit his vast income. Two lived in England—Spini of Florence and Bellude of Lucca—and they loaned a great deal of money to the king, and probably also to his knights and barons. Specie was scarce in Britain and payment was usually made in kind, the staple being wool, which had a ready sale in Europe.

Edward held a Parliament in Berwick, which he had taken into England in 1302, and many Scots were compelled to go there and swear fealty to Edward as the ruler of Scotland. One of those who went was young Sir Alan de Moravia of Moray, but on his return he joined William Wallace in his struggle for the freedom of Scotland, and became his right hand man until years later he left Wallace, and little was heard of him thereafter. The King wrote to the castle of Forres telling the Sheriff that Robert de Brus and Ingelgramus of Gynies could have their lands again. De Brus was soon to be known as Robert the Bruce and the first of the Stewart kings. Gynes may be Geanies in Ross-shire.

Henry de Rye was sent to Scotland to handle the escheats, a provision in English law under which lands without an heir or owner reverted to the king. His area was north of the Scottish Sea, the London term for the Firth of Forth.

As the home of Sir Alan Moray, the province became the focus of the Wallace rebellion. Wallace attacked Forres Castle, burning it and making Henry de Rye prisoner. This is why Edward advanced on Forres, burning the castle of Elgin on the way. When Wallace was defeated and in hiding, John Comyn was virtually ruler of Scotland and Edward sent out detachments of troops to try to capture him. Later he paid homage to Edward and was recognised as having a claim to the Scottish throne.

In addition to living off the wealthy Abbey of Kinloss, Edward also made it a home for disabled and infirm soldiers. He stayed in a house of one of the Canons of the Cathedral and granted the request of his host that the Bishop of Caithness get 20 oak trees for the building of his Cathedral at Dornoch.

At this time the Abbey had an abbot, a prior and a sub-prior and 23 monks. The abbot was entitled to wear a mitre and had a seat in Parliament. They had spacious and comfortable quarters with a parlour in which they met to chat, a scriptorium, a treasury, a hostelry where strangers were entertained, and an almonry where the poor got alms. The monks had a large daily allowance for food, with two pecks of wheat for white bread and two pecks of barley for brewing. The Abbey employed a large staff to look after them and work their farms. The scattered farms, stretching into Buchan, had been formed into a thanedom—a rank slightly lower than a barony. The abbot was thus a military as well as a church leader, and abbots and bishops often led their own troops in war. The church was an ardent supporter of the monarchy.

The province had its *vexillium Muravia,* the flag of Moray. The king's scribes wrote mostly in Norman French and transcribed the local names, which to them would have sounded uncouth and strange, in very odd ways. Elgin was Eign, or d'Eign, Dein, Deim, Deign. So common was this that in later years hisorians used to speculate on the site of this town, coming to the conclusion that it must be Drainic, although no trace of building has ever been found there. Moray was Mora, Morenne, and even Murineeve.

The English officers left in charge of the burghs after Edward's departure were long remembered for their severity and cruelty.

As justiciars in charge of the region north of the Grampians Edward appointed a Scotsman, the same Reginald de Chen who had governed Forres castle, and an Englishman, Count John de Vaux of Northumberland. William Wiseman, who had been Sheriff of Forres, was made Sheriff of Elgin with the title of Viscount, *Vicomes,* meaning then that he was a deputy of an Earl. His brother, Alexander Wiseman, was made Sheriff of both Forres and Nairn with the same title.

Neither Sutherland nor Caithness had castles, so no Sheriff was appointed. De Chen later wrote Edward in London, reminding him of the 200 oaks he had promised him to repair his castle at Duffus, which had been burned down during the insurrections in Moray. These trees were to be taken from the forests of Darnaway and Longmorn.

1306   After the murder of the two Comyns in the Church at Dumfries, Robert the Bruce had himself crowned King of Scotland and hurried to Moray where he held lands around Forres. Here he collected the first of his supporters in his successful war. He was also the keeper of the forests of Longmorn and Darnaway. The Bishop of Moray was one of the most zealous of his party. The Bishop's family were of Pettie, and the people of this estate, as well as others in Moray, rallied to the side of Bruce. His dispute with the Comyns also endeared him to the Moray people who had long been in conflict with the Comyn family. Alan Moray of Culbin was another of his chief officers.

As many Scottish Barons expected Bruce to be as unsuccessful as Wallace, they began to write Edward asking that they be given the lands of those who had joined Bruce, and these were distributed among them.

1325   David, Bishop of Moray, founded a College for Scots at the University of Paris. That University had been founded in 1100 and many Scots students attended there. Scots also went to the universities in Utrecht, Leiden and Gouda in Holland, Padua in Italy and elsewhere. Britain had no universities yet. There is still a Scots house in Paris, and Protestant theology is still one of the five faculties in this university.

1326   The burghs were asked for the first time to send members to

Parliament to sit with the Lords and Bishops. There was no separate House of Lords, as in England, and all Three Estates sat together until 1707 when the Scots Parliament disappeared.

1332   Earl Randolph of Moray died and a Douglas was given the title.

1357   This was a disastrous year for the nation. King David II had been a prisoner in England, although allowed much freedom and attending the court. He was now allowed to return to Scotland on payment of a ransom of 100,000 merks, an enormous sum for such a small and poor country. The Estates had to provide one-third each of this money immediately. Two bailies were forced into a house and put under guard, and under threat of death had to produce a list of the burgesses and the amount each had to pay. To speed them in their task, they were also denied food. This amount was the "stent" on each burgess, and it was an unenviable task for the two men.

1363   About this year Jean Froissart (1338-1410) visited Scotland and stayed six months, being well received by King David and the various barons. He wrote of the condition of Scotland: "There is neither iron to shoe horses nor leather to make saddles, harness or bridles, all these things come ready by sea from Flanders."

By this time the little port of Veere had become the centre for trade between Scotland and the Continent. It was on the island of Walcheren but is now three miles inland. The Scots merchants had stores and agents there, and the little town, now of 1000 people, has many memories and records of this period.

1390   This year saw the introduction of the iniquitous system of "Manrent." This was a legal agreement by which a man bound himself to a master completely, counting on being rewarded for his services, no matter what they were. His patron was often a fortune hunter, willingly acting in any way that would benefit him —in other words, little less than legalised banditry. Whether the Wolf of Badenoch strengthened his forces by this means is not known, but he began to act in a more savage way. His father, the King, had made him Lieutenant of all the country from Moray to the Pentland Firth, but he abused this power. He set out on a number of forays, and set fire to the choir of Forres and many houses, including that of the archdeacon. In the following year he attacked Elgin, burning the cathedral, the house of Maisondieu, the church of St Giles and the fourteen houses of the canons of the cathedral.

A painting in the Council chamber depicts the scene at Darnaway which is said to have incited him to act as he did. The Earl of Moray held a tournament of jousting at St John's Mead, in imitation of the more sophisticated practice of chivalry in France and elsewhere. The Wolf was not invited and was turned away when he arrived with his bands of followers. In revenge he attacked Forres and did other damage in the neighbourhood. The Earl of Moray at this time was John Dunbar, one of the oldest of Moray families, who had married the king's sister. Robert Bruce's nephew, Thomas Ranulf or Randolph, had held the title, and was followed by a Douglas. Ranulf had been given the superiortiy of Forres as well as that of Elgin and Nairn. In the reign of David II (1329-70) the king admitted that his father had done Forres a great wrong by giving these superiorities, and he withdrew them, stating that no person could be interposed between the king and his vassals in the royal burghs. This was recorded in the first Parliament of his reign.

1424   James I took away the rights of the royal burghs to elect their councillors, who had to be residents and burgesses, practising their trades or crafts. From this time forward councillors were appointed at Michaelmas for a year by the retiring councillors. The candidates no longer had to reside in the burgh, but could be gentlemen from anywhere in Scotland. The majority of the dissolved council made certain that none of their opponents were elected, and chose the most wealthy and powerful of the local landowners. Craftsmen were barred from sitting on the council, and thus began the story of increasing corruption which went on until the Reform Act of 1833.

The first act of the Parliament in James's reign was a law against "vagabondage," which was always a problem in Scotland, as the country did not have a Poor Law as England had. The poor were dependent on the charity of the church, which was quite good with most orders until the Reformation, when the wealth of the land fell into the hands of the nobles and their henchmen.

Poverty seemed to be equated with sin, or alternatively a punishment for wrongful behaviour, under the Calvinists. James had succeeded to the throne after a long period of misrule by the

Regent Albany, who had died at the age of eighty. The king intended to put a stop to the many abuses, but his changes allowed abuses of an even worse kind. One law he did pass said that the law applied to poor and rich equally, and a poor man had to be given the free service of an advocate if accused of an offence.

1438   James I was assassinated and was succeeded by his son, James II. He tried to carry out the policy of his father, correcting the wrongs and errors of the regency.

He ordered that distances between towns and various points be measured and recorded. At this time the Scots mile was equal to 1½ English miles. Later the disparity was reduced to 156 yards, and later still the countries had the same, 1760 yards to the mile. The ancient deeds are very accurate when there is a secure base for the measurements, such as the banks of a river, but there was not yet the ability to calculate the heights of objects, buildings, trees or hills.

James II also introduced Lord Lieutenants, who were responsible for defence and order in a county if the king was absent when any trouble broke out. In the past the illness, incapacity, or seizure of the king was not provided for.

1476   The first printing press was set up in England.

1494   First mention of whisky. A friar was granted 6 bolls bere to make aquavitae, a direct translation into Latin of the Gaelic *Uisgebeatha,* "the water of life."

1496   James IV presented Forres with a charter of "Novadamus," purporting to be a copy of the original charter, which the burgh had never actually held.

This charter repeated that Ramphlat was a part of the Common Good, although it had passed out of the town's ownership for almost two centuries. King Robert the Bruce had given Sluie and the forest of Drumine to his nephew Ranulf, Earl of Moray, who had fought by his side during the War of Independence.

This area lay to the south of Ramphlat and passed into the ownership of the Cummings of Altyre through intermarriage with the Moray family. The land north of Ramphlat had been originally given to the Knights Templar who had also aided Bruce, and this had also become part of the Altyre lands.

Grazings, pastures, water rights and boundaries had been a source of disputes and fighting since man first began to keep herds and flocks, and so it was between the town of Forres and the owners of Altyre. The powerful landholders could use *force majeur* against small burghs, and these could look for little support from the crown. Most landowners were hereditary sheriffs and dealt with complaints in their own courts if possible.

In October 1478 the laird of Altyre was appointed forester for the forest of Drumine, and later to look after the forests of the Earl of Moray.

1504   From this date craftsmen could not be sent from the burghs to sit in Parliament. The burgh representatives were now merchants, and they were not long in bringing in vindictive legislation restricting further the craft guilds and their members.

Those merchants who dealt with imports and exports were now becoming wealthy and intermarrying and consorting with the landed gentry. These did not now disdain to put their younger sons into trade and commerce, something which did not happen in England or elsewhere. The ordinary merchants found themselves between this higher society who did not mix with them, and the craftsmen and others in the town with whom they would not associate.

1507   The first printing press in Scotland was set up. The great demand was for the Bible.

1513   James IV was slain at Flodden with the "flowers of the forest." During his reign there had been hopeful signs of increasing prosperity and enlightenment, but this came to a sudden end with his death.

1528   The first martyr, Patrick Hamilton, was burned at the stake. He was the youthful Abbot of Ferne, and had studied at the university of Paris, where the Roman faith was being criticised, and he had also visited Marburg in Germany which was to be a centre of Protestantism. While Patrick was ostensibly burned because of his beliefs, opinion at the time said "the reek of Patrick Hamilton had something to do with the bitter feud between the Hamiltons and the Douglases."

1531   The Lord High Treasurer in Edinburgh paid messengers "to ryn the post at night." This is the first mention of mail carriers and is a sign of the expansion of business and commerce. Before this the chief means of communication was through the movement of churchmen and church letters. There was a constant traffic to Rome and other religious centres, and merchants found it convenient and safer to travel in such company. The best accommodation was to be found in the abbeys and priories, and the roads used were those made by the Romans a thousand years earlier.

1532   James V founded the College of Justice, half the seats plus one being reserved for monks and priests. Scotland did not produce lawyers at this time, and those wishing to enter the profession had to study on the Continent, where Roman law was practised. Thus the legal system took a different path from that of England.

1543   The shadow of the Reformation was now being cast ahead, and an act was passed allowing anyone to read the Bible in English.

1560   THE REFORMATION . . .

This did not take place overnight but was a long drawn out process foreseen for many years. The crucial and last decision of 24th August in this year was to abrogate the Pope's privileges and to stop the celebration of Mass. The priests who did not accept the new state of affairs left quietly. Some went abroad to continue as priests while others took up other work, such as tutors or secretaries with Catholic families. The first Protestant minister in Forres was not appointed until 1563, but services and readings of some kind would have been held until then.

On the whole the parish priests and vicars were humble men, not very well educated nor very intellectual. Some could not read or write and scarcely knew the meaning of the Latin they used in the services. To fill the vacancies, exhorters and readers were appointed until trained ministers were obtainable. The exhorters preached and the readers read and explained the Bible. Many parishes could not find a minister for many years. Edinkillie did not have a minister until 1574, and Dallas had two readers until William Paterson was appointed minister in 1574.

One of the many effects of the Reformation and the disappearance of the priests was a great increase in witchcraft, and it is no coincidence that the first act against the practice was passed within three years of the Reformation.

As a consequence of the Reformation there was now a new attitude to the power of evil. A primitive and corrupted Manichaenism (the religion of Mani who represented evil or darkness, as something capable of thought and volition) had always been prevalent among the ordinary folk of Scotland, perhaps a relic of the early religion, and now they found themselves bereft of all the holy water, exorcisms, sacred relics and the charms and ceremonies provided by the Catholic church. As there was no priest to turn to for protection against the evil eye, disease and misfortune and other ills, people, especially the poor, turned to witches. Formerly these had been considered fairly harmless by the church. Many old women who acted as nurses and midwives providing simple herbal remedies may have been regarded as witches. Some may even have been sufficiently unscrupulous as to take advantage of simple poor people.

Bishops and other high church dignitaries were mostly connected with the best families, and they were allowed to stay in possession of the lands and buildings, keeping two-thirds of the income during their lives. The priest at Pluscarden lived for long in comfort at the Priory, and according to tradition was on excellent terms with his Protestant successor.

The burghs with their long and close connections with the Low Countries were in favour of the Reformation, and many of the wealthier burgesses worked for its acceptance. The Catholic Church was very wealthy; its income in the year before Reformation was £400,000, while the income of the king was only £40,000. There were between three and four thousand clerics, and if the money had been distributed equally each one would have been wealthy.

The landowners had feued great parts of their estates to the church as they always needed money, which they obtained by getting a good sum for occupation of the land with perpetual feu duty. The lairds now saw that by reformation and legislation they would change from vassals to superiors.

By this time the king had appointed laymen to take over the abbeys and lands and use much of the revenues for their own purposes. These were called commendators, and James V's six illegitimate sons held estates in this way.

Many of the monks and priests were immoral, and Pluscarden Priory had been closed some time earlier because of the behaviour of the monks, who were dispersed among other monasteries to be disciplined. Their order was abolished and a new one took over the priory.

At the Reformation, the Bishop of Moray married his mistress in the cathedral at Elgin and settled church lands on his large family at the same time. Concubinage was common as well as other wrongdoing. The monks at Kinloss had long given up work and lived the lives of wealthy gentlemen attended by servants and enjoying a high standard of living.

In Forres, the Town Council took over the church lands and from this time until the last century were responsible for the church. In Kinloss a Mr Edward Bruce was made Commendator and on the death of the abbot Richard Reid took over the lands and was given the title of Lord Kinloss. He had been parson of Tarras but was of good family. His son succeeded to the title, also becoming Earl of Elgin, thus combining the two titles. The elder son of the Earl of Elgin still uses the title of Lord Kinloss.

Richard Reid's uncle Robert was the abbot before him, and was a famous figure. He had imported a skilled gardener from France for the gardens.

Sir Alexander Seaton was made Commendator of the widespread lands of Pluscarden and sold much of them. He later became Lord Dunfermline.

The burghs took over the church schools although many had schools under their own control by this time.

The church had employed many people and these now found themselves without work, and the number of men without any means of support grew, while the charity handed out by the church was also stopped. The Netherlands had for long recruited Scots for defence on land, and France also had regular Scots units, reaching as far back as the Scots Archers, the French king's personal bodyguard. The government now granted licences to individuals to recruit regiments to fight abroad for any country willing to hire them.

Donald Mackay, later Lord Reay, had a body of 3600 fighting on the Swedish side, and Lord Spynie had a regiment of 3000 fighting for Denmark. Among the generals of Gustaf Adolphus were Lord Ruthven, Lord Forbes and a brother of the Earl of Haddington. Lord Irvine led more than 9000 Scots in the French service. Others went as far as Russia, one becoming Marshal of the Russian army which faced Napoleon at Moscow.

1580   It was estimated at this time that more than 30,000 Scots were living in Poland. For centuries the Scots traders had set out with packs of goods on their backs or on horses to wander all over Europe, many settling there. Many Scots names still survive, some altered, others with the same spelling, such as Kennedy. The father of Emmanuel Kant, the famous German philosopher, was said to be a Cant from Scotland. Cant, Younie and some other purely Moray names are to be found elsewhere.

1587 James VI introduced Justices of the Peace on the English model. He decided to appoint "owing to lax justice . . . godly, wise and virtuous gentlemen of good quality, moyen and report . . . making residence within the same to be Commissioners for keeping the King's Peace." These were recruited from the minor gentry now appearing, and were disliked by the people as they were mostly Episcopalians. This innovation also irked the lairds and others who held hereditary sheriffdoms and judgeships who feared that their income from the fines and forfeitures might be jeopardised. These J.P.s never became the "men of all work" that they were in England, and the office has never had the prestige it still has in England.

1595 The Post Office appears in the records, the Aberdeen Postmaster having to wear blue livery. The mails between London and Berwick took eight days in twenty stages. From Berwick to Edinburgh they were carried by runners on foot or occasionally mounted.

1597 The burghs were enjoined to raise taxes for the building of jails, prisons and ward houses. Little was ever done in this way, as prisoners were expected to pay for their food, but few were able or willing to do so. The councils objected to supporting offenders, and to avoid the expense many prisoners were allowed to escape. The jailers were hauled before the council and severely reprimanded, but were rarely dismissed.

The monopoly of trade in the Royal Burghs was abolished to the great anger and anguish of the merchants, who protested vigorously but with almost no effect.

1603 - 1648 During this period many burghs of regality and barony were formed, but few of these erections survived for long. Muirton of Kinloss was one, and held fairs and cattle markets for a short period.

1603 An Act was passed confirming Acts of 1565 and 1579, making the Kirk Sessions responsible for "stenting the parishioners for relief of the poor." These acts had never been enforced, but neither were the harsh laws against begging, except on very rare occasions.

The Scots had a kindliness and sympathy for the poor who had to break the law to survive, and anyone stealing food for survival was not classified as a thief. According to Forbes's *Institute of Scots Law,* he could not be charged with theft if he could carry the meat away on his back.

Wages were half those of England, but poverty did not bring the despair and anguish obvious among the poor in England. Each parish had a quota of beggars who had to wear a long blue gown with a leaden badge provided by the Kirk Session. They carried a wallet or "gaberlunzie" in which to store the articles of food given them, for few could give money. They could not beg outside their own parish, and those found begging without a licence were taken before the Kirk Session who advised them to go elsewhere, perhaps giving them a copper or two. This system of "Gaberlunzie" men continued in Brechin until 1845, and perhaps elsewhere.

Kirk Sessions occasionally sent to Edinburgh or London for twenty shillings of farthings, so that the poor could get a farthing when appealing for help at the church door.

A mounted force, the King's Guard, was set up to execute warrants of the royal council and to collect the fines and make arrests. The king had now gone to London to reign there. He was followed by the nobles, artists, actors and writers, all of whom had to have a patron without whom they could not survive.

Scotland, with her overseas connections, was much more European than England, having very close ties with France, the Low Countries and Scandinavia, and enjoying very good standing in the community of nations. She had not been at war with any country except England for some centuries.

1607   Settlers from Fife and Lothian were given land in Lewis, Harris and Skye as well as Glenelg on the mainland. This was to forward the policy of extirpation of the Highlanders, and explains the presence of non-Gaelic surnames in these areas.

1609   Parliament enacted that the judges and magistrates of burghs should wear a distinguishing dress as well as churchmen and officials. The dresses were to be designed by the king himself.

1610   A policy of settling Presbyterians in Ulster was inaugurated, grants of land and other privileges being given to volunteers. The Irish had been an intractable people since Pope Adrian IV had given their country as a present to King Henry II of England in 1155.

70

It was thought that this "Plantation of Ulster" would assure peace and order in at least one part of Ireland. A considerable number of Scots took this opportunity of becoming farmers with the promise of an ample supply of cheap labour from the dispossessed people. The Scots settlers never gained the social position given in that country to the English. Like so many political cures, this one became worse than the disease.

1611 - 1711   In this century Uppsala University had 132 Scots on its staff. The number of Scots students in the same period is unknown.

1612   Patric Tulloch of Tannachy was presented to the Chapel of St Leonard's, newly erected. It stood on ground across the road from the present Leanchoil hospital.

1616   James VI obtained an act against smoking tobacco. He had already written a book *A Counterblast to Tobacco,* but it did not seem to have had much effect.

Beginning this year every minister had to "keep ane famous book" and record therein the names and dates of all births, marriages and deaths. As there was no way of enforcing this, the records depended on the energy and conscientiousness of the ministers. The many gaps in the registers show that not all were of the high standard expected.

The burgesses found also that their privileges were still being eroded. Until this time, when charged with any offence they appeared in the burgh court to be tried by their peers and fellow burgesses, who were unlikely to be too harsh on a friend and townsman, except for treason, murder or an offence against the state. Now for most offences they were to be hauled before the sheriffs who were bound to the king, and not to the burghs as the bailies were. In addition, the sheriffs were able to put any fines in their pockets.

In the same year it was ordained that schools were to be open to all, the children to be trained "in civility, godliness, knowledge and learning." All barons and substantial freeholders were enjoined to send their sons. This act was aimed at the Highlanders as the children would be taught in English, a language which they avoided if possible.

The population of Scotland was estimated to be 700,000.

1617   The Register of Sasines was set up, so that every transaction involving property was recorded in a central register, giving Scotland an unique set of records.

1621 The French were expanding in Lower Canada, the present Quebec Province, and emigration was encouraged from Britain to Upper Canada, now Ontario, and to Nova Scotia, as a counterweight. Scots were not encouraged to go to the English Colonies, the future U.S.A., but many moved down from Canada.

1624 The Macintoshes in Inverness-shire were dependents of the Earl of Moray and had acted to revenge the murder of the Bonny Earl by the Marquis of Huntly and as a reward had been given lands in Moray. The Earl was now friendly with Huntly and tried to put the Macintoshes off the lands. The chief was an infant but his uncle Lachlan assembled five hundred men and "fell sorning through Moray . . . and divers other parts" helping themselves to food but being careful not to injure anyone.

The Earl brought in a band of Menteith Highlanders, but had to go to London to get the powers of lieutenancy from the king before he could force the Macintoshes into subjection. Some of them were executed but the principals escaped scot free. They were fined, the money to go to the Earl, but he did not get much.

In the same year the Town Council of Aberdeen banned banquets at christenings, forbidding "nae mair than four gossips and four cummers at the maist" to be at the ceremony. "The extraordinary drinking and scolling (health drinking) was a slander to the times, when many were dying and starving at dykes and under stairs for cauld and hunger."

1625 Sir Robert Gordon of Gordonstoun was made a baronet of Nova Scotia, the first patent of its kind. This order of baronetcy was founded by James I and VI to encourage gentlemen to settle in Canada, but few carried out their side of the bargain.

A fast was held in July because of the continuing heavy rain which threatened failure of the crops.

1626 About 4000 young men were shipped from Cromarty to Hamburg to fight for the Protestant cause against the German emperor. These Scots fought so well that they were called "the Invincible Regiment," but few survived the war.

1627 More than 11,000 men were sent to Denmark to reinforce the Scots fighting the emperor. These were not all volunteers as one would expect, for an order issued to the bailies of the burghs instructed them to arrest "idle and masterless men fit to be employed in the wars."

Scotland still had little work and food for the population, and the army was the only way of using these surplus men.

1628   Lord Lovat was appointed sheriff of Forres and was charged by the Government to search for and capture Catholics.

By this time Scotland was already losing the place she held in Europe, no longer having ambassadors or representatives anywhere. With her continental connections she was held in high regard, whereas England until this time had been very insular, and often threatening. Scotland had only once declared war on a continental country, Norway.

1631   Nichol Sutherland of Forres was sentenced to death for the crime of incest with a woman who had been a paramour of his mother's brother. The Earl of Moray was puzzled at this sentence and reported it to the General Assembly of the Church, but the sentence was carried out. The laws of incest were very strangely interpreted by the church, which accepted the marriage of first cousins, but a man MacBean was beheaded for marrying his first wife's half-brother's daughter.

1633   A camel belonging to the king was paraded through Scotland but it could not be shown on the Sabbath, as Sunday was no longer the semi-holiday of Catholic times.

An Act confirmed the privileges of the Royal Burghs in the most ample manner. Only merchant burgesses could trade with France, Flanders and other foreign ports. Only they could sell wine, wax, candles, silks and other imports, and the act declared that those rights "are only proper and competent to the free borrows royall that have a vote in Parliament and to no others."

This was the high water of the monopoly rights of the royal burghs, but an immediate erosion began with the smuggling and illegal trading by the non-free burghs, which were increasing in number, and by the noblemen who were now taking an active part in trade and commerce. The English nobility would not deign to such matters, but the younger sons of the Scots were becoming traders and merchants. An ancient customary exception to the laws of monopoly allowed "nobles, barons and other landed men to bring merchandise from overseas to their awin particular use and behuif," so long as they did not re-sell them for profit. This last condition was rarely observed.

1638   Moray zealously supported the National Covenant, which has been called the Magna Carta of Scotland. In April the Presbytery met in Forres and all the ministers signed, except George Cumming of Dallas. He may have been one of the Altyre family and did not want to cross his chief. Among the gentlemen who signed were Kinnaird of Culbin, Alexander Brodie of Brodie and Hay of Park and Lochloy.

John Hay, minister of Rafford, wrote a book attacking the new services, but printing was not allowed although the book had the approval of his colleagues. The Reverend William Falconer drew up a list of complaints against the bishops.

1645   The plague had broken out in Scotland, and it was reported that on 1st April "This day Kelso with haill houses, corn barns and barnyards burned by fire, caused by the clenging (cleansing) of ane house whilk was infected by the plague." All 306 houses were burned.

This danger of fire was prevalent all over the country, as the houses were of wood with thatched roofs of straw or heather. Kelso was a considerable place with 1400 inhabitants. At that date the population of Forres was calculated as 360, but this is probably on the low side.

In 1684 Kelso was again burned, the fire starting in a malt-kiln, and the flames were spread by a violent wind so that six hours after the fire started every house, shop and barn was gone with the loss of 4000 bolls of grain. An appeal was made to the Privy Council for help, and an order was issued that a collection be made in every parish church on Sunday. Just after this collection, Glasgow had a bad fire and asked that it be allowed to keep the money collected to help their own people. The Privy Council had a sum on hand to help relieve the sufferings of Scots in the hands of the Turks, and this was used until such time as the church collections arrived in Kelso.

Most burghs have records of money being sent to free or comfort some of their people who had been captured and enslaved by the Turks, in the Mediterranean.

The Battle of Auldearn was fought this year between Montrose and General Hurry, whose defeated men were pursued through Forres.

Cromwell united the two Parliaments and of the 430 members in the new Assembly, only 30 came from Scotland. Forres joined Inverness, Dornoch, Tain, Dingwall and Nairn in electing a member, and delegates met at Inverness. The provosts usually undertook this duty and thus peers and leading landowners found it worth while to be provosts although not attending council meetings. One peer, Lord Findlater, was provost of three burghs at the same time and three earls of Seafield were provosts of Forres. Entry to Parliament was entry to wealth, power and political spoils, and it was usually a relative of a peer who went to Parliament as M.P. The Royal Burghs elected eight members in all.

Cromwell gave firm but good government, refusing assent to the persecution of witches for one thing, but inflicting heavy taxation for the building of castles at Inverness, Perth, Inveraray, Leith and Ayr. The owner of Kinloss, a Brodie of Brodie, sold most of the stones of the Abbey to the builder of Inverness Castle.

Lord Lewis Gordon, a supporter of Montrose, ravaged the county, burning Brodie Castle and destroying the huts and nets of the fishermen of Findhorn, whose superior was an opponent.

1649   Rates were now levied on both heritors and tenants, this system lasting until 1957, when the whole burden was placed on the occupier.

Men servants were paid £5 per annum, while a woman received £1 but had also shoes or a piece of clothing; those who worked on farms also received meal and some clothing and, if married, a house for which a new tenant had to provide the roof. This was usually made of tree branches covered with turf, the farmer having a right to the old turf for manure. A cow cost £2 6s 8d, shoes were 3s a pair, and a wooden chair could be bought for 1s 6d. Gentlemen were giving up the habit of wearing swords and carried canes instead.

Forres took out a decree against the white fishers of Findhorn who were sending their catches south without first offering them to the burgesses. The fishers ignored the decree and the burgh resorted to the courts which denounced the culprits as rebels and "put them to the horn" with a fine of £100 in addition. Putting to the horn meant that they were now outlaws. The Findhorn "haddies" must have been highly valued in Edinburgh where the carriage must have greatly added to the cost. The fishers were encouraged by the laird of Muirton who was able to collect the petty customs from them for his own pocket.

In the 140 years between 1510 and 1650 prices had increased six-fold in England, but wages had not risen in step and the working class suffered severely. Scotland fared even worse, Scots money falling to one-twelfth of sterling. Economists refer to this period as the "Price Revolution." One reason given for this phenomenon was the arrival of large amounts of gold from the recently discovered America. As the amount of gold increased its value fell, like any other commodity in excess supply. But only the price increase was noted. Malthus said later that the real reason was not the gold from America, but the growth in population, and economists still cannot agree about the true reason.

Since the Union of the Crowns in 1603 the interests of the upper classes had moved to London. They now modelled themselves on the more elegant and refined squires of England, sending their sons to English schools where they learned the accents of the ascendancy.

1651   Cromwell had captured between seven and eight thousand Scots at the battle of Worcester and ordered that they be sold as slaves to the plantations in the West Indies, most being landed in Jamaica. There they intermarried with negro slaves and Scots names still persist among the coloured people there.

1659   On 16th February a great storm battered the harbour at Aberdeen, sweeping away the "bulwark" which protected the port. Sand now threatened to block the harbour and the city appealed for help to rebuild the bulwark. Forres responded by sending £50, with a promise of a similar sum in August if it could be raised. This was a considerable sum for the times.

1660   About this time there are references to tea, coffee and chocolate as well as asparagus, artichokes and cauliflowers. These may have been brought back by the exiles, many of whom had travelled much in Europe.

With the return of the king new taxes were required, and to forward this a new method was introduced. Commissioners of Supply were appointed to fix valuations and collect the taxes. Each burgh was given an amount to raise, and this was the basis on which royal burghs were organised from this time until county councils were set up in 1889.

There was no form of government outside the royal burghs, and the collection of taxes there was done by the presbyteries until this new system was started.

1661, 1663   Statutes were passed allowing manufacturers to seize idle vagrants and put them to forced labour, and collect payments from the parish of origin of those seized. Since 1535 the parish was responsible for any pauper, and strange paupers were expelled from burghs with orders to return to their native parishes which, of course, were unwilling to receive them.

1661   When Cromwell had united the Scots and English Parliaments he had ordered that all the Scottish state papers be packed in barrels and sent to London where they were stored in the Tower of London. Now after the Restoration they were returned to Edinburgh for the use of the revived Scots Parliament. A frigate had loaded many of the barrels but storms forced it to return and transfer 80 barrels to a Burntisland sloop. This ship was sunk at sea and the papers were lost. No inventory had been taken, but it was presumed that amongst them were many of the early papers dealing with the first burghs, as no record of these exist. Hence the paucity of information about the twelfth and thirteenth centuries.

1663   THE WITCHES:
In 1661 after the Restoration the church was greatly concerned at the prevalence of witchcraft in the country. The restraints put on the prosecution of witches by Cromwell being removed, a Commission composed of 21 ministers, 9 lawyers and 3 physicians was set up in Edinburgh by the General Assembly of the Church of Scotland. One of the leading lawyers of the time was Alexander Brodie who, as a member of the College of Justice, had the title of Lord. He had been a leading figure among the Covenanters and had been one of the party sent to Holland to arrange the return of King Charles II, landing with him in Garmouth.

The Committee set to work by first employing professional witch-finders, the chief of whom was Mr John Colville who had been trained by the infamous Mathew Hopkins, Chief Finder in England, who later was almost himself put to death as a witch.

The Reverend Murdo Mackenzie had been made Bishop of Moray, these titles having been introduced into the system, and he took up residence in Elgin. He and Lord Brodie feared and hated witches and were implacable in their efforts to find them. Brodie was an inveterate diarist, confiding his fears and doubts each night to paper, and it is to this trait that we owe our knowledge of the subject that was so embarrassing that little is to be found recorded. Colville visited Brodie at Brodie Castle to confer with him and explain the infallible methods used in finding witches; these are so distasteful that they are not recorded here.

The Kirk Session sent a report to the Commission in Edinburgh of the presence of two witches in Forres and asking for a licence to proceed against them; this was granted. There is no record of what the witches were charged with, of how they answered, how long they were imprisoned, questioned and tortured. Torture was regarded as essential to discover the truth and those who confessed without torture had still to go through the ordeal to make sure that they had told the truth. Finally, they were put on trial before a special court of country gentlemen and ministers. We know that the lairds of Grange of Kinloss, Muirton of Kinloss, Park in Nairn, Lord Brodie, a Minister and the witchfinder Colville—who also acted as Depute Justice—formed the Court. The Minister would have been either Mr Fullerton of Forres, William Urquhart of Rafford or perhaps, although unlikely, Mr Colin Falconer.

The first test would have been the water trial. For this the victim was "crossbound," the thumbs being tied to the opposite big toes, and then placed in water, preferably still water. Sometimes a blanket was placed below them. If they sank they were innocent and if they floated they were guilty. This test dated back to the laws of Babylon which were taken over by the Old Testament and were therefore of ancient belief. Unfortunately, the innocent were often drowned as few would hurriedly rescue them, in case this was a ploy by Satan to get the goodhearted person in his grasp.

The small ponds made for soaking or "retting" flax were the convenient sites for these tests, and the records of the Baron Courts of Stitchill of 1661 report that in the month of August there had been 120 burnings of witches, and that the ponds were full of drowned bodies. These figures would refer to Scotland only.

At the first trial the Laird of Muirton refused to take part and left the Court. Brodie wrote in his diary that night, "The witches became obdurate and now denied the charges." The Court met within a few days, with all the judges present, but the diary says "Muirton became so scrupulous and would not vote." The third and final trial was on 1st May. Lord Brodie said that all the witnesses agreed clearly but Satan had hardened the hearts of the witches and made them deny the charges. The Laird of Grange agreed to sit as a judge but opposed the verdict.

Both Grange and Muirton showed great courage, for it was no small thing to favour the witches, and laid themselves open to accusations of being accomplices. Churches do not put people to death, but the sentence was automatic after being found guilty and the civil authorities had to carry out the sentence. The two bailies of Forres who had to carry out this duty were most unwilling to do so; as Brodie said, "They were so irritate that there was no peace." But the judges were inexorable; refusal to carry out their decision would bring them within the ambit of accusation.

The bailies would know the two victims, Isobel Elder and Isobel Dempster, residents in the town; poor, ignorant and superstitious, which was enough to condemn them in some eyes but not in all. In addition to this, an execution was an expensive affair and the year's income from the 130 or so Burgh and Outlandish Burgesses came to a meagre £240 Scots.

There are few accounts available but a burning at Lauder in 1649 cost £92 14s 0d Scots, from which was deducted £27 which belonged to the poor victim and which was used to meet part of her execution costs. At the burning of Janet Wishart and Isobel Crocker in Aberdeen in 1596, the requirements included 20 loads of peat, 1 bushel of coal, 4 tar barrels, fir barrels, stake and dressing, 4 fathoms of rope plus the cost of carriage to the hill.

The site of the hangman's gibbet at Forres was on the right hand side of the road going to Elgin near the town and the execution would be there. Lord Brodie wrote that "Park rode with me to Brodie, but no importunity would make him stay the night." Probably he had had enough of the Lord for one day. Lord Brodie showed a ghoulish interest in the witches and earlier had gone to Auldearn to interview the witch Brandon before her execution. He tells how he prayed to have some pity for her but could not do so. Auldearn had, in the year before, seen the trial of the famous Isobel Goudie and twelve other women and three men. They had been accused by the minister of Auldearn, the Reverend Harry Forbes, of such things as tipping him out of his bed at night. All were found guilty; it was never said that they were put to death, but this was unnecessary as it was the inevitable outcome.

The secret and unconscious conspiracy to avoid all mention of such trials in church circles is shown by the remarks of the Reverend Lachlan Shaw who wrote *The History of Moray*. He was alive when the last trials took place and would have read the

79

records of the kirk sessions, yet all he remarks about this time is that to be old, ignorant and poor, was unfortunate for women. No serious work has been written about the subject in Scotland, and no figure can be given of the number put to death. It may be apposite, therefore, to say something more.

The best figures are given by Charles Frazer Black of New York City Library, who spent his life studying old Scottish records. He gives 1800 accusations and 4400 deaths; an accusation often included more than one person. The authorities believed that the witches gathered in covens of 13, and as they were tortured until satisfactory answers were received, their suspicions were soon proved to their satisfaction.

The only Act in Scotland was in 1563, instigated by the Calvinists, including John Knox, and it was repealed in 1736. The last trial was in Dornoch in 1727, and the horror of that one must have convinced many that the time was due for an end to such scenes. The accused was a Jenny Horne and her daughter. The daughter had deformed feet and hands and this is said to have been caused by the mother turning her into a pony which she used to ride to the Witches' Sabbath. Both, of course, confessed and had been sentenced by a hereditary sheriff named Ross. He had been accused of being too lenient with such people, so decided to make an example of these two.

Jenny was asked to repeat the Lord's Prayer and in her stress said "Our Father which *wert* in Heaven," and this was taken as proof of her guilt. It was very cold on the day of the execution and she sat round a fire waiting while the pyre was built. She remarked that so many friends around such a good fire made it the most cheerful sight for many a day. There is some uncertainty as to whether the daughter was also put to death, and the names are in doubt, two others being used, but it is a Scots custom to be careless of names, married women using their maiden names all their lives and if married more than once or brought up by a relative with a different name, can be referred to by any of them.

The Act was repealed in 1736, not without objections from lawyers and others. Twenty years later John Wesley was vehemently opposed to repeal in England when it was suggested, saying "to give up witchcraft is to give up the Bible." The Act was not repealed then but only a few years ago. It also dealt with

80

charming, fortune telling and other branches of arts and craft, and the police were made to look foolish by being forced to deal with such cases.

In Scotland, and probably elsewhere, witchcraft had psychological and social implications, and was not wholly religious. It supplied a need, for at the Reformation Calvinism was introduced and it did not recognise imps, devils, demons, succubi or incubi or evil spirits. There was simply Satan, too intellectual a concept for the people. In the Catholic Church immediate protection was found against charms, spells and the evil eye, with a small sum to the priest. He was equipped with book, bell, candle and holy water, sacred bones and relics, and special texts for the driving away and counter-manding of all such dangers. Now they were unprotected and turned to anyone who claimed to be able to deal with them. In one case in Elgin, the charm used was *in nomine Patris, Filius et Spiritus Sanctus*—"in the name of the Father, the Son and the Holy Ghost," a slightly incorrect memory of what his father had heard in his youth from the Catholic priest. To the Protestants this sounded like the language of the Devil.

This period in Scotland, whilst no more and perhaps less bloody and awful than elsewhere, had a greater impact than in countries where witchcraft had been an offence and heresy for many centuries. The old women in a country where the Pictish religion was animist, would have a good knowledge of herbs and gave a kind of medical service; but what a recipe could do was uncertain and some of the old words given by Pictish or other priests would be used to bring out the full virtue. But Christianity, with the Bible's injunction that no witch be allowed to live, put an end to this. The witch cult in Scotland was derived from heathen practices and was an alternative to the incomprehensible metaphysics of the highly educated Scottish clergy. Dr Alexander Comfort in *Nature and Human Nature* says, "In primitive societies it was the equiva-lent to the theatre, the novel, the Sunday paper and TV as well as the Saturday night booze."

To us who live in a scientific age, where ideas are verifiable and capable of being applied to problems, it is difficult to imagine the earlier times when authority, tradition, magic and guesswork pre-vailed. Darwin showed our relationship with animals. Freud showed us that we have insight into our own motives and mental processes. Everyone has a desire to master nature and blend it in to a better shape. Every race has its dream time, *Tir nan Og,* the lost Atlantis, the Golden Age of Greece, and the Hyperboreans.

To conclude, medicine explains with "meteorism" how bodies can float in times of stress so that the innocent were more likely to do so and be found guilty than the actual self-deluded witch.

The Provost of that time was Francis Forbes of Thornhill but he may have made himself diplomatically absent at the time of the trial and executions. Who the bailies were is unknown, as five councillors held that office spread over the years 1661-1664.

Murdoch Mackenzie, the Bishop of Moray who so zealously prosecuted so many witches, had been a chaplain in the Swedish army of Gustavus Adolphus, King of Sweden. He was so bigoted that he would allow no celebration to be held at Christmas or other religious festivals. On Christmas Day 1658 he visited many houses in Elgin to see if any had dared to have a Christmas goose.

1672   An Act of this year laid the foundations of Poor Law in Scotland, saying a rate could be levied, half on heritors and half on occupiers, which could be added to the parish church funds for distribution to the poor.

1679   The *Crann Taire,* the dreaded Fiery Cross, appeared in the streets for the last time, on its way from Nairn to Elgin giving the alarm that the Macdonalds were coming. The country gentlemen with their retainers mustered at Auldearn, but dispersed after finding that it was a false alarm. The purpose was to get them to rally to the defence of their homes, and thus keep them from going to reinforce the king's host. That army fought later at Bothwell Bridge. The Laird of Culbin had hurriedly hidden all his papers in a wall around his home in case they were burned as had been those of Brodie Castle in 1645.

1680   An elephant was shown in Scotland for the first time. It had been brought to England at a cost of £2000 sterling, and was hired by an Alexander Deas and others for show in Scotland. They refused to pay the hire of £400 as the elephant did not drink every time it was offered water. It was much written about at the time.

1681   Six women were hanged in one day in Edinburgh. Two of them belonged to the Cameronian religious sect, and four unmarried girls were hanged for infanticide. Within a couple of months another unmarried mother was hanged for the same offence. She declared that she had done this deed in order "to shun the indignity of the church pillory." The King's brother, the Duke of York, said he knew of no other Christian country which "rather made scandals than buried them." The ruling classes approved of the law, using the text, "They who sin openly should be rebuked openly."

Bo'ness was affected by a religious mania, not uncommon in that time. They denied all institutions, even the days of the week. They protested against taxes, confessions, covenants, the king and his government and the necessity to have to work for one's bread. Wives left their husbands, and if the men in pursuit touched their dresses, they indignantly washed the piece touched to remove an impurity. Finally 26 women with their children left their homes to live in the fields, led by a gigantic man, Muckle John Gibb, known as King Solomon. Such behaviour was widespread but the non-availability of the kirk records prevents us from knowing what was happening in Forres and other places.

The smoked fish from Findhorn again made news. A weekly post had been started between Edinburgh and Inverness via Aberdeen, but the people thought the postal charges excessively dear. A letter from Edinburgh cost four shillings Scots for each sheet, the envelope counting as one sheet. A son going south for some reason would arrange with his parents that on his arrival he would send an envelope with no message if all was well, and as the postage had to be paid by the addressee, he or she would examine the envelope and seeing no letter would refuse to pay and hand it back to the carrier.

At this time the letter carriers were accused of carrying parcels or packages in which letters were concealed. The charge said that letters were being hidden in clothes and stockings and on more than one occasion had been placed in parcels of "Finnan" haddies. Forres would by this time have a Post Office.

1691   For many years the country had been growing ever more poor and the Convention of Royal Burghs issued a report on the state of the burghs. Some, like Dingwall, were bankrupt, and all but two of the burghs reported dire poverty. The exceptions were Forres and Arbroath.

1696   Some merchants in Forres and Banff were charged with defrauding the Post Office by making up parcels of letters and delivering them to the towns and villages when delivering their commodities and goods by their wagons and pack horses.

1696 - 1703   These seven years were known as "King William's Hard Years." For seven years the harvests had failed because of cold wet summers and little sun. The whole of the country was in a parlous strait and eagerly turned to the plan of William Paterson, the founder of the Bank of France and the Bank of England. This man of genius put forward the plan for a Scots colony on the Isthmus of Panama. Scotland was not allowed to trade with the English colonies in America, the West Indies and elsewhere, and they had to pay taxes on their goods entering England.

The project was sound and if the matter had been left to Paterson could have been successsful to a certain extent, but because of the rivalry, jealousy and corruption so common in the country he was quite divested of any influence or control and sailed with the expedition as an ordinary member.

The site chosen in Darien was a sodden jungle and fever ridden, and this in combination with the hostility of the natives and the blockade of the Royal Navy soon brought the expedition to disaster and death by disease and starvation. The goods sent were unsuitable for sale, including tweeds, knitted woollens and feathered hats. The natives were in any case few, with little to trade with. Two ships had set out at first with 1200 people, and as the survivors of these were ready to sail home another five ships arrived, loaded with similar cargo.

This only added to the troubles, factions being formed which fought each other. Hundreds died and in despair the colony was abandoned, some making for home and others trying to get to America or Canada. One ship only came back to tell the story of the tragedy. Some were lost and others were wrecked. Many became slaves in the West Indies and a few settled for good in the American colonies.

Many burghs as well as lairds and others who could scrape together some money had invested in the company and every penny was lost. Some burghs had pledged all of their Common Good to make an investment. Sir Edward Kinnaird of Culbin, whose estate was completely covered in sand by 1698, had borrowed money from friends and had gone with the ships. He had died in Darien and his son reached America never to return to Culbin. For many years the widow petitioned the king for help, as she was unable to pay the taxes demanded. No help was given and she lived on the charity of relatives.

1696   Gaelic was now beginning to die out, and it was reported
this year that Callander had not had a minister for 20 years, as a
Gaelic speaker was required and none had heard the call.

Duncan Forbes, Laird of Culloden, received as compensation for
the damage he had suffered from the rebels the privilege of distilling
whisky at Ferintosh free of excise duty.

1697   Christian Shaw, the teenage daughter of the laird of Balgaran
in Renfrewshire, claimed that she had been bewitched, and after
a trial five unhappy women were sentenced to be burned. A man
also accused had strangled himself while in prison waiting trial.
This was not a simple-minded or deluded girl, for she later married
the minister of Kilmaurs, proved to be an astute business woman
who made linen thread, and after a visit to Holland made the first
cotton thread in Scotland. She built up a large and prosperous
business in "Lady Balgaran's Threed," the start of the Scottish
thread and cotton industry.

1700   Because of its cheapness whisky was now displacing ale as the
drink of the country. A quart of whisky cost tenpence.

The notorious James Macpherson, hanged later this year in Banff,
terrorised Forres on market days and also Elgin and Banff. He
was accompanied by a band of 30 ruffians, mounted and armed as
well as himself. The two constables of the burgh could do nothing
but hide until he had left the town. So dangerous was this job
that each six months two burgesses were conscripted for the duty.

1701   The River Findhorn made another change of course, turning
east to drown the village of Findhorn, the site of which is covered
by the sea a mile north-west of the bar at the mouth of the bay. For
some time it had flowed into the sea near Auldearn. So great was
the change in the river that fifty years later the owners of the
salmon fishings were pleading for relief as the nets did not provide
any revenue. Only the netting of salmon at Findhorn could have
been affected because the Town Council in 1704 were getting a good
revenue for the fishing in the river. The fishings were let in periods
of 16 days, and the lairds of Burrisyards had one day, while
Grangehall, Tannachie and Durn each had two days. The cost for
one day was £8 per annum.

1704   From 1603, when the king left Scotland, the Scots Parliament
had been run by a small committee—The Lords of the Articles—
which until 1690 was under the control of the king in London.

Queen Anne was more pliant and this year the Scots passed an Act of Security, so that, on the death of Anne, the crown of Scotland would not pass to the Hanoverian prince George, later George I, as had been arranged by the London Parliament.

1705   In retaliation the English Parliament passed an Aliens Act. This said that if the Scots did not accept George, all Scots would be treated as foreigners and would thus be debarred from trade with the English colonies, and would be greatly restricted in other ways. The Scots had wanted a federal state but consideration or discussion of this was refused.

The Customs for the year 1705 brought in £30,000 and Excise only £33,800. The total revenue was £160,000 against the 5½ million pounds in England. Some of the successful Scots merchants and bankers in England or the West Indies had fortunes larger than the total revenue of their native country.

1707   Scotland was prostrate and in 1707 voted for union by 110 votes to 69.

Because of some unspecified trouble in the Town Council, the membership was reduced to 15, and remained at this figure for two or three years.

The first Turnpike Act provided that companies should be formed locally to build suitable roads for the increasing traffic and trade. The name came from the halberd or pike which was hinged on a post to swing across the road as a barrier. In all 350 different Acts were passed between this date and 1844. Before this time roads in the burghs had to be maintained by the occupiers of houses, who had to provide the labour. In the countryside, tenant farmers and cottars whose grounds touched the road had to put in so many days of "statute labour" between seedtime and harvest, but for the rest of the year the roads received no attention. This work was supervised by the Justices of the Peace.

The letter rate was now twopence for the first 50 miles, and fourpence for more than 80 miles. The post runners between Inverness and Aberdeen were paid £30 a year.

This year marked the Union of the Parliaments of Scotland and England, and the end of the country as an independent state. All Scots coin was withdrawn to be replaced by British money. The amount to be exchanged was £600,000 sterling. Coin had always been scarce and traders had often to make their own tokens and

86

scrip. In the north-east these tokens were often made of wood, being easily turned out by the many wood turners. Values of coin were as low as one-thirtieth of the English penny.

The merchant fleet had 93 ships with a gross tonnage of 6000 tons. The largest vessel was only 160 tons burthen, and had been built abroad because of the scarcity of suitable timber.

1708   The first Member of Parliament was elected to the new united Parliament in London. He was elected by the Provosts of Forres, Nairn, Inverness and Fortrose. This panel was supposed to ask the advice of their councils, but many never visited the towns where they were nominally provost. Earl Findlater, for example, was provost of four burghs. The aim was to elect a son or a friend, as membership of the House of Commons was the quickest and easiest way to honours and wealth. No great change seems to have taken place in the intervening centuries. The Forres member was Robert Urquhart whose father, a minister, was the Laird of Sanquhar, or Burdsyards as it was called. He was a solicitor and fought as a captain in Lord Orrery's Regiment at the Battle of Sheriffmuir on the Government's side. He "was wounded in the belly so that his puddings hung out." He recovered and was made a Sheriff in 1724. Later this family fell on hard times and his grandson and namesake is said to have begged at the door of his former home.

1709   An Alexander Nicholson of Dyke took in boarders, young women for his school. A receipt exists for a quarter's fees and board for two daughters of the Laird of Balmachedie, Alexander Dunbar. The amount was £4 Scots. The Scots £ was worth one-twelfth of the £ sterling at that time.

1711   A postal service was started between Edinburgh and Fort George via Dunkeld for military purposes, but civilians could use the service. After the failure of the 1715 Rebellion it was thought that quick communication with the military in the north was no longer required and the service was withdrawn in 1718 amidst public protest. The whole country now had a postal service with a Scottish Postmaster General in Edinburgh. Post carriers got threepence a mile, with four shillings and eightpence a year for shoes. They had various other perquisites but could be fined for late arrival.

1713   For a number of years prior to this date the town council had accused the Laird of Blervie of encroaching on the town's lands on

Califer and annually, when riding the Marches in June, had paused to graze their horses on the growing corn, while the riders pulled off the turves which formed the roofs of the buildings.

Tiring of this harassment the laird took the council to court in Edinburgh, and was awarded damages. These with the costs could not be met by the meagre income of the burgh and it had perforce to sell the estate of Coxton to meet the bill.

There is no explanation as to how this pleasant little estate near Lhanbryde fell into the town's possession. One possibility is that it had been a security for a loan which had never been redeemed.

1720   Provost Dawson had a considerable overseas trade, and one of his ships bringing a cargo to Findhorn went aground near Lossiemouth. The Brodie of Brodie had some property at Kineddar and the provost rented one of the buildings and hurriedly transferred the cargo there. He apparently tried to outwit the Customs men and a special messenger was sent from Edinburgh by the Chief of Excise warning him that he must hand over the cargo to the Customs. The provost seems to have fled the country, for he was ejected from the council for too long an absence. This was the only time this happened.

1724   Potatoes were now introduced to Moray but it took another 30 years before they were grown generally, and another ten years before they were accepted in the Highlands.

1727   A Board for Manufactories was set up to encourage industries. The Sunday Communion Service could still last for 12 hours, starting at 9 a.m. Because of the large number of communicants, many were served outdoors in the kirkyard as the church could not accommodate them. The bailies, accompanied by elders, still "perlustrated" the town to make certain that all who were fit went to church. Offenders were taken to court through the week where the same bailies sat on the bench in judgment.

1727 - 1729   General Wade made the road from Dunkeld to Inverness, 102½ miles in all. A revenue officer, Burt, who accompanied him, reports with malicious glee the naïve astonishment of the natives on beholding their first coach, the first wheeled vehicles they had seen.

1730   The forests in the north and west had now almost been consumed. Only the forest of Rothiemurchus and a few other smaller woods equally remote were left. The timber had been used to make charcoal for the smelting of iron. In this year a furnace was still working in Nethybridge, as it was cheaper and easier to carry the iron ore from the Lech to the furnace than to carry the charcoal and timber to the mines. The finest trees had been floated down the Spey to Garmouth, where it was used in shipbuilding.

1736   The Scots law against witchcraft was repealed.

The General Assembly of the Church of Scotland ordained "if heritors do not present a minister for a vacancy the elders could 'give the call' subject to the approval of the congregation."

Forres is noted as one of the few towns to have a sewing school for girls. These had a right to attend the parish school but parents preferred to keep them at home to help with the housework. The more affluent engaged tutors who visited the homes.

1740   The Forres Guildry Society was started. This was an association of merchants and others, maintaining a pension and sick fund, each merchant paying a considerable sum on entry, which was invested. In the late nineteenth century, only one member was alive, Thomas Kerr, a draper who owned a considerable amount of property and lived at 14 North Street. He gave the funds of the Guildry on loan to the town council on condition that they gave him a pension for life. This loan still appears in the town's accounts, although it cannot be repaid to anyone.

Among the medicines still being prescribed by physicians were the following: toads, eaten as a remedy against dropsy and epilepsy, and rubbed on the skin for the cure of carbuncles. The woodlice known as slaters were used in the treatment of colic, convulsions, cancer, headaches and epilepsy. For dysentery, ague and smallpox, vipers were prescribed, presumably dead, although they would not be easily available. The excreta of dogs, cattle, sheep and pigs was made into a decoction for various ailments.

1741   The houses in the towns and villages were still mostly built with wooden fronts and thatched roofs. A conflagration in Aberdeen swept through very many houses, and it was decided that all houses should in future be of stone. Sandstone and granite quarries were opened in Aberdeen and Caithness, but the local masons used the whinstone from the town's quarries at New Forres. This is a very hard stone, and the Forres masons became well known for the high quality of their work. Forres firms built many fine buildings

89

in the north, the best example still in use being the Dornoch Hotel, the pride of the old Highland Railway.

1745   When Prince Charles Edward was in Inverness he was given the only room in the town which did not have a bed.

1749   The estate of Grangehill of Moy was bought by Sir Arthur Grant of Freuchie, who changed the name of the property to Dalvey, the place where he had been born in Speyside. Freuchie was the village at the walls of Castle Grant, and which later was moved a mile or so south to moorland, to become the burgh of Grantown-on-Spey.

1750   The 1745 Rising, like all wars, had brought many changes in its wake. Perlustrating ceased in the town, and the use of the stool of repentance for moral offenders was decreasing. So dreadful was the ordeal of sitting in sackcloth through long services and sermons of reproach that many girls strangled their illegitimate babies at birth. They were then tried for infanticide and it was common for as many as five to be hanged at one time after trial in Edinburgh and elsewhere, where the High Court sat. The men were able to get away, although Robert Burns sat beside Jean Paton through the ordeal.

An Act of Parliament allowed linen to be woven anywhere in Scotland without payment or let or hindrance. This broke the monopoly of the royal burghs, who previously held the privileges of spinning and weaving flax. The craft survived for a long time; the widow of the last weaver in Forres lived in the row of cottages known as "Wabster Raw" behind where the Masonic Temple now stands. She died in 1912.

1755   The population of Scotland was estimated to be 1¼ million, of which Aberdeen held 15,433.

1760   Farmers were adopting modern methods, and some ploughmen were brought from Dorset to the north to teach farmworkers. Within 40 years the Scots had so surpassed their teachers that they were tempted to England at good wages to be farm managers and gardeners.

1763   A thrice-weekly postal service was started between Aberdeen and Inverness.

1769   The Hereditary Jurisdictions Act became law. This abolished the judgeships and sheriffdoms held by peers and landowners, and which they passed to their heirs or sold. The powers given to them were often abused, and could no longer be tolerated after the 1745 Rising. The holders demanded an enormous sum in compensation for the loss of this income but this was greatly reduced. The Duke of Gordon got £4982 19s 6d for the loss of various regalities and baileries, £18 19s 6d being for the loss of the bailieship of Kinloss. The Earl of Moray, who held the sheriffdom of Moray, claimed £8000 and received £3000. The Laird of Grangehill (Dalvey) demanded £500 for the regality of that estate but received nothing.

This was the first time that many landowners had obtained such sums of money. Cameron of Lochiel in 1745 had been able to call out 500 men for Prince Charles's army but could not raise £50 in cash to buy food or supplies. The money was spent in various ways, many building mansions to replace the two- or three-roomed houses they occupied. Few buildings of any merit existed in the countryside prior to this disbursal. The Earl of Moray, already adequately housed, invested his awards in extending Darnaway forest, planting in the next few years over 12 million oak, larch, beech and other trees.

1773   Dr Samuel Johnson and James Boswell stayed overnight in the town in "an admirable house kept by Lawson, wine cooper from London." This place has not been traced. The principal inn, the Crown, was owned by a man named Brodie. The main stage inn, now the Queen's Hotel, was not built until 50 years later.

They arrived from Elgin in the evening of 27th August and at Drumduan, James Boswell, always attracted by the morbid, glimpsed the gallows there, and hastily jumping out of the chaise ran back and was shocked to see a body still suspended from the gibbet. It was that of a Kenneth Leal who had robbed a stagecoach, and had been left hanging there for six months as a warning to others.

Boswell returned to the coach and sat in silence. Johnson in the dusk could not see his face and diverted himself by talking about witches dancing at the foot of Boswell's bed at night. Boswell was relieved to find that his bedroom opened off that of Johnson. They went on to Cawdor next day, pausing at Macbeth's hillock where Johnson recited several times, "How far is't called to Forres."

1775   The shock effects of the great Lisbon earthquake were felt thousands of miles away. A flock of sheep grazing in a field near Dyke were drowned by an enormous tidal wave which swept inland.

1776   The run-rigg system was abandoned in the burgh and the lands were being formed into larger units, some as large as 150 acres and leased for longer than the former one year term.

1780   Post runners now went to Grantown three times a week and were paid 2s 2d for each journey, plus £2 a year for office duties, the total for the year being £16 8s 0d. They would have travelled by Dunphail.

In Nairnshire farm carts were being made and sold for six shillings and eight pence. They were made wholly of birch, no iron being used, and would appear to have been little more than sleds. In 1743 a farmer bought two for seven shillings, but in 1810 carts cost £10 but had wheels with iron tyres.

1782   A calamitous harvest brought famine, especially severe in the north of the country. January had three floods in ten days, and there was continuous frost for eight weeks after 1st February, with a great fall of snow in March. It lay two and three feet deep for a fortnight. Nothing could be sown until May but little growth followed. Ten days of hot weather in July was followed by six weeks of rain and cold stormy winds. A hurricane in August broke much of the stalks of corn, and on the 17th September the hills were covered with snow. Another heavy snowfall happened in the last day of October, while the stooks still stood in the fields, and this was followed by ten days of hard frost.

Sir John Sinclair of Ulbster, the originator of the *First Statistical Account of Scotland,* obtained a grant of £15,000 from Parliament, of which he was a member, towards the relief of the famine. Hundreds of families emigrated to Canada and the newly formed United States of America. Whole parishes and estates went as a body. Sir John was active in introducing new methods in agriculture, including turnips and artificial grasses.

The years 1740, 1778, 1796 and 1799-1800 were also years of great distress and want, approaching famine conditions.

1784   "Forbes' famous boast," as it was called by Burns, now ended. The family received the sum of £21,580 in compensation for giving up the right to make and sell whisky without tax. This was an enormous sum at that time.

1789   Sir William Gordon Cumming found Altyre House too small for his 16 children and bought Forres House from the Tullochs of Tannachy

92

1792   Parliament passed an "Act for the Protection of Rabbits."
Rabbits, which were a late arrival in Scotland, were being reduced
in numbers by foxes and other vermin, and probably by the
poaching of the hungry and poor residents. The government were
concerned at the possible disappearance of this cheap and
nourishing food. As there was no law against catching them, this
first control was introduced.

1793   A French refugee from the Revolution, the Marquis de
Bailleu, came to live in the burgh. He spent much of his time
with the local gentry in sport and hunting. He later returned to
France and was reinstated in his estates.

1797   The town had now 2987 inhabitants, an increase of 992 since
1755, while Elgin had increased from 4554 to 6306. This was the
result of the 1745 Rising breaking up the clan system, so that the
clan chiefs claimed all the land which previously belonged to the
clan. The new owners brought in sheep, and to do so had to drive
out the people. This move into the towns continued until in 1972
more than 80 per cent of the people in Scotland lived in burghs,
and many of the others lived just on the outskirts.

1798   Mail coaches now ran at an average of 10 miles an hour
between Aberdeen and Inverness, despite having to ford several
rivers, or be ferried across.

1800   A census of agriculture gave Morayshire 16,900 cattle and
58,200 sheep. A ploughman could get £12 for a half year, and a
labourer two shillings and sixpence a day.

1802   The wars with the French needed more men and few volunteers came forward. The Militia Act was passed to raise men. The
Deputy Lord Lieutenants for Forres, Rafford, Dyke, Edinkillie and
Kinloss were responsible for drawing names from the lists of able-
bodied men in each parish, the lists being made up by the parish
schoolmaster. The men had to attend each August at the Court-
house in Forres, when names were drawn. If selected, a man could
either enrol in the militia or obtain a substitute. Failing either, he
was taken before the Deputies and fined, and another name drawn.
This Act continued until 1852.

1805   A new Act required owners of adjoining land worth £100
Scots to make and maintain turnpike roads. The road from
Nairn to the Spey was to be 30 feet wide, a figure decided several

centuries earlier, but often ignored. The tolls for the full distance were 1s 6d for a two-horse carriage, fourpence for a horse and cart, and twopence for a horse and rider. There were tolls at Forres Toll at Drumduan, Gateside of Alves and Newton Toll. Liquor was sold at most toll houses.

1809   Thomas Telford built the first bridge across the Findhorn at Mundole. The Moray Floods of 1829 swept it away, and the ford had again to be used.

1816   During the year, 65 foxes were shot near the town, as well as large numbers of polecats, wild cats and weasels.

1820   A year at Edinburgh University cost £30, a large sum for a weaver or farmer earning only £15 a year. Aberdeen University was somewhat cheaper.

1821   Following the campaign against foxes and other vermin, rabbits multiplied alarmingly and hundreds of pounds of damage was done to the plantations of young oaks. These were being planted everywhere at the insistence of the Admiralty who were concerned at the shortage of suitable timber for the naval war-ships.

1832   A fine suspension bridge was erected at Mundole. The cost of £30,000 was raised locally and pontage fees were collected from all users until the debt was cleared in 1881.

The Reform Act came into effect. During the debates in Parliament a law lord had said, "The Scottish burghal system was the longest lived and the most successful political and economic system ever invented, having existed for seven centuries." From 1150 Forres had been governed by this system which continued in a modified form until 1975. Of the 66 royal burghs formed, Forres was one of the most successful in retaining land and forests given at its founding.

By this Act the few remaining privileges of the royal burghs were removed. They had been so corrupted during the previous centuries that they were not allowed to take on the new duties laid on town councils by the various Health Acts which followed the reforms. It was feared that bribery and corruption would continue until a new generation had grown up. In place of councillors, Commissioners of Supply, Roads and Police had to be elected by the direct vote of householders. It had been hoped that new people would come forward, but in small towns like Forres there were too few men willing to give the time and work needed, so that the offices were filled by the men who were to have been displaced.

Forres Town Council continued also but had few responsibilities apart from the school, the cemetery and the Common Good. In the course of time the Commissioners disappeared and the Council took full charge until the Act of 1929 took away many duties such as education, police and public health, as well as the control of weights and measures.

Inverness, Fortrose, Nairn and Forres shared an M.P. There were now 60,000 parliamentary voters in Scotland, with 72 Members of Parliament.

Prior to this there had been only 500 voters. One-third of the councillors had to retire each year, so that it was possible to change the complexion of the council in a year and a day. This was a most democratic system, responsive to the wishes of the electorate. Other advances in legislation were made at this time, among them the restriction on the working hours of children, and inspectors were employed to enforce this legislation, which was more advanced than that in England.

1833   The Police Act laid down rules for the behaviour and acts of policemen.

1837   The *Forres Gazette* started as a monthly paper; in 1851 it was issued fortnightly and in 1855 became a weekly. Since that time the happenings in the burgh have been most minutely recorded. Forres was fortunate in having a newspaper of its own. For a good number of years it had two, the other being the *Forres News* which was issued gratis.

1843   The Disruption of the Church of Scotland ended the monopoly of teachers in Parish schools. Only members of this Church could be teachers, but now the Free Churches began to build their own schools.

1844   Alarm was felt at the plague of rabbits and Altyre Estate employed a skilled rabbit catcher from Norfolk. Between March and September he accounted for 7000 rabbits, providing a good supply of fresh meat at a time when famine threatened the north as well as Ireland.

Wood pigeons and starlings, both very rare in 1800, were now plentiful and the pheasant, unknown at that earlier date, was now being bred for the moors.

1845   The Forres Water Company was formed to supply piped water to houses.

Until now the Church of Scotland was responsible for the relief of the poor, but the Free Churches did not undertake this duty, so a Poor Law was passed, making the parish do so.

1846   The privileges of the trading and craft guilds were now completely abolished, and as a result the new developing industrial towns were able to import cheap Irish labour. This was the year of the Potato Famine, and emigrants flooded into England and Scotland, reducing wages everywhere. Many Scots emigrated in search of a better standard of living.

1853   The Forbes Mackenzie Act controlled the issue of liquor licences. All bars were now required to close on Sundays, but inns and hotels could serve alcoholic drinks to travellers any time after midnight on Saturday until midnight Sunday. This relaxation was for people who had to go at least three miles for a "bona fide" reason, such as visiting church or relatives or business. When the horse was the only means of locomotion generally, and when many people had to walk, three miles was a considerable distance. The invention of the motor vehicle made a farce of this law and it was eventually withdrawn.

The Town Clerk of Forres issued the last "peat ticket." This allowed a householder to cut his year's supply of peat from the town's bogs or peat mosses. Peat was the main fuel, and in some parts of Scotland the only fuel. Forres, like all or most old towns, had been built in the midst of peat. The names survive—Easter, Wester and Nether Bogton, the Roch or Rough Bog, and Bog Over.

By this time the peat had been used up, and the Laird of Altyre offered the peat rights in the Key Moss, stretching from Dallas Dhu to the Grantown road, in exchange for a piece of the King's Meadows to the north of the town. Within a short time the railway arrived, bringing cheap coal from the brigs carrying coal into the harbour at Inverness. Peat casting was one of the most exhausting tasks of the year, and soon the Key Moss was left untouched.

1854   This year brought the compulsory registration of births, marriages and deaths, and also the Valuation Act which established the rating system whereby owners of property were responsible for payment of rates to pay for local authority services.

HIGH STREET, FORRES, LOOKING EAST (c. 1900)

1857   Forres now had its own police force.

1860   The Findhorn Railway was opened, joining the Highland Railway at Kinloss. When the railway reached Forres in 1854 the traffic through Findhorn harbour had increased, and plans were made to extend the railway to Findhorn. But as the railways linked up with the south by way of Aberdeen and Perth, the regular steamer cargoes were reduced and the ships no longer called at Findhorn. The railway cost £3000 and was built by Messrs William Brand of Dundee. It was closed in 1868. A later "light railway" was planned 40 years later, but the plans did not materialise because of the advent of motor vehicles.

1867   A government enquiry found that one third of the children in the country evaded school, many because of poverty. A new Public Health Act came into operation allowing councils to "remove nuisances, erect hospitals, prevent disease, license lodging houses, form sewage and drainage districts and provide water supplies."

All male householders now had the vote, and the amount of money to be raised by a local authority for any of the new laws was limited.

1872   The new Education Act made school attendance compulsory for all children. The total cost for education in Scotland for this year was £359,717, of which the burghs had to pay £103,550.

In 1974/5 Forres alone had to pay £346,000 for education, more than one thousand times as much as in 1870.

Agriculture had been prosperous following the Crimean War but now began to decline. This was hastened by ten years of poor harvests between 1872 and 1882. Grain had to be brought in from abroad and soon Canada, U.S.A., and Australia were pouring in cheap grain from their new and fertile fields. This kept down the price of the home produced grain which otherwise would have risen in price. In 1857 Scotland had one million acres under wheat; in 1907 the figure was 81,000 and in 1928 this was still lower at 58,000 acres.

1885   At this time Forres, like other burghs, began to receive grants from the government. This money came from the new Goschen formula whereby the allocation for Scotland was based on eleven-eightieths of the sum spent in England and Wales.

97

1889   County Councils were established, Forres being included in
Elginshire. Until this time the rural areas were administered, if
that is the correct word, by justices of the peace and parish bodies.
The law of the lairds, however, most commonly prevailed.

Rates had to be paid partly by the owner and partly by the
occupier of properties. This continued until 1957 when the burden
became wholly that of the occupier.

1890   To meet the increasing costs of education it was decided that
the duties levied on wines, spirits and beers would be distributed
among local authorities, and two years later the distribution of
these grants started.

Dr Robert Douglas's ANNALS OF FORRES
*give a full account of local events and
Forres Burgh Council business during
the period from 1900 to 1933.*

Year 1934

One of the first matters before the Council was the re-turfing of the Grant Park Bowling Green, which had never been satisfactory. On lifting the turf, the contractor reported that only a thin layer of black soil had been spread on the sand base, so that the grass had sought upward nourishment from the fertiliser spread on the surface. New soil and turf were laid but the spring was a dry one and the green could not be opened at the usual date in May. The opening was continually postponed without any reason being given, and there was much criticism of the Council. A policy of secrecy had for long been maintained on all matters, so that councillors who were not members of particular committees had little knowledge of what was going on, and enquiries were usually rebuffed by the statement that it was a matter for the Committee only.

Rumours were rife, the most popular being that the Council had refused to pay the contractor until the green was restored, and he refused to do any more work until paid for what he had done.

The Town's Forester, however, was busy; he drained the football pitch for the Forres Mechanics, and also replanted New Forres. At a cost of £2 10s, an ointment, "Smearoleum," was spread on the young trees to repel rabbits, hares and other vermin. This recourse to science was not successful, and the ground had later to be closed in by wire netting fences. The trees on Alexandra Terrace had to be removed —against the protest of the residents—to allow the road to be tarred.

In March a special train ran to London for the England-Scotland football match. The fare was £1 14s 6d return, meals on the train costing 2s 6d. The train left Forres at 4.20 p.m. on the Friday, arriving Euston at 7.20 a.m., returning that night at 9.45 p.m.

This was a momentous year for cricket as, in September, the Australian Test team with Don Bradman were to play a Northern Select at Grant Park. The cost was borne by Sir Alexander Grant of Logie, himself a former Forres cricketer.

During that week, the town had 55 hours of sunshine, and three thousand attended the game on the first day, Friday, 14th September. Among the North team were Mr Jack Kemp and Lieutenant James Grant Peterkin of Grange, along with Neville Wigram, son of Sir Alexander's friend, later Lord Wigram, and a frequent visitor to Logie House and Forres.

On the Friday, the local team were nervous, scoring 48 against

99

the visitors' 106, of which Bradman scored 7. On Saturday Bradman was bowled by Jack Kemp and was out for 2. Jack himself reached 20 before being bowled in return by Bradman. James Grant Peterkin had 9 and Neville Wigram was 28 not out. The game ended early in the afternoon of Saturday as the Australians were leaving for various destinations, and many latecomers were disappointed to find the teams gone.

The Housing Committee, with more work than most, in its early report said that another 75 houses would be required in the next five years: 50 to replace unfit houses, 15 for overcrowded families and 10 for homeless families. This was not well received as houses were being completed at Roysvale Place at a cost of £420 without a Government subsidy, and they were difficult to let at rents of £25 for four-roomed houses. Two were let to bank tellers, one to a postmaster and one to a solicitor practising in Inverness. Arising from a complaint to the Secretary of State, the Scottish Office demanded an explanation as council houses were intended for those who were unable to provide their own housing, and insisted that the "means test" be applied to these tenants. They were permitted to remain at an increased rent of £30 plus occupiers' rates.

In Tulloch Park 12 houses had been built specially for "slum clearance" and these were let at rents of £10 8s per annum, which included occupier's rates.

At Fleurs Cottage 4 acres had been feued at £10 an acre from Mr Fraser, Knockomie, for council houses. This brought a petition from the residents of Thornhill against the proposal, and the arguments which developed in the Committee brought the resignation of the Convener, Mr Jack Robertson of Balnageith. Many of the Councillors were owners of property or had friends and relatives who owned property, and many members disliked being on this Committee, as there was much pressure from those in need. The Government rejected the proposal for the 75 houses in the next five years, as inadequate, and instructed that the programme be increased and hastened. The Council persisted in supporting the petitioners and this ground was later used for the fire station.

The Mechanics' Institute which housed the Library and Reading Room could no longer pay its bills, and asked the Town Council to take on this duty. As was the practice, a special committee was appointed which considered the matter at length before making a decision. Such committees, selected by the office-bearers, ensured that no one who was very enthusiastic for the subject to be investigated be appointed to the committee. Later in the year the committee reported that the Hall should be taken over, the Reading Room retained, but the Library closed. The loss of the Library was much felt, for although no new books had been bought for many years, books were donated at times, and it was also very cheap.

G. W. Anderson, Chemist and Bookseller, 64 High Street, had a good selection of quality fiction, but the reader of light and cheap fiction could only get this at Katy Munro's in Tolbooth Street. This had started as a sweet shop but soon all the space, including counter and floors, was required for the works of "Sapper," Annie S. Swan and others, as well as thrillers and westerns.

For those wanting the newly issued and well reviewed books, the usual course was to form a group of a dozen or fifteen, each paying a shilling or more per month. A book was decided upon, bought and circulated in the order written on the fly leaf, the last name retaining the book. In this way, such books as Robert Graves' *Goodbye to All That*, Eric Remarques' *All Quiet on the Western Front* and Siegfried Sassoon's *Memoirs of a Fox-Hunting Man* had large sales in remote areas like Forres.

The Provost, Charles Macdonald Fraser, solicitor, of "Woodlea," had held office for many years but he was now a sick man. He had lived most of his life in Forres and had served as a councillor and bailie before becoming Provost. He was a clever, just and charming man who would gladly have demitted office, but as the lifelong friend of the town's benefactor, Sir Alexander Grant of Logie, he was requested to continue. Mr Fraser was also a keen cricketer and encouraged Sir Alexander to donate a pitch in the Grant Park to the Saint Laurence cricket team. During his tenure of office from 1926 to 1940 he carried out his duties as Provost with dignity. He was relieved of the Provost's duty of attending all committee meetings and Bailie Michie Anderson undertook much of the Provost's work.

The Grampian Electricity Company was bringing a supply to the town, and had had discussions with a Lighting Committee about the route the cables would take. The High Street and some other streets were to have underground cables, but elsewhere the cables would be on creosoted wooden poles, which could be used as lamp standards as desired. Part of the underground work was to be in St Leonard's Road where a number of Councillors dwelt, and this inspired Mrs C. M. Edwards of Sanquhar to write one of her frequent letters to the

101

Gazette, asking why. The Provost, whose house, "Woodlea," was in that area, was upset at the imputation and called a special meeting of the Council to try to reverse the decision of the Lighting Committee; he had not been told or had not heard of the Committee's findings. Councillor Mackenzie had been the only member wanting all cables underground and he repeated this at the special meeting; but the Council were committed to the agreement, and any alteration would be at their cost; this they would not accept.

Agriculture was still very depressed and when, in the spring, the farmers put their usual requests for repairs to the town farms, they insisted that something should now be done. The Lands Committee offered them a 10 per cent abatement of their rents on condition that they did the repairs themselves. This they welcomed, for they had labour but little money. Naturally, they did the minimum of work, and in the course of years the condition of the farms got worse, so much so that when one fell vacant, the Council found that they had to abandon it as a farm, the steading being now unusable. This was false economy, as the repairs were a correct charge on the Common Good, which received all the rents. But the surpluses in the Common Good were used to keep down the rates fund, and the consequent shortage in the fund was used as an excuse for not doing necessary work on the lands and forests. Fortunately, later Councils, after the War did much remedial work, and when the Council decided to sell the farms and woodlands, they were in good condition.

Not only the Town's tenant farmers had a struggle; the local branch of the National Farmers' Union reported that it had 33 members paid up and 24 in arrears. As the prices of land were falling, they could not afford to give up farms as this could mean bankruptcy.

At this time, in East Anglia, Handon Great Lodge, with 500 acres, had been sold for £500, another of 150 acres for £1000 and a third of 560 acres for £3200, all with house and steadings in good condition.

It was in this year that the *Gazette,* in reporting a debate, remarked that, as usual, the Town Council was divided into two compartments, one containing Bailie Caldwell and Councillor John Mackenzie, and the other the rest of the Council. Councillor Mackenzie did not necessarily hold the same views as the Bailie but he could not bear to see a Councillor standing alone, and would say, "I second the speaker, but do not agree with him," and thus allow the subject to be discussed.

Another active and intelligent member was Dean of Guild Alec

Merchant, of the Bobbin Mills. He was probably the most progressive member in the Chamber, and put his views forward clearly and strongly, so that passions could arise. Much of this was in the Finance Committee, where any sum to be spent had to be agreed. Fortunately, the Treasurer, James B. Taylor of the Royal Bank, was by temperament ideally fitted to control and calm the members.

At the year's end, the Budget for the next financial year was agreed. It totalled £14,174, of which £3050 was met by Government Grants, and was further reduced by the £1300 not spent as planned during the current year. Running the Burgh cost £4748, but the major part had to go to the Joint County Council in Elgin. This amounted to £9426 (Education £272; Public Assistance £2929; Roads £1160; Lunacy £1044; Public Health £774; Police £568; Miscellaneous £225). Public Assistance took more than a third of the money raised, showing that the poorer an area was, the greater its financial burden.

Among the many other items of Council business during the year was the provision of another eight allotments for unemployed men, so that they could eke out their meagre allowances by growing food, the necessary seeds and tools being supplied; this was at Orchard Road.

The Small Debt Court was transferred to Elgin.

A suggestion from the Scottish National Development Association that the Burgh should buy ground for a civil airfield, was considered and rejected, but it was agreed that electricity be installed in the buildings in Grant Park, but not in the Police Station which, at that time, was in "Balaams Pass," now the Tolbooth Bow. The Shambles would also be supplied. A tenant in a house which stood on the line of the new Castlehill Road had to be evicted, as he refused to move to a new house.

A bequest from the late Mrs Younie was received and added to the charities already held. This new one was of £227 11s and the interest each year was to be spent on a supply of oatmeal, groceries and tobacco with one shilling in money, for suitable applicants.

The Cleansing Contractor, Mr William Hay, Firewood Merchant, withdrew from his contract, and it was given to Mr McLennan Ross at a cost of £803 17s for the year.

£1000 was borrowed to buy steel columns for the new electric lamps.

Work was to start on the wrought iron gates at Castlehill designed by Alastair Macdonald, architect son of Ramsay Macdonald, Labour Prime Minister. The gates were to cost £180, the wall £60 and the architect's fee was £37.

All available Common Good land inside the burgh was rented to Mr Donald Macrae, Pilmuir Farm, at £4 per acre.

With the installation of electricity came a welcome fall in the number of unemployed men in the town; forty were taken on by the contractors, reducing the number on the register to 197.

In November the nomination meeting was held, where two candidates were put forward—Dr Gordon Hutchison and James Auld, Meal Miller. As two retiring members did not stand (John Pullar, St Austins, and J. M. Ross) there was no poll.

Year 1935

Morayshire Motors started the year with an advertisement in the *Forres Gazette* for the new Hillman Minx, in eight body styles, at £159; five styles of the 20/70 at £269; as well as the seven-seater limousine costing £348. At this time, advertising took up only a few square inches of the *Gazette* each week. The Editor had great difficulty in filling the pages and printed anything that was available free, so that such things as "The Letters of Walter Bagehot" ran for many weeks.

Cattle at the mart were around £25 and pigs changed hands at £4 6s 6d. Trade was again depressed with the arrival of winter and 340 were on the register of unemployed. The Bobbin Mills had work for only two or three men, and when the Mills went on fire some time later, they were never re-opened. This was the last of the old industries which had made Forres a busy little town two decades before. Most tradesmen were out of work and there was no need for labourers.

Professor Crew of Edinburgh University was concerned at the fall in the national birthrate and warned that the population in 1976 would be down to 33 million. He advocated that the obstacles to parenthood be removed. These were, of course, poverty and the lack of jobs, which meant that marriages were prevented or postponed. The policy of the Government since the War had been to economise in every field and refused to accept the veiw that unemployment could be cured by spending money.

Professor—later Lord—Keynes was expounding his policy of expanding purchasing power, but those who believed him were labelled foolish and unreal. Apart from the Picture House—where

104

4d, 6d or 1s allowed people to escape from reality for a few hours, there was little entertainment during the winter. The Literary Society met in the Academy with a programme of talks and play readings.

Scarlet fever was still rampant and typhoid fever occurred in Grantown-on-Spey, where there was no suitable hospital and the case had to be taken to Forres Fever Hospital. The County Council sent the bill to the Grantown Town Council, which had to increase the burgh rate by a penny to pay it.

In February, 40 men made their way by cycling or walking to Burghead, where the B.B.C. were to build a broadcasting station. None were taken on as only preliminary work was being done, although a number were taken on later. At the Grain Market, barley could not be sold at £1 8s the quarter and wheat was £1 1s per cwt.

Several accidents at the dangerous bridge which crossed the track of the disused Forres and Findhorn Railway again raised the question of its removal. An offer was made to do so at a cost of £800 but the County Road Board thought the price too high. It was not demolished until R.A.F. Kinloss was built, as large vehicles could not negotiate the sharp turn.

The trial took place in Elgin Sheriff Court of Sergeant Henry Cook, who was in charge of the police force in Forres, for the unlawful arrest of Alexander Austin, Tolbooth Street. This case was featured in the national press at great length. The waitress in Alec Austin's mother's restaurant in Tolbooth Street, had a child, which the parents of the mother took to Austin as the Father; he, in turn, took it to the police station. The policeman on duty refused to take custody of the child and sent for Sergeant Cook. On arrival, the Sergeant asked Austin several times to take the baby to a place of safety which he refused to do. The Sergeant locked him in the cells for a period and then released Austin, who sued him for illegal arrest. A full day was taken for the trial, the decision of the Sheriff being that Austin was awarded a pound damages, but had to pay modified costs of the trial.

Much fun was also afforded the national press at a suggestion by Councillor Havers of Hopeman, that pedestrians on the roads at night should wear reflectors on their clothes and hats.

Miss Grant, a farmer at Alves, organised a concert to raise funds for the Agricultural Benevolent Association, which gave grants of up to £20 to farmers who had to give up their farms, thus ensuring that with the Old Age Pension of 10s a week they could have a home and some comfort. Mr McConnachie of Muirside, Brodie—a very active and controversial figure in local affairs—advocated that farmworkers be included in unemployment schemes, and asked that their wages be paid fortnightly in cash, at least £1 per week with perquisites (house, oatmeal, milk and potatoes) valued at 10s a week. Aberdeenshire farm wages were lower than this.

In February 17 properties were advertised for sale. Albion Villa, Tytler Street, with 3 public rooms, 5 bedrooms, garage and garden, was in the columns for several weeks before it was sold at a reduced price of £750.

The *Elgin Courant,* equally short of news, attacked Forres as "lethargic, with shops open one hour a day less than Elgin." The *Gazette* counter-attacked, accusing the *Courant* of promoting Elgin to the status of a city, and its provost to the peerage.

In March a part of the British Union of Fascists held meetings in the town, a supporter of this movement being Mrs C. M. Edwards of Sanquhar, who had no difficulty in reconciling contrary views. The chief speaker was William Joyce, who later, in wartime, was the infamous "Lord Haw-Haw" and who was hanged as a traitor because of his broadcasts on German radio. He had a small quiet audience at the Museum Square and was asked few questions, which inspired him to say that he judged that they fully supported his views.

The School Management Committee considered applications from 13 poor families for free medical treatment for their children, for which, if granted, they had to travel to Elgin. One unemployed father asked for travel costs, which were at first rejected but later granted.

Three youths appeared in the Burgh Court charged with various offences, and the ringleader was sent to Rossie Detention School. A great uproar followed, with meetings called in the People's Hall in Batchen Street. Allegations were made that the boy was sentenced because of his family and his colour, and a petition was organised, promised as one with a thousand signatures, to be sent to Mr George Lansbury, the leader of the Labour Party. There was a demand that the Bailie be "impeached." The allegations of cruelty and brutality to the boy were made to look silly by the appearance in the *Gazette* of a letter from the "victim" praising the food, comfort and facilities of the Home. The organisers faded into embarrassed silence!

At a football match in Elgin between the town's team and Forres Mechanics, the Chief Constable was punched in the face, the referee received blows, and the teams had to take shelter. After a pause, the game was restarted, ending with a draw of 1-1. Extra time had then to be played and soon two players had to be carried off the field. For many of the unemployed, football was their only outlet and feelings ran high all over the country.

Little was happening in the Town Council, but the Baths Committee reported that a swimming pool could be built for between £4000 and £5000. The opposition to the proposal argued that this would absorb all the money in the Munro Fund, and the running costs would put an intolerable burden on the ratepayers. The report was moved by the Convener, Bailie Macdonald, but when it came to the vote he said that he was to vote against his proposal. There was some laughter at this but it was not a unique occasion. The Convenerships were held by the senior members, but if they did not agree with the majority of their Committee they could refuse to present the report. As the proposer had also the last word in the debate, in addition to the first words, they would not give up their privilege. No reference was made at any time to the possible revenue from those using the pool, or from the Education Authority in sending school children for swimming lessons.

Moray County Council decided to build six houses of corrugated iron, for cheapness, two of them in the Forres area.

In June, the Silver Jubilee was celebrated by sports in the Grant Park. Here, a microphone and loudspeaker were used for the first time by the radio dealer, Mr James M. Younie. Mr A. H. Macdonald, Town Clerk, made the announcements and introduced the speakers. The Town's oldest man at this time was William Green—in his late nineties—who still followed his trade of jobbing gardener. The Town Clerk asked him to examine the microphone, which he did without remark. He was then asked if he had enjoyed himself and just at that moment the microphone was switched on inadvertently; there was surprise and laughter when William's strong language at the discomfort of sitting on a hard chair was broadcast. With his usual aplomb, Mr Macdonald coached the ancient to say something more suitable. The Press was somewhat confused and the *Daily Express* reported that the concourse had been addressed by "Sir William Green."

After the Games, the Council and others went to the top of the Califer to see the Provost light the giant bonfire. Many stayed until it was dark enough to see the 74 bonfires stretched all round the coast from Caithness to Banff. Bonfires were the traditional way of

107

marking an occasion, and had previously been lit in Roysvale or Grant Park. But when the bonfire was made for the celebration of signing the Peace of Versailles in 1919, two small girls had put a match to it before the Council arrived. So annoyed were they by this slight to their dignity that the culprits were arrested and taken to jail, where wiser counsel prevailed.

A year or so later, the family of one of the girls emigrated to Australia and it was said that they were too embarrassed to remain in the town; but they were neighbours of the writer, and he saw no sign of concern or guilt in any of the family.

The Mechanics Football Club was in a good financial position, having received no less than £50 from Falkirk on the transfer of Mr Kenny Dawson of Batchen Street to that team. The ubiquitous Bailie Caldwell attended the Annual Meeting and moved that the unemployed no longer be allowed into the pitch free, as in many towns they had to pay sixpence. This was opposed, as the 300 or so unemployed made the attendance at a game more impressive for the visitors. The Bailie was proposed as Chairman for the following year but said he was already on a great many bodies.

Mr Fraser of Knockomie gave £3000 for a Nurses' Home at Leanchoil in memory of his wife, and Sir Alexander Grant paid for the installation of the X-ray apparatus.

The *Gazette* gave a full report of the trial of a Mr Gray of Lhanbryde who had lit the bonfire there before the correct time. The report ended with the gnomic remark, "One does not know if William Gray subscribes to the insane creed of the Communists."

On the May holiday at Inverness, 2000 people travelled by train, 80 to Forres. Railwaymen were the largest body of workers in the town, and they now added their voices to the demand that the second half of the cut in their wages, ordered by the Government in 1931, be restored. The lowest paid, porters and surfacemen, received less than £2 per week. It was stated at the end of the year that six million workers had received pay increases totalling £18 million pounds; this was an average of £3 per person per year.

Unemployed juveniles had to attend evening classes before they got any benefit and the Education Committee complained that as soon as they qualified for benefit, they were seen at school no more.

Inverness Town Council had a heated discussion when a member, Colonel Henderson, complained that a man who had joined the Territorials before the War, and served all through the War—including the Battles of Vimy Ridge and Festubert—had now to live in a house of one room with his wife and seven children. The Housing Convener explained that they did not have a house large enough for this family, and to put them in a smaller house was to break the law on overcrowding. Such rigid adherence to the letter of the law was not uncommon. Some still looked upon applicants for council houses as much like beggars and paupers, responsible for their own plight.

A beggar in Forres, John Tough, was arrested and given twenty-four hours to raise money for a fine of £1 5s, which was patently impossible, and was re-arrested and sent to prison for 14 days.

In the summer, a cloudburst at Tomatin had washed away a bank of the Findhorn and for some days the river water was very muddy, only eight grilse being taken in the nets during that week.

Moray County Council restored the cut in the roadmen's wages. The amount was 2s 6d: the roadmen worked 60 hours per week.

The Joint County Council had to spend £36,897 for the relief of the able-bodied poor, while the Government gave £8500 towards the costs.

William Briggs & Co., started a Depot in Forres, taking on 12 men.

At Budget time most Councillors became very economy minded, and Bailie Caldwell wanted to know how many employees the Council had. The figures varied from 10 to 15 so a report was called for. The Provost explained that Mr Rankine, the Burgh Surveyor, had no assistant, no office and no clerical assistance. He also had to do the skilled work on the town's water supply, such as joint pipes and repair valves. The town's men were spread over different areas, controlled by different committees. The Forestry men had to do repairs on farms or fences, work in the Park and help with such things as snow clearing. Mr Rankine was also Firemaster, Clerk of Works, Shambles Superintendent, Water Manager, Sanitary Inspector, and many other things.

Miss Linton, an elderly lady, was injured when dismounting from a train and died in hospital as a result. The platforms at Forres Station were abnormally low, 30 inches from the carriage floor and 22 inches from the lowest running board. The Railway Company promised action, which came about nearly twenty years later.

There was a better attendance than usual at the nomination meeting; the questions now being raised in the Council about housing and other matters had aroused interest in the electorate. Two Councillors did not wish to return to the Council and only two new names were put forward—George F. Anderson and A. H. Forbes.

Both were natives who, after an absence of some years, had returned to live in the town. Both promised to press for improvements in housing and sporting facilities for the young. The retiring members were John W. Ross and James Morrison.

A legacy from the estate of the late Lord Forres allowed the Forres District Nursing Association to pay off their debts. Lord Forres was formerly Sir Archibald Williamson, Liberal M.P. for Moray and Nairn for many years. He had developed many great railways in Argentine, where he had named a station "Forres," but after his death this was replaced by a Spanish name.

The Burghs had complained for five years about their unfair representation on Moray and Nairn Joint Council, where they were outnumbered by the landward members, although the Burghs made a greater contribution to the rate income of the County. The Secretary of State gave the Burgh of Elgin three extra members, but this still did not give the Burghs a majority. In 1929 the counties of Moray and Nairn had been obliged to combine, and to make this more acceptable politically the county of Nairn was given nine council members and the Burgh of Nairn six, in the new County Council. The imbalance was never corrected as an Act of Parliament would be required to alter the Nairn figures.

Councillor Dr Hutchison was the principal speaker at the Smoking Concert in the Cluny Hill Hydro after the Annual General Meeting of the Golf Club. He painted a gloomy picture of the town—"no industry, no pay day," every back lane and alley should be closed down, "scrap the lot" was the theme. The blame he placed on the centralisation of local government in Elgin. He also spoke of the money in the Munro Baths Fund. In the discussion which followed, Mr James Anderson, Schools Inspector, wanted the money to be distributed among the sports bodies in town, and feelings began to run high. A Mr A. M. Low of Glasgow complained that he had come expecting to hear of golf, and described Dr Hutchison as "a combined black and red shirt wanting to put the world in order, beginning with Forres." Eventually, harmony was restored and the concert continued.

At Christmas Messrs Geddes were advertising men's shirts from 3s 6d to 7s, whilst Thomson & Co. had sherries from 3s 6d to 6s per bottle.

The Railwaymen's Ball on New Year's Eve had formerly been the social highlight of the year and the National Union of Railwaymen tried to revive past glories with a Whist Drive and Dance; the tickets

110

for whist and tea were 2s and for the dance 1s 6d. This was a far cry from the half guinea of pre-war days.

Because of the bad weather, the Soup Kitchen was opened a week earlier, again in the charge of Police Inspector Neil.

At the last Council of the year the members were divided on the purchase of new cleansing carts, horse-drawn but four-wheeled, at £133 each. A local firm offered to supply similar carts at a lower price, but the Convener, Dr Bruce, urged that they accept the offer before them, saying that the carts would serve for 30 years.

The Rector of the Academy had received the gift of a radio for the school, and enquired who was to pay the annual licence of 10s. The Council said that the Education Committee would have to take the responsibility.

The local Sub-Committee for Public Assistance said that the boots provided for poor rural children were too heavy for them. Dr Bruce, who was chairman, thought that a 3 in. sole was about right but that delicate children could perhaps get something lighter.

At New Year, the insurance stamp for men was increased to 5d and the 2 lb. loaf went up to 6d.

The year had been a very wet one, with 755 mm. (30.22 inches) of rain, compared with the 350 mm. (13.5 inches) for 1934, but there had been slightly more sunshine—1407 hours against 1376 hours; January brought six inches of snow.

Year 1936

At the beginning of the year, Bailie Caldwell again asked that the Minutes of all Committees be available for the members, so that they would know what the Council was doing. A Councillor moved the previous question which meant that until this was voted on nothing else could be said. The motion was carried, which meant that the matter could not be discussed until at least six months had passed.

Housing was now taking up more time and receiving more attention from the new Councillors who had entered the Council to press for more houses. None of the new Members were property owners, which was most unusual. A survey had been made of the houses in the burgh and part of this was now issued. This showed that there were 1200 dwelling houses, of which 128 were overcrowded. The

111

number of houses in 1911, when the population had reached its peak at 4811, had been 1083. The overcrowding at that time must have been much worse, as families were also larger, many of the poorer people having to sublet part of their homes to get money for the rent.

The Convener of the Health Committee, who had instigated the survey, thought that Forres had come out of it rather well compared to some other towns, and complacently opposed the building of small houses for families of two or three, saying that they would soon be overcrowded by the tenants. This meant that such families would have little chance of getting a house, as the regulations said that no family would get a house larger or smaller than their needs. Despite protests the majority decided that 80 houses would be enough for the time being. The Department of Health did not agree and insisted that the figure be increased to 145, with a proportion of small houses in addition to the 4- and 5-apartment houses planned. Only the living room and bedrooms were counted as apartments, but all had to have a separate kitchen and bathroom. A further survey was made and this showed 56 houses (with 78 families) ready for demolition.

Notices were sent to the owners of these 56 houses and the following month the Health Committee removed the names of nine owners who said they were to modernise their houses as soon as possible. Some of these were not demolished for another 30 years, when the Council had far greater powers. New houses in Bogton Road were let at weekly rents of 6s for a three-apartment, and 6s 9d for four apartments, inclusive of occupiers' rates.

The owner of Graham's Cottages in North Road died and the Council bought the property for demolition; but so great was the need that they were modernised as far as possible and, at the time of writing (1973) are still occupied.

Later in the year permission was given to start on 42 houses on the site of the "Lang Raw." The owners, Miss Ross, "Seaview"; Mr R. Murray, "Drumnamarge"; and Mr Daniel Murdoch, Fish Merchant, refused to sell at the prices offered and a court of arbitration was held. This fixed a figure somewhere between the prices asked and offered. This was the first case of compulsory purchase of land.

Members pressed for more information and learned that 114 houses had no water supply and 268 houses had more than two families. Dissatisfation increased with each extra piece of information, and more action was promised. The walls of secrecy were crumbling!

FORRES, FROM THE CHEMICAL WORKS (c. 1900)

To pay for the new houses, bonds to the amount of £20,000 were issued at 3 per cent for seven years. This was a good investment and they were quickly taken up, although the older members felt that this was an intolerable burden added to an already large debt.

At Easter the Academy Philatelic Club held its first meeting and new rules were issued for the staffing of schools. The Scottish Education Department announced that it would be considered unsatisfactory if there were more than 50 pupils habitually in the control of one teacher. In the advanced division the maximum would be 40 for the first three years, and 30 pupils in subsequent years. This would come into effect on the 31st August of that year.

A public meeting was called by Bailie Caldwell to choose a parents' representative to the School Management Committee, of which he was Chairman. Only Councillor Auld—who was already a representative—attended but Rev. W. Wishart sent a note to say that he would like the position, to which he was appointed. Mr Auld had no children and Mr Wishart's two sons were at boarding schools in the south. Towards the end of the year this committee had a full attendance of all its 18 members, to discuss the raising of the school leaving age to 15. There was opposition to this from the members from rural areas, as the proposal would mean centralising many small schools which did not have room for the necessary new classes, such as cookery and practical woodwork rooms.

The Education Committee in Elgin recommended that future supplies of chemicals for science classes be obtained from wholesalers, whose prices were 25 per cent lower than local suppliers. The Moray and Nairn Chemists' and Druggists' Association repudiated this, claiming that they were only 10, and sometimes only 5 per cent above the wholesalers. But the Committee adhered to their decision.

The Office-Bearers of the Town Council dealt with the distribution of the charity money held by the Council, the largest source being the Jonathan Anderson Trust. The income from the Trust's investments had fallen to only twopence, and they decided to sell these stocks and invest the proceeds in the Savings Bank, which paid 2½ per cent. They had to cut the usual annual £2 per needy person to £1, and even then some names had to be deleted for lack of funds.

The death of George V and the accession of Edward VIII was announced with all the usual ceremony at the Cross. Later, when the new King announced his abdication, the *Gazette* gave an unusually full and frank report of his association with Mrs Wally Simpson—

113

much more than the national press. This was the first that most local people knew of the affair.

The railways were now feeling the pinch from the increasing competition of buses and private cars and made belated efforts to improve their condition. At the beginning of the year a special train ran for the rugby match at Edinburgh. The fare was 13s; and on 30th January an evening train was run to Inverness, the return fare being 1s.

The Mechanics Football Club won the North of Scotland Cup from Inverness Thistle, and over 600 travelled by a special train to see the game at Inverness. Others had gone by ordinary trains and so great was the crowd returning that the Forres Pipe Band met several trains but missed the one by which the teams travelled. More cheap fares were announced, including one to Glasgow for the day at 13s, and one could visit Rothesay for £1 4s 6d, which included train, steamer, breakfast, lunch and high tea. On Thursdays the day fare to Aberdeen was 5s 6d and by the Sunday train to Grantown for 1s, and Aviemore for 1s 6d. But they could not equal the comfort or the convenience of private cars and private hire buses.

At the junction of North Road and Caroline Street the roadway fell in, to expose one of the old town wells, with a 65 foot shaft; it was filled properly this time and the roadway reinstated.

The Forres Cage Bird Society was resuscitated after many years and an Annual Show fixed for 5th December. The Forres area had always been noted for the many varieties of birds, and during the depression a number of men had eked out their relief benefits by trapping birds and sending them south by train to the markets. This was illegal but no prosecution ever took place; the most frequent bird sent was the siskin.

Another body formed at this time was the Forres Townswomen's Guild. At a meeting in Castlehill Church, Mrs Murray of Moy House was appointed the first President, and the membership soon totalled 180. The Guild asked for a rent of the Academy Lecture Room at the reduced rent for educational bodies, but this was resisted strongly by Bailie Caldwell, who pressed them to take the Mechanics' Institute; eventually the Council let this at a reduced figure.

A horse-drawn rotary brush sweeper was bought from Dundee Corporation, who were giving up horses. It cost £13 and rotted away quietly in the Burgh yard. It was meant to sweep the snow from the streets, but when the fall came all horses were required for the snow-ploughs to draw the carts loaded with the snow to be dumped in the Mosset Burn.

Mr R. K. Forsyth of Kincorth Farm had drawn the attention of the District Council to the insalubrious state of the Town's dump at Monkland, but the County Sanitary Inspector said it did not constitute a nuisance under the Act, but that he would act against the many middens in the village of Kinloss. Following this, the proprietor of the dump, Colonel M. Grant Peterkin of Grange, wrote the Town Council giving them notice to quit at the end of the term of let. The Town Clerk noted that Colonel Peterkin's letter was dated two days later than the legal time, and advised the Council to ignore it. This dump lasted the life of the Town Council, ceasing in 1974.

At the February meeting it was proposed that the Burgh Surveyor, Mr John Rankine, get a foreman or an assistant. On this occasion the "previous question" was again moved and carried; the subject was postponed for at least six months. But a majority decided at the same meeting that cattle would no longer graze in Roysvale Park, which was to be reserved for Junior football. Encouraged by this victory the Council accepted a motion by Dr Hutchison that "a public convenience be erected at the Cross or the West End before summer." Councillor Forbes was also successful in getting agreement for a boating pond to be made in the Burn Green between the two lower "jaws" or "weirs." This was enthusiastically supported by Dean of Guild Merchant who offered to present two small rowing boats which an ex-serviceman could ply for hire.

The Burn Green at this time was the only open space for children residing north of High Street, but this place was also used as a drying green for the washing from the Hand Laundry in the "Big Hoose" at Dunedin Place, and the blankets from Taylor's Weaving Mills. During the debate on this, Bailie Macdonald suggested that a swimming pool also be provided but it was not clear whether this was to be at Burn Green or elsewhere. Thoroughly encouraged by their successes, a further proposal was carried that a chute and swings be erected at Grant Park at a cost of £40. However, the older and wilier members acted swiftly. The convenience was remitted to the Public Health Committee, where it died quietly. At the next meeting the opposition had consolidated its ranks and the proposal for the boats was sunk without trace, by the quotation of impossibly high costs of insurance against the death by drowning of children falling out of the boats. The chute and swings were postponed for many years, also because of the cost. Although Standing Orders said that any Council decision could not be reversed for six months this was ignored and the decision rescinded.

At a later meeting, Dr Hutchison was again successful with a motion that "sporting facilities" be improved. This was also fruitless as the wording was not specific enough, and so gave reason for not implementing the decision.

The County Road Board declared that the ancient suspension bridge over the Findhorn would have to be replaced as it could not carry modern traffic. This was a graceful structure in very beautiful surroundings and there was an effort to retain it as a feature for tourists. But the estimated cost of maintenance, which would have to be borne by the town, was too great, and a new bridge was built in time for the outbreak of war. The first estimate of £28,000 was much exceeded, but it gave welcome work, along with the B.B.C. station at Burghead.

Easter was the coldest of the century and the summer was late: there had been bonfires on the ice at Blairs Loch. The number of unemployed reached 450 this year; men were taken on to move the ice and snow from the roads. Because of the lack of work, Dean of Guild Merchant asked that the Government declare Forres a "distress area" as it had done for Nairn. The Provost thought this would be of little use as there was no industry to assist.

Permission was given for the Horticultural Society to erect a tent in Grant Park for the annual flower show, and charge for admission. No charge could be made for entering the park itself, by the terms of the Deed of Gift.

The Ladies' Linen League reported a successful year's work in repairing and supplying linen at Leanchoil Hospital.

The cleansing vehicles were now fitted with rubber tyres, joining the dairy and coal carts on their now silent way along the granite setts and cobbled streets.

The Council also had the problem of the police station, which was sited in "Balaams Pass" or "Tolbooth Bow." This had been adversely commented upon by His Majesty's Inspector of Constabulary. The 1929 Act said that all police stations were the property of the county councils, but this was an inseparable part of the whole Tolbooth, and the County Council were glad, therefore, to disclaim ownership.

The Salvation Army opened a new Hall in Urquhart Street, and the fact that it was now an acceptable body was proved by the Provost attending the official opening wearing his chain of office.

Shopkeepers, to the number of 40—the highest figure known—attended a meeting called to solicit their support for the Forres

116

Amateur Athletic Association, who were organising a Gala Week during the Glasgow Fair in July. Support was also promised for an Amenities Association, which would develop and advertise the attractions of the town for the tourist trade. A Committee was formed to do this, the members being—Messrs G. R. Mackenzie, George Philp, Ben Grant, A. H. Forbes and R. K. Forsyth, the latter as President.

Plans had been obtained for the improvement of the Mechanics' Institute, now to be known as the Town Hall. This had been discussed with Sir Alexander Grant, who had recommended Mr Alastair Macdonald, son of the Prime Minister, Ramsay Macdonald. Hoping, as always, that Sir Alexander would meet the bill, the Council appointed him Architect. His experience had been in designing cinemas and this influence is obvious in the main hall. A gallery, supported by shapely iron pillars, had run round the three sides of the stalls, with excellent views of the stage. These were fronted by artistic wrought iron railings. This was replaced by a sloping hanging gallery. When the work was finished, Sir Alexander was asked to express his opinion on it, describing it as excellent but doing nothing more. The cost, at £300 a year, was finally cleared thirty years afterwards.

Sir Alexander had, earlier in the year, given Nairn Town Council an interest-free loan of £28,000 to allow them to modernise the harbour and he now gave the Nairn people another £3000 as a gift to modernise the baths. He had obviously got tired of being looked upon as an easy means of relieving the burdens which the ratepayers of Forres should meet. But, until his death, he was still looked upon in this light by the older members.

The Council now had to face the cost of road repairs. The roads had been neglected and were in a deplorable state. The Roads Committee wanted St Leonard's widened and repaired at the Gable Inn, as well as the main road from Rosefield to Drumduan Lodge. Bailie Caldwell argued that the money must go to repair the Grantown road and to make a footpath from the Toll to the town. The Dean of Guild pressed that Gordon Street, from its junction with North Road to the Gasworks, get priority; he could scarcely cycle on this part to his Bobbin Mills! Bailie Caldwell said that because of the enormous cost of this road he had scored it from the list, but Bailie Michie Anderson said that at least £600 should be spent on it, although it would need £1000 to make it good.

117

A member of an old Forres family—the Reverend Alexander Fridge—had died in the south and his widow sent a sum of money to found a charity in his memory, the interest to be distributed annually among ten deserving residents.

Mrs C. M. Edwards, in addition to being an indefatigable writer of letters to the *Gazette,* had many other interests. A meeting of her Litter League was held. She praised the cleanliness of the streets and then opened a parcel of litter which she had collected in a small area. The annual income of the League was 10s 5d, and the meeting ended with a sketch and songs.

Intimation was received from New Zealand that the late Arthur S. Murdoch, a native of the town, had bequeathed £30,000 to Forres for the purchase of the fishing rights on the river, and also £1000 for Leanchoil Hospital. There was much excitement among the anglers in the town, but later letters disclosed that a brother of Mr Murdoch had a life rent of this money, and after his death it would accumulate for some years. It was nearly twenty years before the rights could be bought. The money crisis of 1931 reduced the value of Australian and New Zealand money, so that the £30,000 and £1000 became £25,000 and £750 respectively.

The Gala Week in July realised a surplus of £135, which was retained by the Amenities Association. A "Flannel" Dance had been organised in June, to raise money for unemployed, but had a loss of 14s. Such unchaperoned dances were not yet accepted by all parents.

A circular from the Home Office outlined plans for air raid precautions in the event of war. This was the first official mention of such a possibility, although many thought war inevitable, but they were in the minority. But the warning had its effect; the price of scrap metal began to rise, as did other prices and, consequently, demands for increases in wages. The passivity and acceptance of hardship of the post-war years was disappearing, and interest in local and national affairs was obvious. Criticism of the Town Council became vocal.

An increase in the salaries of the officials was agreed, the Town Clerk's to rise from £290 to £350 a year; the Town Chamberlain from £200 to £275; the Forests and Cemetery Superintendent from £143 to £170. There was consternation at the following month's meeting when a letter was read from Mr Souter, demanding another £10 as Town Chamberlain; this was granted.

In October, Dallas Dhu Distillery started up after a lapse of six years, and on the last day of the year at the Mart, barley was sold by the farmers at £2 per quart; this was the first time this price had been reached since 1919.

The Department of Agriculture announced that the value of the perquisite of farmworkers was 16s for each hundredweight of oatmeal; 1s for each gallon of milk; £3 15s for a ton of potatoes and £6 for a house. The workers did not accept this figure as potatoes were on sale in Forres at £1 15s per ton.

A "New Deal for the Highlands" was announced by the Government, to which the *Gazette* sourly remarked "Under London Leadership." Dairy workers received a good increase, men's wages rising to £2 8s 6d per week and women up to £1 12s 6d according to grade. But the week was still long and the starting hours early.

At the meeting of the Forres branch of the National Farmers' Union, membership had again fallen, with 28 members paid up. Mr McConnochie was re-elected President and referred in his speech to the depopulation of the land, saying that Dallas alone had lost 30 pairs of horses, each pair giving whole time work for a man, and they had not been replaced by tractors.

A report from the Secretary of State underlined this decline. Since 1913 the cultivated land in the North-East of Scotland had fallen by 18,449 acres, and the people employed on the land, from 35,334 to 22,336, a reduction of 13,000. No new industry had appeared to absorb them and they had emigrated, either to the south or overseas. The value of the farms in the same period had fallen by 22 per cent.

Horses were now so rare that the occasional appearance in the street of a beautifully groomed horse drawing a smart cab with a liveried and top-hatted driver drew attention. This was the equipage still used by old Mrs McKessack of Struthers for shopping.

The farm of Whiteinch had now been carved into small holdings of from four to five acres, each with its new house. These were being let to ex-servicemen at rents of £5 10s or £6 10s. The farming community had opposed this development, claiming that they were not viable units, but this was not put to the test. The establishment of R.A.F. Kinloss later brought jobs to all in the area.

Another sign of better times was the number of advertisements appearing in the local papers. A few years earlier they were rare, but now Donald Macintosh of Inverness was advertising pianos and organs with free delivery and payments as low as 19s a month. They ranged from £8 10s for a "solid walnut" up to £28 for a "Lestel mahogany overstrung." Geddes of Forres were selling "costumes for maids and smaller women" at £1 15s 6d and £1 3s 6d.

The Cluny Hill Hydrophathic Company owned the Golf Course and at the annual meeting of shareholders the Chairman said that the numbers of town players had increased, bringing their fees up to £351, an increase of £5, while visiting players' fees were down by £3 to £287. The cost of maintaining the course had been cut by £177 to £776 so that the net loss on the course was now only £148.

Angling Association fees were nearly doubled to £1 1s.

In the month of May, farmworkers were brought in to the Unemployment Insurance system, but not private gardeners, game-keepers or domestic employees. If workers were engaged by the half year and not by the week, the employer paid a reduced rate.

There were changes in other spheres too. At this time, the Duke of Richmond and Gordon sold the whole of the Burgh of Huntly, along with the lands, plantations and estates of Gartly, Rhynie, Cairnie and Drumblade; in all, 400 feus and 68 farms, which had been in the thanage of the Dukedom for centuries.

But there were still traces of feudalism in Huntly. In 1935 a bank clerk there had asked permission to marry; the Bank rule was that no one could do this until his salary was £200 a year. The young man, a Mr Notman, wrote that his father was willing to make up his salary to this sum; this the Bank rejected. Mr Notman's salary was £160 and when it rose to £180 he applied again, saying his fiancée had lived in lodgings for six years, that his father was giving him £20 a year, and gave the date of his wedding. The reply was a letter of dismissal. As an ex-bank clerk he had a stigma and was unable to get a job. The Bank refused to discuss the matter with the press.

At the November nomination meeting the Hall was two-thirds full, the best for many years. The discussion and speeches lasted 90 minutes. No election was needed as Mr J. C. Robertson refused to be re-nominated, and his place was taken by Mr Fred C. MacBeath, butcher. The burgh rates increased by 1s, the Joint County Council requisition being blamed for the increase.

The Joint County Council had no bye-laws preventing the erection of wooden shacks and shelters. Colonel Grant opposed the introduction of such bye-laws because this would mean that the Council would be required to build more houses.

For Christmas, the shops were advertising "Finest Back Bacon" at 1s 7d per lb. and "Best Streaky" at 7d.

120

Year 1937

The new year started with mild weather, quickly followed by some of the worst snow storms for many years. With the better lit streets, the old custom of bringing in the New Year at the Cross was revived and a number of youths collected, soon to depart for the first footing.

The first week had 240 registered unemployed but as the snow came on this soon increased. The slight increases in the price of grain which had brought cheer to the farmers dismayed the poultry breeders and egg producers, who claimed that they had little profit before but were now losing money, and that they would soon be out of business. Despite the high figure of unemployed there was the usual shortage of tradesmen, especially in the distilleries now getting busier. Maltmen, stillmen and mashmen were in demand and short supply.

The Council dealt with the celebrations for the Coronation but did not make them public, so that until a week before the 12th May there were complaints that nothing was being arranged. But arrangements had been made and the day went well with the usual parades, games and speeches. The Council promised that they would again guarantee the Flower Show for a loss of £10, and at the same meeting decided to take over from Sanquhar Estate the private road which ran from Sanquhar Road to Burdshaugh. This is now the road in front of the Academy; the cost was £534.

The Labour Party had been very active for a number of years and especially so at the previous General Election. The National Party had drawn up a new policy and the local Party met to discuss it. One after another members resigned during the talks after disagreements and at the end of the meeting the local Party no longer existed.

In February there was a rare occurrence for Forres, a strike, the first since the General Strike of 1926. The firm was Messrs Ross & Sons, St Leonard's Works, which made portable buildings, sending them all over Britain. The 22 men stopped work and published a letter giving their case, and after a week on strike their demands were met. They asked for 2½% increase on piece work and 10% more for time work. The firm had just developed a house which was erected at a total cost of £100. A number were built in Burdshaugh Road next to the Mosset Burn, and were given a certificate from the Town Council, who considered they had a life expectancy of ten years. All

121

are still in existence and, on changing hands, do so at prices as much as fifty times their cost. The principal of the firm, Mr James Ross, had ideas on building much in advance of his time, and it was a loss to the town when he died at a comparatively young age.

Skins of moles, weasels, stoats and rabbits were still in demand and regular consignments were being despatched, principally to Leeds. A number of men earned money by trapping these, the molecatchers being almost full time doing so.

Following flooding at the Waterford Mills the Council agreed to cut back the east bank to the line of the original piles at a cost of £24 13s, the Mills agreeing to pay £10 of this.

In February Dr Hutchison put forward more specific proposals for improving the sports facilities. Among them were, a grandstand for the football pitch, grass tennis courts in Grant Park and badminton in the Town Hall. Council Forbes suggested a swimming pool. Bailie Cormack, convener of the appropriate committee, deprecated a hasty decision and asked that proposals be remitted to his committee for more consideration; these were never received.

At the Farmers' Union meeting, Mr McConnachie gave, as usual, a long and interesting speech, in which he went out of his way to praise the graders of dead meat in the slaughterhouse—Forres Shambles. They were, he said, much more expert than in the establishment he had formerly used. He had, for some time, been very critical of Forres, having been one of the first motorists fined for parking overlong on the street! The citizens felt they were forgiven.

The Amenities Association was now firmly established and called a meeting, with the Provost in the chair, to discuss policy. The Provost pointed out that the chief beneficiaries of the Association's work—the shopkeepers and bar and hotel keepers—were noticeable by their absence. Mr R. K. Forsyth was made permanent President. For the next three years they did a great deal of good work, signposting and improving paths and walks, drawing up lists of accommodation, designing a new guide book, and organising the yearly Gala Week, until the war interrupted this work for a number of years.

Major Tryon, the Postmaster General, told Parliament that in view of the serious economic state of the country he could not consider returning to the penny postage for letters and halfpenny for postcards at this time.

As the School Canteen closed at the end of winter, the Superintendent said that a record number of needy children had been fed, 5500 meals having been eaten.

The Council were shocked when told that the cost of modernising the Town Hall was now £3500 but it was much more than this before the work finished.

The owners of Ben Romach Distillery spent £1500 in beautifying the grounds of the works.

On the 1st April the new Unemployment Assistance Board took over most of the responsibility for maintaining the able-bodied poor and workless. This meant a considerable saving to all local authorities.

There was a proposal that chutes and swings be erected in Roysvale Park, to be paid for from the Common Good. There was a long silence after the proposer sat down; then Councillor John Mackenzie seconded the motion—who, as the *Gazette* tartly remarked, "seems to support any progressive proposal when heard." Dr Bruce approved in principle but was concerned with the safety of children, as erecting this slide was asking for trouble. Bailie Cormack agreed and said that this could be part of a larger project in the future. Dean of Guild Merchant thought that the Grant Park would be a better place, although all games—except cricket by the St Lawrence, and bowling on the Green—were prohibited. When voted upon, two supported the motion and nine voted for a later development. It was 1972 before any amusements were installed in the Roysvale Park.

An offer to rent Roysvale Park at £15 a year was received, and the majority considered that this was too large a sum to forego, so the previous decision to reserve it for Junior football was rescinded.

The Police Board decided to reinstate an Inspector in the town. The last Inspector had retired in 1931 and the reduction in status was one of the economy moves of that year.

Sir Alexander Grant died, his funeral being the largest ever known in Forres. His passing was a blow to many of the older members who had known him well, and who had depended much—many said too much—on his generosity. Some had counted on his paying the costs of the Town Hall, and hoped that this was provided for in his will, which was not the case.

The spring was so dry that the anglers had to give up, although the firm building the Findhorn Bridge were grateful for the abnormally low level of the river.

During the summer the Lovat Scouts were in camp at Kinloss. This was one of the few cavalry regiments left in Britain and their manoeuvres, especially their sports, drew large crowds of spectators.

News leaked out that 375 acres of land from the farms of Langcot.

Doonpark and Muirton had been bought for use as an airfield for the Royal Air Force. The Countess of Moray called a meeting to resuscitate the Auxiliary Red Cross Unit which had been in existence during the first World War. This, she said, was at the request of the Government.

The annual nomination meeting in November had to be held in the small hall of the Town Hall, as the main hall was occupied by the builders. So great was the attendance that members of the audience had to sit on the stage behind the row of candidates, which caused some confusion at first. Only two candidates appeared although there were eight vacancies to be filled, as Dean of Guild Merchant was moving to Inverness and Councillor George Anderson to Elgin. Dr Bruce presided and spoke long and gloomily of the state of the Common Good. Mr William Taylor, Bolton Cottage, was proposed from the floor, and mounting the platform, he also spoke. There were actually eleven candidates on the voting form. Six of the retiring members were re-elected and Mr Taylor and Mr John Cowie, locomotive department clerk, were the two new members.

The burgh rates were reduced by 1s in the pound, the decrease being due to a reduction in the County Council requisition, whose burden of public assistance was greatly lessened by the Act mentioned earlier.

The only newsworthy item in the paper, in the last issue of the year, was a case in the Burgh Police Court. On his Sunday off, the "Boots" at the Carlton Hotel had presented himself at the Commercial (Queen's) Hotel as a "bona fide" traveller from Tomintoul, on his way to Kinloss. He was thus able to buy spiritous liquor. On Sundays, one must have travelled at least three miles before being considered to need a drink. This was a relic from the days when travel was on foot or horse. The Bailie said that, as a hotel worker, he would be well aware that he was breaking the law, and said he must deal with him with the greatest severity and fined him 15s 6d.

Year 1938

The advertising campaign in the previous year, by the Forres Gas Company must have been successful, for the company now planned to instal new plant to double the gas produced.

124

The tenants of the land earmarked for air stations received notice of what ground was to be taken, and were told that it would be only for emergency use, no buildings having to be erected. This decision did not last very long for with the increasingly threatening behaviour of the Germans, the Government decided that they would require a series of air stations along the east coast of the country where the ground was suitable. This step was the beginning of a process which stopped the decay and depopulation in Morayshire. If it had not been for the arrival of the Royal Air Force at Kinloss and Lossiemouth, with the many satellite airfields, the county would have gone the way of all the other northern counties. Thirty years later, the villages and parishes of Banffshire had populations smaller than those of 1801, although at that time the population of Scotland was only a third of its present level.

At the year's first Council, Dr Hutchison asked that steps be taken to protect the private houses in St Leonard's "in juxtaposition" with the timber works there. As the houses would be damaged if the works took fire—which he thought was very probable—their value was falling. There was a pause while members considered whether the Doctor was serious or not—always a problem. Councillor Cowie took it that he was, and seconded the motion. Bailie Cormack asked what authority the Council had in the matter and the Town Clerk said none. But the Doctor insisted on a vote being taken, when he was defeated by twelve votes to two.

Dr Hutchison had been a noted orator and debater in his student days, and his main interest in the Town Council was as a forum where he could exercise and display his skills. He put forward many proposals and spoke to the members in a manner much different from that usually found in local government. If he was successful in getting his proposals accepted—which was often because of his fluent and persuasive talk—he would then ask permission to withdraw the motion.

Only on one occasion was Dr Hutchison dealt with in the same manner. During an elaborate speech he was interrupted by a Councillor who claimed he was "bemused by the idioglottic vocabulary of the speaker" and asked for enlightenment. Somewhat taken aback, the Doctor asked if he could "have a gloss." The interrupter referred him to the pages in *Alice in Wonderland* where the eponymous heroine had a conversation with Humpty Dumpty.

The *Gazette* noted that new Councillors were now ignoring the old convention that a new member was silent in Council for the first three years, although he could join in committee discussions, and here was Councillor Cowie speaking and putting forward a motion for discussion at the February meeting.

Speaking to his motion, which was on housing, Councillor Cowie compared many of the houses in town to rabbit warrens, which should be replaced. Bailie Cormack supported him and applied this remark especially to the houses in North Road, which were among the oldest. Dr Bruce tried to move an amendment to this, but was unable to frame one which did not imply that the Council should defy the law. He did say, however, that since 1919 over £8000 had been spent on new houses, and asked the proposer why he had not warned the electors of the burden of debt he proposed to put on them. He claimed that 240 houses had been built, but the figure was considerably less than that, but accurate information was never made available.

Later, Dr Hutchison raised the matter of the trade of the town. He took exception to traders in neighbouring burghs—meaning, of course, Elgin—taking away trade by sending goods through to Forres by bus, paying the bus cost and, if the goods were ordered by telephone, refunding the cost of this also. But he also said that the local shop-keepers were not "pushful" enough, closing for lunch and keeping shorter hours than elsewhere. A member pointed out that visitors liked the quiet relaxed way of life in the town, while another said it was also referred to by some as "Sleepy Hollow."

The proposer received little support, but again insisted on a vote, and was defeated by eleven votes to three, proving perhaps that there was some complacency in the town.

Satisfaction was expressed with the Chief Constable's report for 1937. This showed that Forres had only 63 offences for the year, whilst Nairn—of much the same size—had 201, and Elgin, three times larger, had 376.

About this time the Reverend George McWilliam of Auldearn, who was Chairman of the Education Authority, told the Presbytery of Inverness that it was now time to bring coloured missionaries from such places as Bengal, Manchuria and Africa, to evangelise Scotland.

Despite the spread of films, the live theatre was not quite dead; in one week in the spring the town had the Forres Players putting on a comedy, *Call It a Day,* while a professional company produced *Follies of Scotland.* The prices for both shows were 2s, 1s 6d, 1s and 6d.

The Amenities Association had been very active since their formatin and now asked permission to erect seats in the West Pilmuir and to lay out an eighteen-hole putting green in the Rose Garden. Approval was given for the seats but the second proposal was rejected. At its next meeting the Association complained that the Council had given no financial support, and insisted that it was the duty of the Amenities Association to raise money for anything they wanted to do.

Thiry-two out of thirty-five applicants for free medical treatment for their children were granted by the School Management Committee on the grounds of hardship. Three were refused and the Committee named one applicant who had a weekly wage of £2 15s. To make matters worse, he was employed by the Scottish Co-operative Society. There were still many who looked on this organisation as a tool of Moscow.

The Town Council continued to press the County Council to retain the suspension bridge, which was to be demolished as soon as the new bridge was ready. One argument was that if war came the old bridge would be very useful if the new one was destroyed by a bomb. It was also argued that the maintenance cost would be small, mentioning that £5 might suffice for painting it. The County Council at last relented and said they could have the bridge if they, the Town Council, would maintain it. Quite unabashed, the reply was that this could not be done because of the cost of maintaining it.

It was now time to implement the Home Office instructions about air raid precautions, and Bailie Michie Anderson was elected to take charge of this. He and a small Committee very quickly built up an organisation that stood up to all the stresses and strains of the war, although the town was, fortunately, never attacked, and the Bailie was in charge until the service "stood down."

The Amenities Association complained to the L.M.S. Railway Company about the dangerous state of the platforms, their lowness causing many injuries and bruises. Within a week a reply was received promising that they would be brought up to the necessary standard within two years but, again, the war intervened.

The Drill Hall was now in daily use. The newly formed Voluntary Aid Detachments of the Red Cross and the strengthened company of the 6th Battalion of the Seaforth Highlanders were now drilling and training. Councillor Colonel A. D. Macdonald had called a meeting to get new recruits for the company, and brought it up to 163 men. Morayshire was the smallest county to have a Territorial Battalion of

127

its own, and an appeal for men on that ground was sufficient to bring in recruits.

There was severe frost on 10th May, damaging potatoes and much of the fruit blossom. This was the coldest and wettest May so far recorded.

The Post Office was to lay cables through the High Street and the Council refused permission as the street had been dug up three times within a short period. The Secretary of State had to instruct the Council to grant permission, otherwise the Post Office would have had to resort to legal proceedings.

The Empire Exhibition opened at Bellahouston Park in Glasgow, and drew large crowds. Special trains were run at cheap fares, the first of these, starting at Inverness, carried 800 passengers, including 130 from Forres. The fare for the 340 miles journey was 13s 6d. It left Forres at 2 a.m. and gave a full day in Glasgow before arriving home in the early hours next morning.

As a result of Hitler's threatening attitude, Mrs C. M. Edwards of Sanquhar had for a time stopped her weekly letters to the *Gazette* in Hitler's praise, but now resumed. In one she attacked the Government for being a military ally of France, which, she claimed, was sending aeroplanes to the Spanish Government; this meant we were supporting the Spanish Republicans. This was too much for the tolerant Editor, who replied to her in the same issue, asking if Italy and Germany did not only supply aeroplanes, but also men and ammunition, to Franco, whom the Editor described as a "Nazi Bully."

The past season had been a good one financially for the Forres Mechanics Football Club, which had fielded a wholly amateur team, but had a poor showing in the league tables, having gained only seven points. A new grandstand was needed, and as the grass was in excellent condition it was decided to let it for sheep grazing during the summer and earn some money.

The Housing Convener asked that house building be slowed down as costs were rising, and houses formerly built for £300 would now cost £500. This was a sign of the rise in prices and wages brought on by the demands of materials in case of war. Grain prices also rose, but after the Munich settlement they fell again.

The Education Committee said they were interested in obtaining ground from the Town, in Batchen Street, for a new Police Station and an addition to the Primary School, to relieve the overcrowding of that rapidly deteriorating building. The Council refused as they needed the area for housing, and added that they did not think it right to put a Police Station so near a Primary School, when no allowance had been made for playing fields.

Mrs Edwards wrote complaining that her husband had feued land at Burdshaugh for houses, but now the tenants of these houses were using some of the ground as a dump, and were also polluting the burn. Councillor Will Taylor said that his laundry drew water from the burn for some purposes and confirmed that there were many foreign bodies in it. The Burgh Surveyor was instructed to take the matter up with the police.

Two wooden, four-apartment houses, were ordered from Sweden as an experiment, to be erected in Albert Street. If these were satisfactory another 100 would be bought, but again the war intervened.

In the House of Lords, attempts to halt rural depopulation were not assisted by the Scottish Peers who opposed a Bill to provide houses for agricultural workers, because of a clause making it necessary to fit such houses with bathrooms; fortunately, they were defeated.

The Air Ministry asked for a supply of thirty-five thousand gallons of water daily for Kinloss airfield, where work had now started, giving employment to almost every able-bodied man in the area. The County Council deferred building any more houses, except in New Elgin, because of the rising costs.

There was silence in the Council when the Town Clerk read out the requisition from the County Council, which totalled £8424. After this pause, the Provost asked had no one any thing to say. There was again silence until Dr Bruce remarked that "everyone seemed to have paralysis in the lingual organ" and, at length, vehemently showed that he did not. Since 1930, he said, Forres had paid over £76,000 but had received not a pennyworth in return—no school or other facility— but £48,000 had been squandered on a "marble hall." This was the County Building in course of construction, also delayed by the outbreak of war.

The Munich crisis caught Forres unprepared, as was the whole nation. Church services praying for peace were held, and something akin to panic appeared in some authorities, who had done nothing about the measures advised by the Government. It said that trenches need not be dug in the North, but householders should dig small shelters for their own use. Many rushed to enrol themselves with the various services. Air raid sirens were installed at the Gasworks, operated by steam from the boilers, and 64 air raid wardens and 20

129

Special Constables were enrolled. A number of gas respirators arrived and had to be assembled for practice. These could be assembled by a party at a rate of 80 per hour, but G. R. Mackenzie, Chief Warden, and James Baigrie, Hallkeeper, devised a tool made for them by William Reid, Engineers, which could assemble 276 an hour. However, the authorities banned the use of this device.

In all, in addition to the wardens and rescue party, there were three first-aid parties and nine ambulance drivers. The First Aid Post could call on 70 men, including 50 rescue men, and a number of V.A.D. (Voluntary Aid Detachment) women who drove ambulances and staffed the headquarters and the hospital. More men were required but the position at Forres was comparatively good.

Despite the fear and worry, there was still time for lighter moments, and the tale went round of the rescue party leader, suddenly faced with a visiting and examining party of army officers and doctors, who answered the question shot at him, "Tell us all you know about burns?" with an immediate "He is Scotland's National Poet."

Neville Chamberlain returned with Hitler's promise of "Peace in Our Time," which brought immediate release from tension, although there were those who did not believe the promise.

The Golf Club reported a further fall in membership, from 67 to 58, but a financially good year, with an income of £41 13s 8d, giving a credit balance at the end of £5 2s 8d.

A Scottish Office report showed that Forres led the North-East Burghs in overcrowded houses, 12·4 per cent of all houses being over-crowded. Elgin had only 5·6 per cent and Aberlour none. The latter figure was a sign of the depopulation of upper Banffshire. Keith and Lossiemouth were somewhat below Forres.

The Council nomination meeting was one of the largest in memory, but very quiet with few questions. The *Gazette* claimed that the audience was overcome by the ornate decoration of the hall, seen for the first time. Only two of the retiring Councillors appeared on the platform, the others adhering to the old habit of waiting to see how many were nominated before handing in their own nomination papers. The two on the platform—Bailie Cormack and Councillor Forbes— were joined by Mr William Thomson, railway signalman, who was nominated from the floor. On the election form there were eight candidates for five seats. A newcomer was James S. Paterson, Burn-vale, another railwayman.

On Remembrance Day, 11th November, the Provost laid a wreath at the War Memorial, but there was no other ceremony. The parades, with pipe bands and troops, had gradually stopped, and it is surprising that the ceremonies after the Second War, which had many fewer casualties, were maintained until the Town Council disappeared.

Mr McConnachie, again President of the Farmers' Union, fulminated at the Government for their neglect of the farmers and their land, talking about "persecution of the Jews," he declaimed, "We will soon be as bad."

At the year's end the Council decided to build eight stone houses in Castle Street, and a Swimming Pond to be sited at Castlehill, next to Burdshaugh Farm, with a Gymnasium at a cost of £5662. This would be an open-air pool and the Munro money was to be used. Dr Bruce did not think this was possible because the word in the donor's will was "Baths."

Year 1939

New Year's Day fell on the Sunday, so that Monday was the public holiday, but the townsmen were called out to clear the snow which had fallen on Sunday; it had been a number of years since snow had fallen on this date. There was curling on the Pond and skating at Blair's Loch for a time.

The Pipe Band had paraded at 11 p.m. on Hogmanay, and did not play after Sunday had arrived. The Council had relented and allowed the street lamps to remain lit after 10 p.m., and this allowed the revellers at the Cross to recognise and toast their friends, thus extending the revelry in the streets.

Several new laws had come into force, including one preventing any young person from working more than 48 hours in any week, or working more than five hours without time off for a meal.

At the first Council meeting of the year there were a number of unusual items. A survey would have to be made to see how many evacuees could be accommodated in the case of war. This was done rapidly and showed that with 1115 habitable houses in the burgh, 532 children and 30 adults (most likely teachers) could be sheltered. Ground at Applegrove was up for sale, and this was suggested as a better site for the swimming pool than Castlehill.

Lady Grant of Logie had given £17,000 for the erection of a maternity wing at Leanchoil, and this fortunately was completed in time for the influx of many more people, including wives of the personnel at R.A.F. Kinloss. There was a sudden decision that Kinloss would be a fully-staffed station and wooden quarters were hurriedly put up. Contractors moved in and the town was suddenly busy. New water supplies had to be laid, runways made, farm buildings demolished and the residents moved out. More than 600 civilians would be needed when the works were completed, and 40 uniformed men arrived in April. The first aircraft accident in the area was on 18th February, near Culloden Moor, when a twin-engined bomber crashed on its way from the South to Evanton; it was one of a formation of nine. The pilot, Sergeant Orbell, had compound fractures in both legs, but the other three members of the crew were unhurt.

At the School Management Committee, Mr McConnachie objected to the proposed classrooms for woodwork at Dyke School. This, he claimed, was a waste of money, for rural children were not interested in such work, and asked that the money for the new rooms be used instead for the digging of air raid shelters. Without these shelters, he claimed, rural school children would have to remain at home during any war.

National Service came into force, and youths reaching the age of 17½ were enlisted. Many young men volunteered for units of their choice rather than be allocated to units and services needing men, or into the Civil Defence Corps.

Mrs Edwards received a setback with news of Hitler's further aggressive actions in Eastern Europe, and dealt with non-political matters in her letters, for example, the cutting of trees at the Oak Woods, and the enormous number of naturalised people in the country, whose loyalty to Britain she doubted—but their colour was not mentioned at that time.

The *Gazette* began to deal with items of news from areas remote from Forres. China and Japan caused great concern. There was speculation as to which would win supremacy and be a potential threat to world peace, supported, as they were, by vast populations.

The sum of £21,000 was allocated for a new primary school, but work was not to start until 1945.

The more conservative members of the Council were shocked by the suggestion that the curfew no longer be rung. The bell tolled for five minutes at 8 p.m. warning the residents to put out their fires and go to bed. It also rang for the same time at 6 a.m. to arouse them for work. This custom had lasted for centuries, from the time that all buildings were made of wood and the danger of fire was great. The arrival of war later in the year silenced the bells, never to be rung at this time again. The ringing of bells was to be a warning of invasion, and when this danger disappeared five years later, no one thought of restarting the practice.

There were 30 items on the February agenda, but the meeting only took a few minutes, as all the matters were remitted to committees.

Local football seemed to be having difficulties with its office-bearers. Many letters appeared in the *Gazette* which were difficult to follow without some understanding of the background. The past season had been a very unsuccessful one, no fewer than four Presidents had been elected and dismissed, along with other changes; committee members were sworn to secrecy.

Owners of commercial vehicles were warned that their vehicles would have their fuel rationed on the outbreak of hostilities, and daily the inevitability of war began to be appreciated, except by the optimistic and vocal section of the Press.

The Golf Club celebrated its fiftieth anniversary, with Dr J. M. Brewster as President.

In March, the post of Town's Forester, Cemetery Superintendent and Keeper of Grant Park, Rose Garden and Castlehill, with responsibility for the repair and maintenance of the Town's farm property and fences was advertised. The salary was £150 per annum with the Cemetery Lodge rent free. Mr Clark Macdonald was the successful applicant. Sites for council houses at Cassieford, Pilmuir and Fleurs Place were discussed. The price of the 12½ acres at Cassieford was £1000 and Dr Bruce asked that this site be ignored as the price was too high; he favoured the Pilmuir as the ground belonged to the Town.

The County Council objected to the requirement that central heating should be installed in rural schools; this, they thought, along with bench work, was a waste of money. The Moray Constabulary was increased by 12 men, mostly retired policemen, as the existing force could not cope with all the work being done.

The roundabout where the six roads met at Castle Bridge was formed, and was the source of many police court cases, as many motorists refused to obey the signs.

An unusual appeal appeared in the paper; this was for donations

133

of eggs for the patients in Leanchoil Hospital. Only paying patients got all meals and those not paying had to have their food supplied by friends and relatives. Many of them were single men who had no friends locally to supply them with food.

The high wall running along Orchard Road from Castlehill Road to the Brewery Bridge was in danger of collapsing on to the roadways and action had to be taken. Suggestions varied from removing the most dangerous parts to knocking it all down, leaving the stones lying on the grass to avoid the expense of their removal. When reminded by the Town Clerk that the ground was let for cattle grazing, it was agreed to erect a fence inside the line of fallen stones.

At the May Licensing Court, Inspector John Ross said the police were dissatisfied with the growing custom of licenceholders closing and locking the bar doors at closing time, thus preventing the police from examining the premises. He asked that they be instructed by the Licensing Magistrates to throw all doors open at this time, as was done by one hotelkeeper. He reported also that some licenceholders joined in a game of darts with their customers, and one actually gave a small prize to winners. He drew attention also to the growing habit of "bona fide" travellers standing their friends drinks, which was strictly against the law. The Magistrates agreed to support the police efforts to stamp out such practices, which arose from the new prosperity and the number of incoming workers living in hostels or in rooms, with few places to go except bars.

Councillor John Mackenzie gave notice of his resignation because of ill-health and died very soon afterwards. He was an excellent Councillor, kind and helpful to new members, but he could speak forcefully when necessary without arousing any rancour. The Council decided to wait until the November elections to replace him, but by that time War had arrived and elections were cancelled. By then also, two other members had gone so that the Council entered the war short of three members.

With the arrival of aircraft and much night flying, complaints became frequent, until the war again brought silence on this subject. Empire Day was celebrated in the Grant Park and, as it coincided with the Centenary of the Savings Bank, the Bank Chairman joined Dr Bruce in making a speech. This was the last time the Empire was celebrated in Forres.

Dr Bruce reported that he had supported the County Council in deferring the inoculation of children against diphtheria, believing that the suggested cost would be better spent on improvements to the Infectious Diseases Hospital at Spynie.

The summer had been hot and dry, with temperatures reaching 85° F. in June, yet within a few days there was hail, and snow fell on the hills. Following this hot dry period the forest at Kintessack took fire and burned for three days, destroying the houses and village hall. Cameron Highlanders and men from the R.A.F. had to be brought in to fight the blaze. About two square miles of woodland were burned and Cluny Hill could not be seen from the town because of the smoke.

In August, work began on the demolition of the farm steading and houses at Waterside and Mundole, to form a field for emergency landings. This later became Forres airfield, a satellite station with fighter planes to protect Kinloss. (Waterside was farmed by two sisters, the Misses Moir). The road from the Pilmuir to Balnageith was closed, as was the right-of-way from Tenby Cottage to the Nairn road.

The St John's Operative Lodge of Freemasons celebrated their bi-centenary. It had always been a strong Lodge numerically, and no procession was complete without a contingent from this Lodge, with their morning suits, white ties, top or bowler hats, jewels and decorated Masons' aprons, and carrying their banner. The various trades, joiners, bakers, hammermen and such bodies as the Free Gardeners and Oddfellows, also had their painted banners. This would have been the last such appearance in public.

In the third week of August three holidaymakers, angling in Blair's Loch landed 28 trout weighing 15 lbs.—the best catch for many years.

The holiday traffic added to the growing congestion on the streets, and the bus companies complained that the delays caused were disorganising their services. These services were very good; at some time of the day there were hourly buses to and from Elgin and Inverness.

During August, and earlier, the Forres Pipe Band had been hired to play at Lossiemouth, Grantown-on-Spey and other holiday resorts in the area.

The issue of identity cards to everyone was completed and the air raid warning sirens were taken from the gas works and placed on top of the Tolbooth, where they could be heard from every part of the town. When the schools re-opened after the holidays, the children were issued with civilian type respirators. There was much protest in the rural areas when those attending air raid precautions lectures and

135

training were told that there would be no duties for them in the countryside.

The sudden signing of a Treaty of Friendship between Germany and Russia shocked those who had held firmly to the belief that the war would only occur if Hitler attacked Russia. There was some panic buying of food and storing of petrol and other essential materials, but some newspapers stridently expressed their opinion that there would be no war. When it did start, on the morning of Sunday, 3rd September, and in London the air raid sirens shrieked, many ran for shelter while the news bills proclaimed "There will be no war" in large red letters.

The Prime Minister, Neville Chamberlain, announced over the radio at 11.15 a.m. that hostilities had started. Not everyone had "wireless" but the news soon spread. The High and Castlehill Churches were having a joint service at the High Church (St Leonard's) and notes were handed to the Ministers in that church and in St Laurence Church.

The news was received calmly, almost fatalistically. There was no singing of patriotic songs, nor waving of flags or speeches as on 4th August 1914, which so many still remembered very clearly. Then, for weeks, bands of children marched through the dark streets singing.

The Forres company of the 6th Seaforths (Territorial Army) collected at the Drill Hall, where a large crowd watched quietly while the soldiers mounted buses to take them to some secret destination.

All commercial vehicles were requisitioned by other units of the Army who were encamped at Roysvale Park. For some days, no delivery vans were available and the people in the country were left without meat and bread, until such vehicles were released.

On the following Wednesday, in the Burgh Court, some cyclists appeared to answer charges that they had, on the previous Saturday, cycled without lights. It was an offence to do this but the Bailie, sensibly, only admonished them.

On Saturday, 2nd September, the St Laurence cricket team had had their best score of the season, 141 runs in a match against Ross County. But, in the first soccer match of the season, the Mechanics had been defeated at Borough Briggs four against two. The Flower Show in the Grant Park had been a great success and the *Gazette* gave a recipe for making "Banana Delight"—fruit which was to disappear for six years.

136

On the Friday of the first week of war 71 children and two teachers arrived by train from Granton. Many more had been expected and the billeting officers had made arrangements with willing householders to shelter them for the duration of the war. The train was very late and the station was in darkness. The Town Clerk was the Billeting Officer and there were pathetic scenes as the children were handed to their unknown foster parents. Within a few days, many had returned home, especially those who had been accompanied by their mothers. The anticipated air raids had not occurred, and they were not accustomed to a small town. Within a few weeks, almost all had gone. In even less time, wartime conditions were accepted as the normal way of life. There were no lists of dead and wounded as there had been in the first days of August 1914. Shops closed early and social life slowed down because of the blackout. The Education Authority would not bear the cost of putting blackout curtains on all schools, so as the winter advanced the schools closed earlier, and there were no evening classes or badminton.

In that first week Forres had its only air raid of the whole war. A German plane, apparently off course and trying to find its bearings, flew over the town and dropped a small bomb in Altyre wood, making a hole in the rough ground and reportedly killing a rabbit.

Years 1940 to 1944

Very few records of local events appeared in print during this time. Reports of anything which might suggest that there were forces in the area or remotely concerned the forces or production could not be printed.

The people of Forres endured the blackout, the scarcity of many things, the strain and uncertainty of war, as did the rest of the country. In some ways they were fortunate, for Scotland was self-supporting in food, as England and Wales were not. While the same rationing applied all over the country, such things as eggs, milk and potatoes were never in short supply in the north. Most people had relatives in the countryside where even fuel to warm one's home was in good supply. But they had the same fears and worries, and they were nearer the war than many. The wives of the pilots and air crews came to live in the district to be near their husbands, so that most of the local people knew some of them. It was impossible not to feel for the service wives when their husbands left on missions. The dangers of these were soon shown when early in the war a large bomber in difficulties tried to land in Roysvale Park and crashed into Fern Villa in Tolbooth Street, removing part of the roof and setting the house on fire; but greater than the loss of the side of the house was the knowledge that nine young men were killed.

The Cluny Hill Hotel, Ben Romach Distillery, the Town Hall and the Drill Hall and other places were requisitioned and filled with soldiers. Huts appeared everywhere—at Sanquhar, in the Grant Park and around the town. Sanquhar House, Altyre House and Darnaway Castle were military hospitals.

Not only British servicemen were to be seen. After the fall of France the Polish Air Force was re-formed at Kinloss, and a month or two later the Norwegian Artillery took over Rafford, where they lived in tents through a wretchedly cold winter. Many of these were men off the whaling ships who had been on the Antarctic seas when war broke out and sailed to Britain rather than go to Norway, now occupied by the Germans. These Nordic men were more easily accepted than the Poles, as most of them spoke at least some English. Arm flashes could be seen from many countries—Czech, Free French, South Africans, New Zealanders and others. Most exotic was Private Alfredo Hilario Camisuli, who had the word "Gibraltar" on his shoulder flash and wore the kilt of the Seaforth Highlanders, although his home was Santo Domingo in the West Indies.

In the town, the Picture House and the British Legion Club—then in Caroline Street—were the only places of entertainment, while a Canteen was run in the Bank Lane Hall. Dances were held in the village halls and at Kinloss, where friendships were made, leading to many marriages. For the first time, dances were held on Sundays.

In May and June 1940, after Dunkirk, the Home Guard was formed with the Town Clerk, Mr A. H. Macdonald as Major, and his brother, Councillor and Colonel A. D. Macdonald, in command. Both had done gallant service in the First World War, as had the backbone of the Home Guard, some of them having seen service in the Boer War forty years earlier.

In October, Provost C. M. Fraser resigned and Dr John Bruce became Provost.

When Germany and Japan declared war on the U.S.A. it was only days before the first Americans appeared in the district; from the

American Air Force at first, but later Infantrymen. Some of their wives managed to follow, and there were few houses which did not have men of other nationalities in their homes, either as guests and friends or as sub-tenants; every house was crowded.

As the fortunes of war began to turn, the whole area was made into a training area for the invasion of the continent. The sandy beaches along the coast were similar to the beaches of France and Italy, and through the night—and often through the day—hundreds of men and vehicles passed through the streets of the town. The village of Broom of Moy was accidentally bombed in a practice attack and had to be evacuated. The inhabitants had to crowd in where they could. The Canadian Forestry Corps cut trees all over the country, and occasional units of Indian Mounted Artillery could be seen with their mules, as they fanned out in exercises from Grantown-on-Spey and other hill places where they were stationed.

The local company of Territorials, the Seaforth Highlanders, had been with the units left to defend St Valery, to allow the main army to escape from Dunkirk, and were captured as a unit with many dead and wounded. Only a few were able to avoid capture and get back to Britain.

Lord Beaverbrook, as Minister of Supply, campaigned for metal to keep the munition factories in production, appealing for every scrap of iron or other metals. Many gave up their cooking utensils, and the Council felt that they must give the large muzzle loading cannon at Nelson Tower. The sum of £18 was received for these, but it cost much more for men and horses to drag them to the railway station.

The Germans had increased the intensity of their air raids in the south, and another influx of children was expected. So crowded was the town with the wives of R.A.F. and Army personnel that accommodation for only 20 children could be provided. These settled much better than the earlier arrivals, and some married and stayed permanently in the town.

Both Kinloss and Waterside air stations increased in size, and the water supplies had to be augmented. The work was done by the authorities and, again, no plans nor intimation were sent to the Town Council. Electric cables were also laid, giving rise to near fatal accidents in later years, when excavations were made for new buildings.

Thirty hurricane lamps were bought for emergencies and, in November, an order was made making it compulsory for all civilians to wear their gas masks from 10 a.m. to 10.30 a.m. on the first Monday

139

of every month; this rule was ignored by everyone. To save light and fuel, shops had to close earlier in winter, and fuel stocks had to be built up during the summer.

At the end of the year, Dr Douglas, who had been Medical Officer of Health for the Burgh for many years, retired; he was the author of *The Annals of Forres*.

During 1942 and 1943 everything was subordinated to the war effort and only routine matters, such as the paying of rates and the collection of rents and rates, could be dealt with in the Burgh Council. The defeats of our armies all over the world, and the fear of invasion, made everyday matters of little importance. Staff were recruited from those unfit, or too old, for work of national importance. There was a shortage of all materials.

With the defeat of the German Afrika Corps, in which many local men took part, the war outlook became more hopeful, making it possible to think of peace and the future.

In January 1944 the Burgh Surveyor, Mr John Rankine, died; he had passed the age of retirement but stayed on. He was an excellent practical man, who had started work as a plumber but became responsible for the many duties of his job. He was Water Manager, Firemaster, Slaughterhouse Superintendent, Health Inspector, and also designed houses for Forres and the Burgh of Kingussie. He had no assistant or clerical help, nor did the Council provide him with an office. His plans and methods he carried in his mind, and they died with him.

Mr James C. MacNish came from Galashiels to take up the position, and had to painstakingly gather together the scattered threads. When the war ended he had to start afresh with the problems left by the military authorities as they left no records or plans. His salary was £300 a year with a War Bonus of £50.

The Scottish Office advised the Education Authority that it was now time to look for sites for post-war building of schools. The owner of Applegrove had decided to sell it, as he was now ready to give up market gardening, and it was bought as a possible site for a new school; the price was £850.

The Market Green and the Town Hall were now returned by the Army. The Hall was in very poor condition after being occupied by troops since the outbreak of war, and required major works to get it back into usable order.

In July, after some disagreement, it was decided to co-opt

eight members to bring the Council up to its statutory set of seventeen members. Those appointed were: Peter Garrow, a long-time critic of the Council at public meetings and in the columns of the *Gazette*; Pat Mackenzie, ironmonger; William Mackenzie, St Leonard's Bakery; John W. Mustard, grocer and son-in-law of Peter Garrow; James W. Thomson, Principal Teacher of English in the Academy; William Thomson, railway signalman; William T. Watters, S.C.W.S. Manager; and James M. Younie, radio dealer.

A grant of £2493 was received to pay for the reinstatement of roads damaged by the military traffic. Pindlers Croft of five acres was let at a rent of £30. Trees were planted at Drumduan and Cluny Hill; those previously planted had been destroyed by the pine weevil. The Army unexpectedly requisitioned a small area of the Grant Park opposite St Crispin's and erected huts here. The last of these was not removed until July 1973.

The Scottish Development Department now stated that they no longer thought that Cassieford was a suitable site for municipal houses and asked the Council to look for another site for 100 houses. This was the plan of 1939.

The Amenities Association was revived and made an appeal for a new school and public toilets. The Forres Mechanics Football Club returned to the Mosset Park, where corn had been grown during the war, and decided that as soon as the harvest was in they would put the pitch in order.

New legislation took away more of the powers of the Councils of small burghs and transferred them to the County Councils. These applied mostly to public health acts. Sir Robert Grant of Logie— following in the steps of his father, Sir Alexander—purchased the golf course, with Edgehill and Clovenside, and presented them to the town.

At the end of the year the Council decided that the new houses would be erected on ground belonging to Sanquhar House and what is now Anderson Crescent and Macdonald Drive.

In the spring of 1944 the forces quietly disappeared. D-Day the date for the invasion of France was near. Then on the 6th June the landing in France took place. Forres airfield had been left empty except for a corporal, and about six days after D-Day several trains arrived at Forres station with prisoners of war and non-combatants, hundreds of them, quite unexpected at this early date. There were some Germans and other enemy troops but the greatest number were

141

"slave labour," men and boys. The solitary corporal could do nothing with this horde of starving men; they raided the neighbouring fields, where the farmers, Mr Wilfrid Scott of Whiterow and Mr Stewart of Thornhill, had been growing potatoes, carrots and other vegetables, and ate them raw. Several acres of carrots disappeared in minutes. During the day the Red Cross took over and arranged the men in squads of four, with one man in charge. The latter was given a pound and sent to forage for food in the town. The shopkeepers had never seen such a sight before; gaunt, starving, unshaven men, in tattered clothing, with no English, proffering money and pointing at the meagre stock of food on the shelves. Frozen foods were unknown but there were packets of prepared pastry, and these were snatched up as eagerly as anything else, some packets being eaten raw on the spot.

But soon things were organised, the Germans and other troops being taken away to prisoner of war camps; the fit men and youths were clothed and formed into units. The numbers were secret but it was said that seventeen units of Polish Grenadiers were formed at Forres, many of them returning to the continent to help finish the war. The camp became a centre for dancing and continental-style entertainment and many marriages took place. There are still many families with Polish names in the district.

Year 1945

The first weeks of the year were bitterly cold, accompanied by flooding. The river mouth was frozen and this ice held back the flow of water, increasing the area flooded; in the end the Army had to blow up the ice. The cold weather continued into February, and was felt more by the rationing of fuel. This ration was 20 cwts. of coal for each house for the months of February, March and April, but not more than 10 cwts. of the ration could be taken in one month. The rationing of petrol prevented cars being used to collect firewood and fallen timber; bicycles and prams were pressed into service for this purpose.

The thousands of troops accompanied by their families in many cases had shown up the lack of public toilets, and one of the first tasks of the Council was to find a quick remedy. Three possible sites were chosen; between the Tolbooth and the Cross; in the Public Assistance Office in the Tolbooth in the room facing on to the High Street, and in Gordon Street. The County Planning Committee would give permission lasting only for five years so these sites were abandoned.

The Education Committee met the Council to discuss a site for a new primary school, and asked for the use of Grant Park, a request refused out of hand.

The war in Europe came to an end on the 8th of June, to everyone's relief, but without the hysteria which had seized the people in November 1918 when the First World War had ended. War still continued in the East against Japan, showing no signs of coming to an end, although the general belief was that the Allies would finally succeed. When hostilities did come to an end in September, the Government seemed totally unprepared. All the wartime restrictions were continued including the total ban on street lights and the showing of lights from houses. But this was ignored whenever possible, and the air raid wardens and police who tried to enforce the ban were ignored. The problems of peace now became obvious after five and a half years of hardship and sacrifice. There was an insistent demand for action to deal with social problems.

The town's water supply barely met the needs of the area including the Royal Air Force station at Kinloss which had been made permanent and was now expanding. The Councils of Forres, Nairn County and Moray discussed a joint plan for drawing a supply from Lochindorb, but the Town Council withdrew, deciding instead to augment the supply from the Romach. The two counties then decided on a reservoir at Clunas to supply Nairnshire only.

The burgh labourers were still paid only £3 15s 0d a week and men everywhere began to demand higher wages. The town's cleansing carts were still drawn by horses, and skilled horsemen were now difficult to obtain, as motor transport was taking over.

As it was not possible to continue hiring two horses with drivers, and provide four burgh workmen to act as sweepers, a motor vehicle was purchased. A public toilet was erected in Caroline Street at a cost of £950.

The election, in abeyance since 1938, was held in November, with thirteen candidates for the same number of vacancies, so no poll was required. The nomination meeting was well attended, demand being made for the early provision of houses. Many men, married during the

143

war, were now returning home and naturally wanted a home of their own. Forres had not been very active in building houses in the pre-war era, and the shortage was very noticeable. This pressure on the Council to build more houses continued for 20 years, election meetings providing opportunities for the homeless to voice their demands. The police had always to be there in force to control those attending.

The Council had never had a clear policy for letting the few houses which became vacant. When a vacancy occurred it was advertised and applications invited. The Housing Committee made its decision in secret, and refused to make public the name of the successful applicant. Inevitably he was accused by the unsuccessful of having obtained the house by lies and deceit, and naturally kept silent until such time as he and his family had occupied the house. Even Councillors were refused this information, and one was threatened with some process of the law when he informed the Convener of the Housing Committee on the morning after the meeting that he was aware of the name of the new tenant. Only Councillors who promised to adhere to this policy of secrecy were elected to the Housing Committee. One who made an appeal to the Secretary of State was told that the allocation of houses was wholly within the province of the Town Council.

Provost Dr Bruce had held the office during the war years and now retired, Bailie Michie Anderson succeeding him in the Provost's chair.

A campaign was being waged for a new Scottish University, and Inverness asked for support from the northern burghs to have it sited there. This support was given but Stirling was eventually chosen.

Whisky was one of the few items not rationed. The quantity available was so small that it could not be divided equally, and as the festive season approached long queues appeared outside the licensed grocers during legal selling hours, which were the same as those applying to bars and hotels.

In the Council the new members clashed with older members who were not used to being hurried. One of the first occasions was when the renting of Roysvale Park for cattle grazing arose. This was the only place where football or other games could be played by the general public, as the Grant Park cricket pitch was wholly reserved for the St Laurence Club, and the bowling green there was leased to two separate clubs. Only strolling was allowed, and cyclists were frequently taken to court for using the paths or the grass. Apart from the time when troops camped during the war in Roysvale, it had been used for grazing. An attempt had been made as early as 1906 to retain it wholly for pleasure purposes. All subsequent attempts had failed, as the revenue from the grazings went to the Common Good, and this fund was used as much as possible to reduce the amount collected in rates. This attempt was again unsuccessful but junior teams were allowed to play at certain times, sharing the park with cattle.

A Parents' Association was formed to press for the much needed primary school. The first floor of the Academy on High Street was now in a dangerous condition, and the primary pupils occupied the ground floor beneath it. The School Management Committee denied the parents use of the school for a meeting and refused also to meet them.

A list of those killed on service during the war was drawn up, embodying 57 names, a much smaller number than those lost in the First World War. These names were to be engraved on the existing War Memorial, but this was finally done by the Rotary Club, who also raised the necessary money, as the Council seemed unwilling to take any action.

Councillor Peter Garrow, who had long advocated a swimming pool, using the Munro Baths Fund, put forward a motion that a pool should be placed inside Forres House; after a full debate he was defeated by nine votes to seven.

The Water Committee recommended that the old style annual visits to the water supply at Loch Romach and Remichie be resumed in 1946, and so this became the chief, and normally the only, social function held by the Town Council.

Year 1946

This was the first year since 1936 without war or threat of war. But the whole nation was exhausted and there was little of comfort apart from the return of men and women from the Services. Each week saw more men and women returning, now married or preparing to marry, and now looking for their own homes. They found that staying with friends and relatives on a semi-permanent basis was much different from spending a few days' leave. Houses were overcrowded and needed repairs but materials were scarce and expensive. All were harassed by shortage of fuel and the other necessities of life, including clothing and furniture.

The new Labour government—the first to have a majority in Parliament—passed much legislation in a very short time. Much of it was deemed revolutionary, and included the compulsory purchase of land for new houses by local authorities. Increased subsidies were also given for housebuilding but the lack of materials and the reluctance of many councils to buy land by compulsion held back much progress. Everything was in short supply except money, and as a result "black markets" in all kinds of goods flourished. In Forres, as in most market towns, the full shortages of further south were not felt. Most people had friends in the country and it was possible to get ample amounts of eggs, milk and poultry, and even butter.

But as the months rolled on rationing was intensified. The U.S.A. had poured in supplies of all kinds during the time of war, but these now ceased. The Marshall Plan was not put into effect until 1948, and Britain now had to pay for everything obtained abroad. This austerity was not borne stoically as in the wartime, and no guilt was now felt as before when the accusation was made: "You are harming the war effort and helping the Nazis" when getting more than one's entitlement of scarce commodities.

Since 1939 prices had risen by fifty per cent, while wages had gone up at a slightly higher rate. There were now few unemployed against the million or more in the pre-war era, and there was more money available. Income Tax was reduced to 9s 3d against the 10s of the war years. The National Debt had multiplied by three times, reaching the enormous figure of £23,636,000,000, and the Government took over the Bank of England. The war-time controls over the railways, mines, electricity, civil aviation and road transport were extended for a period of five years, until such time as they could be nationalised. The Trades Disputes Act of 1927 was repealed as this was the highest priority in the Government's programme. This had banned sympathy strikes, and very soon the workers were using this freedom against the government that had given it to them.

A New Towns Act authorised the building of many small towns to give living space to many thousands of people. The National Health Act, which came into effect in 1948, banished the fear of illness and the consequent doctors' and druggists' bills. But against that, bread had to be rationed and the rations of sugar and fats were reduced.

Almost all food was now controlled and continual trips had to be made to the County Food Control Office in Elgin. A birth, an illness, a visitor, or even a change of residence, required a trip to the food office. Ration cards had to be returned in the case of a death or the provision of extra food or milk ordered by the doctor for an invalid. Buses were few, overcrowded and often very late so the Council requested that a Sub-Food Office be opened in the town. This was refused, but a Food Advisory Office was opened at Forres House, where the Fuel Overseer reigned, and this helped somewhat.

Many hundreds of Polish servicemen passed through the Waterford and Balnageith camps. One regiment shocked the good townspeople by marching along High Street and South Street with bands playing, banners flying, and . . . horror of horrors . . . with fixed bayonets. Mr Macdonald, Town Clerk, hurriedly found the liaison officer and instructed him to let the Poles know gently but firmly that this was a privilege granted by a royal burgh, and unlikely to be given even if requested. It was not done again and was never asked for.

The Officers' and Sergeants' Messes at the camp were popular resorts for the local people, especially the ladies. The strangers had a romantic European appeal, and many married local girls. When given the chance of staying in Britain a surprisingly large number chose to stay. The Board of Trade later said that Forres had received more certificates for aliens setting up in business, in relation to its size, than any other place in Scotland.

Most of these settlers who also included Baltic peoples, Russians and a few Germans, did well, bringing new skills to the area. Some left for Canada, frankly admitting that they were using that country as an entry to the U.S.A. Others bought farms or entered the professions, some changing their names to permit quicker absorption into the community of their choice.

Continued pressure on the Housing Committee forced the members to introduce a system of allocating houses by a points scheme. But this had still to remain a secret, as the Committee members claimed that otherwise some applicants would not hesitate to canvass members of the allocating committee. The Council accepted this, as non-members of the Housing Committee could tell applicants that they knew nothing of the system and could not intervene.

Not long after this innovation a house fell vacant, being given to the person whose name was at the head of the list. After the tenant had taken occupancy it was discovered that he did not live in Forres.

147

There was a great furore but the committee were unmoved. It took many years before the system was made public.

Three new councillors were elected this year, some being members of the newly-formed Parents' Association.

The children at Dyke School went on strike because of the total absence of water there. The supply had always been precarious and now it failed altogether. Witnesses stated that the toilets were in a dreadful state but the chairman of the Schools Management Committee in Forres said he had visited the school and had not noticed anything unusual, but other members rather more observant disagreed. Water was taken to the school by tanker until such time as the supply was restored.

One of the newly-elected councillors, Stirling Kirkland, a bank manager, asked that committee conveners report the decisions of their committees to the statutory meeting of the Town Council, so that all could know what was being done. He and other newer members were dissatisfied with the secrecy that prevailed and forced the matter to a vote, being defeated by ten votes to seven.

The Golf Course Committee contained all the keen golfers in the Council who were inclined to treat the course as if it were a private club. They decided that two members of the club should attend all meetings in the Council Chamber, and as a result aroused great indignation among the non-golfing councillors. By a slow process of rejecting every suggestion from the Golf Course Committee and refusing to vote any money for the running of the course, these unofficial members were removed.

The weathercock on the Tolbooth steeple ceased to function, and remained optimistically and misleadingly pointing south-west. It had been erected in 1848 and was found to be worn to a paper thinness, and was replaced by a new cock. The old one lay in the clock loft, hardly worth carrying downstairs for scrap. When twenty years later an American lady visiting the Tolbooth asked if she could buy it, it was flown across the Atlantic and now faces the sea from the roof of the owner's house in Norfolk, Virginia, the home of the widow of an American naval officer who had been killed in Vietnam.

At the end of the fishing season on the Findhorn, the lessees, Messrs Sellars, reported that the fish catch in the nets was the lowest recorded, only one-third of the normal annual catch being landed.

Much of the Council's work was concerned with bringing back into good condition all the town's properties which had been neglected during the war years. The Town Hall, Clovenside and Edgehill had all been occupied by troops, as had other properties such as the Cluny Hill Hotel and Ben Romach distillery.

Repairs to private property, if costing more than £10, had to be licensed by the Council. Forres House had been the centre for the air raid precautions organisation and had been affected by dry rot. Thousands of pounds had to be spent during the years trying to keep it in order.

Plans were made to build 93 houses at Fleurs, later to be Anderson Crescent and Macdonald Drive. Prefabricated houses were being made in factories and 50 were sent to Forres. The Council had to pay £26 per annum for these and had to let them at £22 per annum to the tenants. These houses were given a life of only 20 years although they were well equipped. All were replaced in the course of time. Many were bought very cheaply and re-erected elsewhere with brick, stone or cement walls and are still very desirable homes.

Year 1947

The Housing Committee had always kept a firm hand on its expenditure, refusing to do anything but the most essential repairs and trusting that the tenants would do what was necessary if the Committee would not do it. As a result, the Committee now found themselves with a good surplus in the housing accounts, and asked the Department of Home and Health—as it was then—if they could use this surplus money to pay off some of the housing debt. This was refused and they were told that the money must remain in the Repair Fund.

In February, the baths in Forres House were reopened for the use of the public. During the war the whole building had been taken over by the air raid warden service and also used by other wartime bodies.

Many things were discussed and numerous motions put forward; notice of these had to be given a month ahead, and as many as nine—covering a wide range—would be on the agenda for the monthly meeting. Some of the decisions reached were carried out but others were referred to a Committee where they were often ignored or

149

subjected to so many delays and changes that they were made ineffective.

The Mechanics Football Club had restored the playing pitch to good condition, and they now asked the Council for permission to erect a grandstand, as the ground belonged to the Council, who charged only a nominal rent. Permission was granted and, in law, the grandstand became the property of the Council as landlord. The Grant Park Bowling Club asked that they be allowed to play on Sundays but this was refused, as was permission to take cars into the Grant Park so that spectators could watch the game. Councillor Garrow wanted the ford at Plasmon Mills to be concreted to make a smoother path for cars, since he ran a taxi service. This also was rejected but done later when the footbridge was moved downstream for greater convenience of the increasing number of people living in the Fleurs area.

After many years of neglect the Council visited their farms at Pilmuir and the Califer. The condition of some of these was deplorable. The tenants had neglected them although they had been given an abatement of their rents on the understanding that they kept the farms in good condition. This may have been caused by the difficulty in obtaining materials and workmen during the war. The Bogs of Blervie farm buildings were beyond repair, and were abandoned, and the farm let as a grazing only. The remaining farms were put in order over a period of time, thus absorbing the surplus in the Common Good. This fund ought to have been much larger but the Treasurer was inclined to take as much from it as possible, and so reduce the rates levied on the residents. This kept the rates of Forres very low as compared to other burghs of a like size. Government grants were also available for farm lands and buildings and they were applied for when work was done.

In reply to a request from the County Council for a site for a new police station, land at Castlehill was offered.

The Golf Committee recommended that a professional greenkeeper and player be employed, and one was obtained at a wage of £2 10s a week, with free rent of the house and the shop attached to the Clubhouse. (This committee was set up when Sir Robert Grant gave the town the gift of the course and the houses at Clovenside and Edgehill.)

The Secretary of State urged that the town join in the Lochindorb water scheme. The Council refused as they considered that this would suffice only for a short time, and a greater supply would be necessary.

This was a wise decision, the Provost, Michie Anderson, being considered an expert on the subject of water supply.

Offers were taken for the demolition of the various air raid shelters in various parts of the town, which were now unsightly and unhygienic. The first price was £818, but the Secretary of State refused permission to accept this, and later an offer of £505 was obtained. So well were these shelters made that it took several times as long to destroy them as it had taken to build them.

The first amusements for children were placed in the Grant Park—a chute and a set of swings. The cost was £300.

Dean of Guild Garrow put forward a motion condemning low flying during the night, as the war was now over. Apart from some opposition from Dr Hutchison, who had served with the R.A.F. during the war, this was agreed, and the Town Clerk was instructed to write to the Air Ministry.

A proposal to build a bridge over the Mosset at the ford was rejected. The town's forests were now "dedicated" under a Government scheme to encourage the planting of trees. This meant that annual grants were given for trees planted but this had to be done under the general control of the Forestry Commission.

The November elections again roused much interest, with eleven candidates for five seats; this was the first and only occasion when some candidates stood with Party labels. All were decisively defeated. The year ended with "load shedding" in the electric supply, shops, as a result, closing early. The supply was cut off every Thursday from 8 a.m. to 11 a.m. and again from 3 p.m. to 5.30 p.m. for the months of January, February and March.

New flooring in Burmese "jurgan" was laid in the Town Hall. The old floor had been laid on old locomotive springs, giving it a resilience which earned it the reputation of being the best dancing floor in the North of Scotland. The springs were to have been replaced but a majority of the Council decided that this should not be done, thereby saving £600.

This year, Christmas celebrations returned to their pre-war gaiety with a number of parties and dances. So great was the demand for the Town Hall that a system of allocation had to be devised. At first, the Saturday allocation was done by lot, but priorities were fixed which gave the greatest number of lets on this day to sports clubs and other bodies. The hall was not made available for dances run for profit.

Although the war was over, there were still a number of prisoners

151

of war in camps in the neighbourhood, including Muirton and Kinloss. These were employed by farmers on a daily basis. On Christmas Day 1946 the Germans at Muirton were visited by the Moderator of the Church of Scotland. Probably because of this, about 20 of the men were invited to lunch on New Year's Day at the farms where they worked.

In January, one of the worst gales recorded struck the town, causing much damage. The metal shaft of the weathercock was twisted and the new one had to be refitted by steeplejacks who also repaired other minor damage.

At the height of summer the High Street was again disturbed, one-way traffic being operated on the High Street and Orchard Road. The granite setts and cobble stones, laid 70 years earlier, were now removed so that the roads could be asphalted. So often had they been opened for the laying of water, gas, electricity and sewage pipes, as well as telephone cables, that most of the granite had been moved more than once. The skilled trade of pavior was now unknown, and replaced setts made the road difficult to walk on and very rough for vehicles. The road engineers promised that once the work was finished traffic would flow quietly and swiftly. This was never achieved, as the increasing number, and haphazard parking, of vehicles on either side of the street brought chaos. The increased number of manhole covers mostly loosely fitted, added to the noise. Towards the end of the work the workmen were rarely seen but still the diversion signs were in place. Exasperated by this, Provost Michie Anderson ordered them to be removed without asking for sanction.

A District Welfare Association was formed, the pioneer work being done by Mrs Jean Mackintosh, later a Councillor and Bailie. Its primary aim was a modern home for old people. The existing home at Burnside had been built a century before as a cholera hospital, but cholera was wiped out at that time by the installation of piped water and a sewerage system, and it never had a cholera patient. It was bleak and inconvenient and showed its age. Mrs C. M. Edwards, who had almost abandoned her esoteric politics and had returned to the Conservative fold, was the first President of the Welfare Association.

The British Legion bought the Congregational Church as their Club Rooms and now had enough money in hand to renovate and alter it. The huts at Waterside, Balnageith, Whiterow and Sanquhar, vacated by the Polish Army, were now occupied by homeless families. Many of these came from a distance, as far away as Glasgow, to get

PAST-PROVOSTS AND BURGH OFFICIALS

Provost A. Michie Anderson
1946-1955

Provost R. B. S. Braid
1955-1962

Provost P. J. F. McKenzie
1962-1965

Archibald Macdonald
Town Clerk

James C. McNish
Former Burgh Surveyor (1944-74)

George Forbes
Burgh Surveyor

Dr John M. Brewster
Dean of Guild

Councillor Ian A. Campbell

Graeme W. Fulton
Bailie

Councillor Hugo K. Kennedy

Councillor Alexander A. Logie

Richard F. McIntosh
Bailie

Councillor Kenneth MacLennan

Councillor Martha B. Morrison

Dr Douglas J. Murray
Treasurer

Councillor Norman C. Redman

Alistair Sinclair
Bailie

Councillor Gordon W. Smith

Councillor David R. Vallance

Councillor William S. Wallace

Councillor Charles K. White

some accommodation. The County Council, in whose area the huts were, was asked by the Government to take them over and, in the course of time, rehouse them. This it refused to do and asked that the Burgh take them over, which the Burgh Council refused to do. Some of the squatters were problem families, not welcomed by any authority.

Later, the Town Council asked for permission to go on with a further housing scheme, and were told they could erect a hundred houses if they agreed to use some of them for rehousing the hut dwellers. This was accepted and, when housed, the squatters fitted in admirably, except for one family. This one was evicted and moved to another neighbouring burgh, which has had to endure them even to the third generation.

Year 1948

This year made an inauspicious start, with the Town Clock failing to strike midnight to bring in the New Year. There were a good number of revellers, the pipe band played, but only after some minutes was it realised that the New Year had arrived. Somewhat disconcerted, the band made a start for home, then turned in to the Museum Square where they played for some time.

A unit of the Gordon Highlanders was expected to move into the vacated army huts to check the inflow of squatters, but it did not arrive and units of the Polish Army from Banff were sent.

The policy of secrecy adopted by the Housing Committee came under attack again, supported by the newly-elected members. They had been successful at the polls with their promise of reforms in the system of allocating houses. Councillor Mrs Mackintosh had six motions dealing with various aspects of the problem, but all were defeated.

At a meeting of the County Council a letter was read from the Government asking that some of the roadmen be dismissed, as the grants for road work were to be cut; it expressed the hope that the dismissed men would take jobs on farms, where there was a shortage of labour. Farmworkers were now unwilling to take work where they had to live in tied cottages, with their lack of facilities. They were

153

moving into the towns and villages, exacerbating the shortage of houses there. The County Council agreed to dismiss 11 of their road squad, but later decided to take no action on the letter.

The Farmers' Union asked that children over 13 should get leave of absence from school to harvest the potatoes which, they pointed out, were extensively planted this year at the request of the Government.

The British Legion opened their new premises. The Managers of Leanchoil Hospital learned that they would be dispensed with under the new Health Act, as the hospital would be run by a Board sitting in Elgin and managing all the hospitals in Moray.

The sanitary conditions at 91 High Street was the cause of a dispute in the Council. A letter was received from the Department of Health enquiring about this property, as they had received nine complaints from the tenants. There were 14 houses on one side of this close and five on the other. The five nearest High Street had a w.c. but the pipe ran into a cesspit only four feet away; this was not cleaned out regularly so that it overflowed. The Provost explained that the Council could only warn the proprietor when a complaint was received, when it would be cleaned and then neglected again. Pressed to take some action, the Provost held that none was possible, as they could not condemn the houses until the people had gone.

In April, the Town Clerk's salary was increased from £350 to £500, and the Town Chamberlain was offered £450. He refused to accept this as, with the condition attached to it, he would have a decrease in his income. Under the old system he received a percentage of all rents collected; after discussion he was given another £50.

The grazing at the Golf Course was let for £100, Roysvale Park for £40 and Applegrove for £23. An attempt to stop this was unsuccessful.

For the first time, the town now had a foreman in the direct works department.

During the celebrations of the anniversary of the Battle of Britain at Kinloss, the air station was affiliated to the Burghs of Forres, Elgin and Nairn. Provost Anderson was handed a missive by Group Captain A. E. Dark; Group Captain Marlow had initiated this earlier. This was the first official contact between the Council and the Royal Air Force.

The houses which had stood so long derelict on the north-east side of Batchen Street were now demolished. To do this, they had to be bought from the owners.

154

Mr John Bowie, a native of Forres, was appointed Greenkeeper and Golf Professional; he came from Boat of Garten, where he had held the same position.

Moray received a number of Jugoslavs from Munster in Germany. They were men who could not return to Yugoslavia and 650 of them had been at the camp since the end of the war. The Germans and Italians in Britain were now being returned to their home countries. Italians had been at Dallas Camp since their capture and, with their pleasant ways, had made friends even during hostilities. With British conditions and Red Cross parcels they were more fortunate in this respect than the local people, and this had often been the subject of comment. A popular tale was that of the little girl who, when asked by the minister of Dallas what she would like to be when she grew up, returned the answer, "An Italian prisoner of war."

Much space was given in the Press to the reports of the meetings of the Youth Panel. This was set up to look after young people and arrange sports and other pastimes. The Minister of St Laurence Church was one of the leading members, while a member of one of the youth clubs took pleasure in flaunting his atheism on every occasion. This resulted in much time wasting in ensuing exchanges and the Panel made little progress. The Amenities Association revived the Forres Amateur Athletic Association.

The Forres representative on the Moray Food Control Committee in Elgin complained that onions were unobtainable in Forres. It was explained that the Ministry of Food sold the onions wholesale, at a standard price, all over Britain. This meant that distant retailers had to pay freight charges from the distribution point at the docks, but could not charge for this, as the retail price was the same as elsewhere, so they did not take onions to sell at a loss. They asked that they be allowed to charge a farthing a pound more.

Provost Anderson and Bailie Campbell had inspected the property at Clovenside, given to the town by Sir Robert Grant, along with the Golf Course, and recommended that nothing be done. This proposal was resoundingly defeated by 12 votes to 2. The houses were brought up to standard and occupied.

A proprietor of two houses in a close in High Street asked that they be condemned. The tenants could then occupy them without payment of rent and rates, while the proprietor also would not have to pay owner's rates. The Council would not issue an order as this would mean the two tenants would have to be rehoused.

155

The Gala Week was revived and was very successful, showing a surplus of £800. This was in spite of the canvas having been blown away in a gale before the games, so that no charge for admission could be made, and only a collection was taken.

August brought the worst floods for many years, no trains being able to pass Mosstowie for a week. The newly-erected Bailey Bridge at Broom of Moy was under several feet of water. The War Department made a payment of £500 to repair the damage done to the burgh roads during the war by army vehicles. Name plates were ordered for all the streets and roads in town.

Glenmore Lodge was opened as a public sports centre, the first step in the development of the Aviemore area for winter sports.

An attempt was made to amend the housing points scheme, without avail. The *Gazette* described the debate as the most remarkable ever known.

The Scotch Whisky Association announced that the whisky trade was dying because of the competition from foreign drinks, which were more deleterious.

The November elections had now ceased, the time being altered to May, and the retiring Councillors had to continue until then.

There was another cut in the sugar ration, a poor portent for Christmas. Turkeys and poultry became very scarce. Price controls had encouraged a black market as the number of suppliers was unknown. Dealers from the south called on farmers and poultry breeders, and carried away their purchases. The food position was worse than it had been at any time during the war; few, if any, delicacies were for sale, trade and money had been poor all year, and the fog and frost did not help towards enjoyment of the holidays. The one bright spot was the news that St Laurence cricket team were the champions for the second year in succession.

Year 1949

This was a year of waiting. The Labour Government had been in power for four years, and economic problems looked as if ready to swamp it. A great mass of legislation had been passed, much of it affecting housing, and all branches of government were trying to

156

digest and apply it. A General Election was now imminent—or in the very near future—and the Council, like all others, was going warily.

There had been a national drive to collect waste paper, which the Council did, and thereby earned a good sum of money. As a result, newsprint was more freely available and the *Gazette* reverted to its pre war size. The Editor offered the back page to R.A.F. Kinloss for use as a station magazine. As there was at times a dearth of local news, this may have been a considerable help to him.

One of the first items of the year was the bitter complaint of Councillor George Smith, later Provost of Elgin. It was about the darkness of the streets of Elgin; only gas lamps were used and coal was very short so that lamps were often very dim.

One of the few changes in Forres High Street took place when the old property at 156 High Street was demolished to make way for a new office for the Aberdeen Savings Bank.

The Provost had written to the constituency's Member of Parliament, Captain James Stuart, to ask his help in getting an allocation of houses for the burgh. The housing list had been closed for some time, when the names numbered 250, but pressure had grown so great that a supplementary list had been started to placate the angry and frustrated homeless, and it quickly had 150 names. Captain Stuart did his best, but all he could press from the Scottish Secretary was six houses.

During a fierce gale, the Bobbin Mills took fire, the conflagration being visible for many miles. The Forres Fire Brigade had to call for help from the Brigades of Elgin, R.A.F. Kinloss and Nairn. Fortunately, there was a good supply of water in the Mosset Burn. Only a few days earlier, the printing works, offices and home of the caretaker of the *Gazette* had also been burned. From this time the *Gazette* was printed in Elgin.

Much of the extra space now available in the paper was filled with reports of sport and of the churches. The Y.M.C.A. hall in Cumming Street was crowded every Sunday evening, and the speakers were reported very fully.

The Amenities Association decided to spend £450 on a nationwide advertising campaign to bring tourists to the town. Fruit growing was being developed along the Moray Firth and a Moray Firth Fruit-growers' Association was formed, two hundred members being enrolled between the Spey and the Ness.

In the spring the number of regular blood donors had reached

157

47, the best of any collection centre in the north; the number increased every year.

The British Railways winter timetable showed 19 trains arriving and 21 leaving Forres Station every day. On Sundays, two trains ran each way between Perth and Inverness. These Sunday trains were very well patronised, intending passengers coming from as far east as Keith and Buckie; it was a favourite walk on a good Sunday afternoon to see the thronged concourse and to watch the sixteen-coach trains being pulled by two of the most powerful steam locomotives and pushed at the rear by a third. The rear engine was not coupled and when the train reached the summit at Dava it stopped and returned, in reverse, to Forres.

Each day 22 buses ran between Inverness and Elgin, with two extra on Saturdays.

At Kinloss, houses had been built for married personnel, and there were now 50 of these occupied and more were planned. The Forres representative on the Education Committee in Elgin pressed for some provision to be made for educating children from these homes, as Kinloss was badly overcrowded. The only new school to be built was allocated to Bishopmill.

The Moray and Nairn Police Force was amalgamated with those of Banffshire, Aberdeen County and Kincardineshire, to be known as the Scottish North-Eastern Counties Constabulary, Chief Constable Strath of Banffshire being put in command.

Sweet rationing came to an end in May and within two days every sweet had been purchased and the shelves were empty. It was some months before supplies were enough to meet the demand.

There were allocations of bananas and the Moray Food Control Committee warned that any shopkeeper using the bananas to make the ice-cream delicacy "banana split" would be prosecuted. At this meeting, a licence was granted to an applicant to open a retail food shop, the first allowed since 1939.

The first May elections were due and ten candidates stood for six seats. The County Council elections, which were held every three years, also had some contests in Moray and Nairn, four places being contested, being 20% of the seats. In the Edinkillie electoral district the voting reached 75%, the minister, the Reverend L. Beattie Garden, being the successful candidate.

There was a rumour that 7000 acres of land at Dallas and Pluscarden were to be requisitioned for army training. The farming community enlisted the aid of the whole community to protest at this, and nothing more was heard.

The progress in building 17 houses at Anderson Crescent was painfully slow, bringing in many complaints from house seekers. Sometimes only one man was engaged at a time and pressure was ignored.

A new public convenience was planned at Castlehill at a cost of £1500, but rejected by the Council because of the cost. When this was raised later it was found that the Deed of Gift of the ground did not allow this type of building. The magistrates who were responsible for car parks proposed that the recently-cleared site in Batchen Street be made into a car park. Tests showed that large vehicles would have difficulty leaving and entering High Street at its junction, and an alternative site was found on the other side of High Street on ground owned by the S.C.W.S.

The Mosset Burn was eroding the Rose Garden and an expert was called in from the Scottish Office. He advised building a low stone wall, but a wooden revetment was made instead, being cheaper.

The July Statutory Council meeting had such a short agenda that the business was completed in five minutes, although the next meeting was not until September.

When the Budget was announced, the Treasurer said that the rates would be held at ten shillings and asked that all building be stopped because of the costs. Permits were required for private house building and none were being issued.

The pound was devalued at this time and cuts in Government grants looked certain. The Banff, Moray and Nairn Building Trade Employers' Association wanted to stop bonuses being paid in the building trade and asked for public support; they claimed that "the practice of paying bonuses made workers unhappy."

The Labour Exchange was moved from Gordon Street to temporary premises at Tytler Street, where they remain up to the present time.

The streets of Findhorn were lit this winter by electricity; there had been nine oil lamps before the war, when they were extinguished, never to be lit again.

Altyre House Hospital was closed and later became part of Gordonstoun School. During its time as a hospital it had dealt with 5000 cases.

A motion to provide playing fields for the youth of the town was not opposed and Roysvale was decided as the best place.

Year 1950

The New Year started with very mild weather, the best anyone could recall, and this encouraged the revellers to spend longer than usual at the Cross. Some indulged in dancing, the jollity increased by a vendor of paper hats.

The Falconer Museum had become very popular, the attendance for the previous year being given as nearly 2000. Unemployment began to increase following the economic crisis and the cuts in public spending.

The main business at the first Council of the year was consideration of a proposal by Councillor Rutherford that a bus shelter should be built in High Street. Many complained of the long wait in the open, exposed to the winter weather. The proposal was supported by all on condition that the cost would be borne by the bus companies. This the latter refused to do, and no shelters were ever built.

There had been many complaints of late delivery of Christmas mail, much of it some days after Christmas. The Post Office was notified about this by letter and the assurance was received that arrangements would be improved for next Christmas, denying that the delay was caused by mail being diverted via Aberdeen instead of coming direct. Added to the letter of complaint was another, that the mail from the train arriving at 4.50 p.m .on Saturdays was made available to callers at the Post Office at 6.30 p.m., leaving only ten minutes before the office closed.

A General Election was announced for 23rd February, and all local business was pushed into the background until it was past. Captain James Stuart, the Conservative Member, was returned for the seventh time, his majority increased by 3000. This was claimed as a sweeping victory, but the vote for his opponent also increased by the same amount. As the population had not increased, obviously many more people had turned out to vote.

The following month another attempt was made to get the grazing cattle out of Roysvale Park, but again there was no success.

The May Licensing Court was held without any change, but the County Court sitting in Elgin granted a licence to a restaurant on the beach at Lossiemouth. This was the first of its kind in Moray and was strongly opposed by the police. Work was restarted on the County Buildings in Elgin; this had been started pre-war but no work had

160

been done since. It took a further two years to get it ready for occupation.

The May nomination meeting had a very large attendance, but not one question was asked, the candidates being heard in silence. A national warning was given that load shedding would be necessary next winter and that all who could, should lay in a stock of fuel.

The Old Age Pensioners' Association was formed, the Bank Lane Hall being made available by St Laurence Church for their meetings.

The police recommended a system of one-way streets to alleviate the traffic problem. Urquhart, Tolbooth and Cummings Streets, with Castlehill, had traffic leading off High Street, but the streets going North off High Street were unchanged.

The Provost reported that permission had been received to build 12 houses in the 1950/51 financial year, and that grants were now available for the improvement of old properties. This was a moderate scheme but it was regularly improved and widened in scope, and became an important element in meeting the demand for homes.

Bailie Cormack resigned and Councillor Forbes took his place on the Bench. Bailie Cormack had served for 25 years, and took a special interest in the Town Hall.

Most of the sports bodies in the town met the Council to discuss the provision of facilities, but nothing positive resulted. The County Council purchased Auchernack for use as an Old Folk's Home, to replace Burnside. It was owned by ex-Provost Dr Bruce, who sold it to them for only £1500. A great deal of work was needed to make it ready for 12 residents. The month of May saw major changes in food rationing. The points system was abolished and such things as biscuits, jellies, tinned fruit and rice were unrationed, as was petrol. The freeing of petrol gave a further boost to road traffic and travelling shops became more common.

New regulations controlling the intake of foreign workers came into force. This did not affect many in this part of the country; the new arrivals were mostly women from Germany and Austria to work in the textile mills, where labour was short. The Letts, Lithuanians and Estonians who fled from Russian rule were left unaffected by the new rules, but most of them had been absorbed by marriage or had emigrated.

The demand for the use of the Town Hall for dancing increased and the new Convener introduced further priorities for several months ahead. The new technical classrooms for Forres Academy were opened

161

at Russell Place in North Road. This helped to lessen the over-crowding of the school, which had also to use the Town Hall, Bank Lane Hall and St John's Hall. The Finance Chairman of the County Council was appalled at the increasing cost of transporting rural pupils between homes and schools. In 1947 this had cost £1860, but now it was £9000. As schools were closed more transport was needed, so that in 1970 the bill amounted to £87,000.

The burgh rate was reduced by twopence; this was achieved by deferring work which later cost more. At all times the Councillors were under constant pressure from house seekers; it was agreed to add to the lists the names of those who had applied but had been rejected. This provided a more accurate estimate of the number of houses required, with the result that the Department of Health agreed that another 16 could be built, and a further 12 in 1951. In addition, the Scottish Special Housing Association was to build 100, but the first of these were reserved for squatters. It was not the original intention that these should be built in Forres; they had been allocated to Elgin but that burgh said they did not want them, so they were offered to Forres. The Housing Committee recommended refusal, but the Council voted to accept them.

A survey of applicants showed that the need was now for smaller houses, as families tended to be smaller. There was still considerable emigration, especially to Corby in the Midlands, where new steelworks had come into operation, with houses freely available. A special effort was made to recruit workers from Scotland. This loss was made up as before by rural dwellers moving into the town for work and better houses. There were few rural dwellers in such areas as Grantown-on-Spey, so that there was no shortage of houses, and engaged couples could get a house on marriage. In Forres, and other burghs, nobody without a family had any chance of a house, except on health grounds. Moray County Council found it difficult to get tenants for some of their more remote houses, because of the cost of travelling to work, and because of the rent. This was £32 for an agricultural workers' house.

The burgh was invited to take part in the Festival of Britain which was to take place on the South Bank of the Thames. A suggestion was that an excerpt from Shakespeare's *Macbeth* might be performed, but nothing satisfactory was ever formulated. However, the town did feature in the Festival, as the Ministry of Works made a full-size replica of the Sueno Stone. This brought two students from the U.S.A. the following year, to examine the Stone more closely and get

162

its history, as their Professor thought he had the key to the meaning of the carvings. As nothing was ever heard from him it would appear that he did not hold the key.

September brought some flooding, but the river only affected the Waterford Mills and Ben Romach Distillery.

A branch of the Scottish Country Dancing Association was formed, as interest in this art revived.

Work was started on Glenlatterach Reservoir, which was to be the main supply of water for the county.

Eggs produced in Moray could now be sold in the shops. Prior to this, only eggs collected in Aberdeenshire were available, while the local eggs went to some unknown destination.

At the annual meeting of the Pipe Band, the Treasurer reported that the last financial help given to the Band by the Council was in 1934, and Councillor Ferguson promised to raise the matter. This he did, also suggesting that £52 might be given to the Scottish National Orchestra, without success.

Year 1951

The year began with a smallpox scare, 600 men having to be vaccinated at Kinloss, where a suspected case had been landed. Vaccination against this disease was no longer compulsory, but there was no outbreak.

The New Year arrived with hard frost, so that few lingered for the customary celebrations. This winter was the coldest experienced since 1894, and because of the icy roads the bus service to Findhorn had to be suspended. The heaviest snowfall was in March. Many had complained about the conditions underfoot, but later it was found that 160 tons of salt and sand had been spread within the Burgh boundaries.

Permits were received for another ten houses to be built, and four permits were issued to private builders. At the same time, the amount of money to be spent on repairs to private buildings was limited to £241 for the quarter; the amount for the second quarter would probably be the same. No work of this kind could be done without the permission of the Burgh Surveyor.

Dr Hutchison raised the subject of the broken sewer at the point where it ran into Findhorn Bay, asking that something be done about the objectionable smell which affected the nearby farms. The sewer was exposed at low tide, and had been broken by tanks during practice for the landing of Allied Forces in France in 1944. This was a military zone but the Army did not report the breakage to the Council and no record was available as to when the damage had been done. When the damage was noted the troops had left and the authorities refused to pay compensation as no proof was available. The Council considered that they had enough to do with their money inside the burgh boundaries and took no action. The County Council feared that if attention was drawn to the nuisance they might have to put it right, and were as inactive. When the Moray, Banff and Nairn River Purification Board was set up many years later, pressure was put on the burgh to make the necessary repairs. The burgh still refused, claiming that the sewers also served Findhorn and the R.A.F. station at Kinloss, which was now a considerable size.

The Forres Sewage Purification Works started up in 1973, those at R.A.F. Kinloss somewhat earlier, whilst Findhorn was left untouched, although the River Purification Board had obtained a Tidal Waters Order, making it an offence to discharge untreated sewage into the Bay.

A Film Society was now showing 16 mm. films in the Town Hall, which were not shown commercially, at least in small towns like Forres.

There had been many changes in the Council since the war. Members coming forward were now more interested in positive action to improve things, rather than to practise economy for economy's sake. Seven candidates appeared on the platform at the May nomination meeting, but again it was quiet, without questions.

To get land for housing the Burgh had to extend its boundaries, which meant a public inquiry headed by the Sheriff Principal from Edinburgh. The 300 acres extension brought the total figure up to 900 acres, with 100 persons who now became resident in the burgh. There had been no census in 1941 because of the war and the 1951 census gave the population of the Burgh as 2236 males and 2438 females, which was less than in 1911, when the area was smaller. The county showed an increase of 18 per cent compared with 1931 and with a greater preponderance of males. This was a reversal of the traditional pattern, where females outnumbered males at almost all ages. The change was due to the presence of the two large service stations at Kinloss and Lossiemouth, and army units at Pinefield Barracks in Elgin. The population of Banffshire had fallen by 4772, compared with 1931, a drop of 8·7 per cent.

The Medical Officer of Health for Moray was concerned at the increased number of cases of tuberculosis, 39 new cases being reported during the winter; the number of cases had dropped every year from 1900 until now. The reason was, without doubt, the shortage of food, poor housing and the lack of adequate heating in many homes.

There were heated words in the May Council at the lack of progress in the construction of houses, sometimes only one man being seen on the site. There was a demand for the appointment of a Clerk of Works to watch progress, but this was denied and, instead, the Architect was asked to meet the Housing Committee.

A new type of aircraft arrived at Kinloss; this was the Shackleton, which was used in a maritime rôle.

Because of the increased cost of newsprint, the *Gazette* was increased by a halfpenny to twopence: wages and costs were rising generally.

The Rector of Forres Academy, Mr A. B. Simpson, retired at the end of the year and the school was divided. The 1926 building on the south side of High Street became the Academy, with a new Rector— Mr J. B. Skinner—whilst the old building, the former Academy—built after the 1872 Act made education compulsory—was named the Forres Primary School, with Mr T. T. Davidson as Headmaster. These arrangements did not alleviate the overcrowding and three huts had eventually to be built in the playground of the Primary site. A party of Academy pupils had gone to Paris at Easter, the first school trip overseas.

A new industry, grass drying, started in a building erected at Plasmon Mills. This operated for a few years until new methods and kinds of animal feeding were developed.

A Rotary Club was formed and the Rafford Sports restarted after being in abeyance for 20 years.

In October, the Old Age Pension rose to £1 10s for men and £1 for women. Auchernack Old People's home was officially opened.

The Council had made several appeals for money to pay for the addition of the names of those who died in the Second World War to the 1914-18 War Memorial. Only £48 had been obtained and the Council would take no further action. Bailie Forbes proposed that the

165

Council make up the fund to the amount required, but this was voted down. The Rotary Club then took the responsibility and collected enough to get the work done, the cost being £500.

A General Election was held in October, Captain Stuart again being successful. He was appointed Secretary of State for Scotland, and in this post did all he could to help Forres, the housing position being much improved, with the maximum financial help from the Government.

Twenty Weir type houses were being erected, and Provost Anderson criticised the increase in price of each house from £1350 originally quoted to £1650 charged. This time a Clerk of Works was appointed to check on progress and work.

There was something of a war scare at this time and Moray was 229 short of its establishment of 340 for Civil Defence. An appeal for more volunteers had a poor response.

Year 1952

There had been much talk of a factory to make wood pulp and paper from the quantities of trees which were now reaching the size required. The most likely place was Inverness or Forres, and the town decided to make an effort to get this course of employment. It was remitted to Bailie Forbes to pursue the matter and, after discussions with all the interested parties—forest owners, banks, sawmills, road and rail transport—the necessary information was gathered. After some time a firm in South Africa became interested: an approach was therefore made to the Secretary of State. Unfortunately, he had to say that nothing could be done to forward this project, as the Government had decided that all timber of this size had to be reserved for use in coal mines as pit props. Ironically, the Coal Board at this time decided to use a new type of steel prop, and there was a surplus of timber. A factory was finally placed at Fort William. It was said that this was for political reasons as much of the timber had to be carried across Scotland. One firm of carriers set up in Waterford Farm, giving some employment.

166

The Forres Literary Society, at one time the most popular and active of bodies, was revived after a lapse of 12 years. It survived only for a short time as its reappearance coincided with the arrival of television.

In February, the King died and Queen Elizabeth was proclaimed, with due ceremony, at the Cross. The British Legion was granted a licence and the St Laurence Cricket Club tried for the last time to obtain permission for cars containing spectators to park around the pitch.

The annual nomination meeting was poorly attended, and only a few of the retiring members appeared. Three new candidates stood but the poll sank to 41 per cent of the electorate.

Two rights-of-way were closed, one from Councillor's Walk to Pilmuir Farm, and one from Orchard Road to Sanquhar Road and Braeback through Applegrove. The County Council were now the guardians of such rights, but would not take any action.

The Railway sent their remaining horses to Glasgow, and replaced them with a motor vehicle. A horse was rarely seen in the town thereafter.

The Nelson Tower had been taken over by the army in 1939, followed by the Home Guard and then the Air Force. It was now returned to the Council who reopened it during the summer.

The Forres Rifle Club bought some huts at Balnageith for a rifle range.

There was a scarcity of labour, the unemployed register being almost clear. National Service was still taking the young men away for two years. Burnside Home was empty and as no use could be found for it, it was demolished and the space leased to Messrs Christie as it adjoined their offices. The Post Office wished to close the East End Post Office but protests were strong enough to persuade it to abandon the idea. There was a proposal to turn the Market Green into a car park, but this failed to get the necessary support. Building permits were offered for 31 houses on condition that squatters were housed in them, and when this was accepted a further 33 houses were allowed for occupation by people on the town's housing list.

The rates were increased by tenpence, a considerable rise, but wages were also increasing and most people were in work, so there were almost no complaints.

A number of United States Navy men took up residence in the Carlton Hotel for some months. They were to train the R.A.F. in the use of Neptune bombers, extremely sophisticated aircraft, but following some disagreement between the two Governments, the men were called back to the States, taking the aircraft with them.

The month of September was the coldest recorded for thirty-four years.

Forres House, since its receipt, had been a continual drain on the town's money. Outbreaks of dry rot were frequent but the building was used for many purposes—Library, Baths, Red Cross stores, School Dental Clinic, Hallkeeper's House, Waiting Room, Toilets and, in addition, a good rent was paid by a firm of architects. The Boy Scouts and Girl Guides used rooms rent free. Each proposal to spend more money on the building was criticised.

For the first time a large illuminated Christmas Tree was erected in the Market Green. In the following years it was placed between the Tolbooth and the Cross, and finally in the Museum Square. The tree was always gifted by one of the neighbouring estates—Darnaway, Logie or Dunphail.

The town's workmen were enrolled in the superannuation fund for the first time. The growing civilian population at Kinloss, many of whom stayed in the town, began to influence the provision of shopping facilities. Shops stocked a greater variety, improved their premises and looked more prosperous.

The year ended as quietly as it had begun.

Year 1953

Until the turn of the century, when it was made into a golf course, the ground at Muiryshade had been known, because of the poverty of the soil, as "Scraphard." The Cluny Hill Hydropathic Company had made this change as an alternative attraction to the medical and herbal baths which were not now as popular as they had been in Victorian times.

When the Council were given the Golf Course by Sir Robert Grant a Golf Course Committee was formed with the keen golfers in the Council as members. The course had, therefore, had a good deal of money spent on it and was becoming very popular. The Club, separate from the Council, had by various means accumulated £600 which they wanted to use in improving the amenities of the clubhouse. This was a long low dingy building, one of a collection of buildings on the course, the best house being retained for a Greenkeeper and later a Professional who combined both jobs.

Among the improvements was the provision of an electric water heater and a cooker. The Council supervised the work but, when it was completed, the Club complained that there was no cooker. A Ladies' Committee controlling the work cancelled the order for the cooker for the clubhouse, deciding that the cooker purchased and installed by the Golf Professional in his own house could be used by the members, although the two buildings were separate. The male golfers were not pleased, neither was the Professional's wife, and the cooker was re-ordered and fitted.

The Ministry of Works, who were responsible for the Sueno Stone, refused permission for the Council to build on the area of ground around the stone, and asked the Council to take over this land and maintain it as an open space for all time; this they refused to do.

The National Trust asked that local authorities commemorate the approaching Coronation by renovating and preserving some old buildings of interesting character. The Council decided that they would restore what was known as the "Keith Bread Shop." This was a quaint semi-circular building at the bottom of North Road with one room downstairs and a small one up a narrow circular stair. It had been built by a Keith baker who wished to supply bread to the navvies building the railways, and who could not get premises in Forres. His bread was brought by a horse and cart daily from Keith. When the decision of the committee was made known to the Council there was much embarrassment when a member pointed out that the building had been pulled down some months before, despite his protest. His objection was based on the fact that his grandfather had lived there after the navvies had gone.

On 31st January there was a gale of the greatest severity. Many roads were blocked by fallen trees, as was the railway. The complete forest on the Hill of the Wangie at Dallas was flattened, the most spectacular of many other damaged woods. The anemometer at Kinloss registered a wind speed of 117 miles per hour. The same gale wrecked the Belfast-Stranraer ferry, with the loss of 130 lives. The wind blew directly up the Mosset Burn, raising large waves and throwing masses of water a distance of 40 yards. Planes at Kinloss were damaged and loaded wagons in the goods sidings were blown on to the main line. High tides coincided with the gale and Kinloss

Schoolhouse and cottages were flooded with sea water. At Nairn, the Golf Course was covered with sea water to a depth of three feet. So much timber had been blown down that a consortium of timber merchants and sawmillers was formed to get the timber cut and removed as soon as possible. It had to be sold at a very low price.

The Golf Club was again heard in the Council Chambers. They had spent the £600 they had raised and claimed that the Provost had promised that the Council would double any sum they gathered. The Provost had been asked to open a Fête organised by the Club, but said that he must have been misheard.

In February, Mr Archibald Macdonald had been appointed Deputy to his father, the Town Clerk. This continued a link between the Town Council and the firm of R. & R. Urquhart, Solicitors, this office having supplied Town Clerks since 1834. The Burgh Prosecutor, Mr Harry W. Leask, had also served the Burgh since 1911, when he was appointed Deputy to his father.

The Department of Agriculture stated that there was a deficiency of 70 farm workers in Moray, but refused a plea by the farmers that young farm workers should not be called to National Service, as they rarely returned to farm work when their time was up.

Another outbreak of dry rot in Forres House again caused disputation. The Post Office began the morning delivery at 7.30 a.m. instead of 8.30 a.m. following a re-arrangement of duties. The first sodium vapour lamps were introduced on the High Street. There were protests at first as "they made people look like corpses," but they were soon accepted and extended all over the town.

The British Legion put a second floor in their premises so that they could transfer the billiard and card tables from the Caroline Street premises which were then sold. These premises were bought by Forsyth's Dairy as a garage for their vans. The path from High Street to the Thomson Monument was planted with flowering trees, to commemorate the Coronation. There were the usual games and sports in the Grant Park.

No tenant took up the offer to buy their house at a price fixed by the District Valuer. The Councillors attended the ceremony of unveiling the plaques attached to the War Memorial, bearing the names of the dead of the Second World War.

The Labour Government had democratised the Territorial Army Association by making it necessary to have a member of the Town Council on its Committee. Forres was one of the burghs which had to provide a member, the law also saying that he must be under the age of 50. Only one member qualified, Bailie Forbes, who complained that he was being called up for the second time! This provision was wisely rescinded later.

The nomination meeting brought out a goodly number of "hecklers." The shopkeepers had been protesting at the one-way streets which, they said, were bad for trade. There were eight candidates for six seats, and two retiring members who supported the traffic regulations were defeated.

There was trouble at the Slaughterhouse as the contractor had ceased killing animals, having hurt his arm, and would not employ anyone to carry on. The Council had to take over the operation of the Slaughterhouse, the Burgh Surveyor being made Superintendent.

The foundation stone of the new primary school at Applegrove was laid by Principal T. M. Taylor of Aberdeen University.

County Council houses were no longer restricted to farm and agricultural workers. The Council bought ground at Fleurs Place from the Plasmon Mills, and made the first purely sports ground in the town. The High Church (St Leonard's) celebrated its Jubilee.

Drumduan Estates was offered for sale to the town, but the majority were against purchase although the ground would have been useful for a cemetery and for housing. Purchase had been rejected some five years earlier when it was offered for £1590. The purchaser had sold some thousands of pounds' worth of timber and now asked a price several times higher than he had paid.

Year 1954

The New Year celebrations were quieter than usual, and the whole year seemed to continue on this note. At the first Council meeting of the year the Provost said that they had not had much success in implementing their house building programme, but the Housing Committee would persevere with it.

There was much discussion in the Lands Committee on the wisdom of spending much money on the town's farms. To bring only two of the farms to the necessary modern standards was to cost £2600. The

171

suggestion that some of the Common Good property be sold to get sufficient funds to repair those that remained was looked on as something akin to sacrilege. In all, £10,000 would require to be spent, and any balance left from the money realised could be used to purchase better properties.

Despite the claims for economy in the Council work, the townspeople seemed to prosper, the Actuary of the Aberdeen Savings Bank making complimentary remarks about the large amount deposited in the Bank during the year.

The newly-formed River Purification Board held its first meeting. The Forres Mechanics football club announced that it was now free of debt.

As new houses became available the housing waiting lists were cleared and it was agreed that only one list would be needed in future. As a result, there was no longer any pressure from applicants for houses at the May nomination meeting. The questions were mostly frivolous and the proceedings were completed in ten minutes.

In June the police moved to their new quarters in Victoria Road. Dr J. C. Adam pressed the Moray Hospitals Board of Management to buy Newbold House, which was soon to be on the market, and would be admirably suited for a home for geriatric patients. The provision of such a home would have freed many hospital beds required for other patients. The Board accepted the need for such an establishment but said that nothing could be done at that time owing to lack of funds. The matter would be given high priority, but nothing was ever done, although the matter was raised regularly by members.

There was an ever increasing contact with R.A.F. Kinloss. Many of the wives and members of the families of the personnel were now working in the town, while the number of civilians also increased at the air station following its steady expansion. The station presented a summer house to Auchernack for the use of the residents there.

Following the resignation of Dr Hutchison for domestic reasons and the death of Bailie Campbell, two members were co-opted to the Council. These were Mr W. T. Watters, who had already served on the Council, and Mr Peter Mitchell, manager of the Savings Bank. Bailie Campbell had given long service in the Council. A keen golfer, he took much interest in the golf course and introduced many improvements there.

The Cluny Hill Cemetery was reaching the end of its accommodation, and some members put forward the proposal that the provision

172

of a crematorium was more in line with modern thinking, in view of the growing demand on the limited amount of land. This was rejected as 'gruesome,'' some members objecting to the matter being discussed. Another effort was made to persuade the majority to purchase Drumduan at the low price of £1500.

Glenlatterach Reservoir was now ready to go into use; it was hoped that this would solve the problem of water supply in Eastern Moray. A branch of the Inner Wheel movement was formed. This body did a great deal of work for charity and the older people in the community. Another attempt was made to get the sheep off the golf course but was defeated by ten votes against six for removal.

The Council saw the first comprehensive plan for the town which was, in general, accepted as satisfactory. It was agreed also that tenants in council houses could erect garages. Bye-laws were passed to control and prevent pollution in waters within the burgh.

Interest rates were very low at this time; the Government agency, the Public Works Loan Board, was lending money for 5 years at only $2\frac{1}{2}\%$, for up to 15 years at $3\frac{1}{4}\%$ and up to 60 years at $3\frac{3}{4}\%$. The stone-built traditional houses at Fleurs were completed, some of them having taken almost five years from the start to occupation. The Council decided that they could no longer afford this type of building, as each one cost £1600. Burnside Home was demolished and the bridge at the Plasmon Ford was finally moved down stream.

Year 1955

The year started with mild weather but by the time February arrived the frost was settling in. It was one of the coldest spells in memory, roads being frostbound and trains frozen. The snow lay so long that the Government put into action "Operation Snowdrop." Planes and helicopters were used to drop food for both people and livestock. So serious did matters become that the Norwegians mobilised army reservists who, with their skis, were to be landed in isolated areas and help rescue the housebound residents. On the eve of the day they were to leave Norway the frost broke.

Until Provost Michie Anderson took office, there was little comfort for any councillors not actually in the Council chamber, which had a large coal fire. When committees sat in the room, members not on

173

the Committee which was in session had to wait on the draughty stairs, sometimes for hours. The courtroom was there but it was even colder than the passage, and held only wooden benches. Provost Anderson let the members use the "Provost's room"—a little place behind the courtroom. This was a big improvement, and later a waiting room was made upstairs; finally, the courtroom was gutted and made into the Council chamber, while the old Council room was made a comfortable waiting room.

The nomination meeting was poorly attended, with only one candidate, a retiring Councillor, appearing on the platform. Provost Anderson announced his retiral from the Council. He had served 30 years, ten of them as Provost, and had a vast knowledge of local government and local history. Fortunately, this was not lost to members, who always had recourse to him when in doubt about the proper way to deal with any problem. Councillor B. S. Braid was elected Provost.

The prolonged talks between the Council and the Fire Service ended in agreement that the new Fire Station would be sited at Fleurs. Provost Braid and other members described the state of the Tolbooth and the rooms as deplorable. These were redecorated, the leather-covered but old and worn seats and chairs were re-covered, new curtains and electric heaters fitted. The stone stairs were covered.

The Hydro-Electric Board began to provide a better supply, as more hydro generating stations had been built, and new cables were available. The Department gave permission to build houses at Castlehill on condition that the site at Cassieford was not used for this purpose.

The Forres Mechanics Football Club reached the peak of their affluence, income for the year reaching £3514. This was the result of the work of the President, Councillor John Falconer, and it was not surprising that he was elected for the third year in succession. The team also did well on the field.

Another General Election came round and again Captain Stuart was returned. The proprietor of the scrapyard, Mr Gordon Williamson, offered the yard to the town for £4000, but the town was not allowed to offer more than £600.

Mr George R. Mackenzie, Calshot, was awarded the British Empire Medal in recognition of the work he had done as Chief Warden during the war. He was also active in many other bodies and organised the Blood Donors' Group into the largest in the north.

174

He did not care for public office but later his wife and son were Councillors at the same time.

The new railway station was opened, tiny compared to the old wooden station with its covered overhead bridge leading to all four platforms. The bus services were now being affected by the increased ownership of private cars, so that services were reduced.

A distressing drowning accident brought gloom to the district. A mother and niece with six of her children going to have a picnic on the sands near the Old Bar at Auldearn got lost in the fog and were caught in the incoming tide, which flows very fast at this point. The father, who had lingered some way behind, could not find them.

After the bitter cold of the winter and spring, the summer broke records with heat and sunshine. In July, the temperature at Forres registered 87·4° F. and at Elgin it was higher. Forest and grass fires were almost a daily occurrence. Steam locomotives were still in use and on the steep gradients on the line over Dava the labouring engines threw out red hot coals with the blast. Landowners complained of the small compensation they got, as values of timber and properties had risen much since the rates had been fixed many years earlier. The River Spey was at its lowest level since 1868, but Loch Romach was able to meet the demands of water users.

Dr Hutchison asked for a report on the town's staff and this was debated. Outside workers totalled 26 with an indoor staff of 11; as the working week was getting shorter his effort to get the staff reduced was unsuccessful.

Another outbreak of dry rot in Forres House re-opened the dispute as to the value of further repair work.

The television signals were poor and complaints brought the promise of a new station at Rosemarkie in the Black Isle. There were also complaints about the high price of meat, steak being 7s per pound in Forres but only 5s 6d in Elgin. With several supermarkets operating there, competition was much greater.

The burgh rates were increased by 2s, more money being needed by the County Council for education, police and roads.

The nation was in one of its periodical economic crises, and the area chosen for cuts in spending was school building.

A hurricane had devastated the West Indies and an appeal for funds was made in Britain. Early in the nineeenth century a number of Forres men had made their names in the islands, and as the fathers of two were Provosts Hoyes and Kynoch, the Council agreed to give

175

£25 to the fund, although the Town Clerk warned them that neither the rates nor the Common Good money could be used. Later, the Auditor refused to pass this item and the members who had voted in favour were to be surcharged. However, an appeal was made to Captain Stuart, still Secretary of State for Scotland, who had it quashed.

The Salvation Army said there was now no need for them in Forres and felt they should move to the cities, where there was greater poverty.

The *Gazette* remarked that Christmas Day was now overtaking New Year's Day as a festival.

Year 1956

This year, using money left by Mr Arthur Murdoch, the Council bought some of the angling rights on the river. Only the pools owned by the lessees, the Sellar family, could be bought at a cost of £15,000, leaving a balance in the legacy which was to be a source of conflict in future years. The Council handed authority for administering the rights to the Angling Association, asking only for an annual report and, if necessary, an annual meeting of the Trustees with representatives of the Association. This arrangement ran smoothly most of the time.

The Housing Committee adopted a policy of disposing of as many unsatisfactory old houses as possible. This was a slow process as many of the proprietors were unwilling to see their houses demolished, although the Council were prepared to give improvement grants for those that could be so improved, with the proviso that they must not sterilise surrounding areas which could be used for erecting new homes.

Dean of Guild Mackenzie forecast a gloomy future if no new industry could be brought to the burgh. He thought two main sources of employment, the gas works and the railway, would be centralised in Elgin, and that the future of the laundry, which employed about 30 women, was also uncertain. The gas works and the laundry were eventually closed down, but the proposal to transfer 42 men in the locomotive department was postponed. But when diesel locomotives

176

were put into service in the Highland region—the first region in the country to go over to this form of power—the whole locomotive department was closed down.

The allocation system for council houses was again altered. The policy of secrecy was changed, thus removing the main cause of discontent and complaint. The burgh workmen were now on a 44-hour week with a wage of £7 8s 6d. The expenditure of local authorities had again to be cut at the behest of the central government. Despite this, the salary of the Burgh Prosecutor, Mr H. W. Leask, was increased from £30 a year to £100. The figure of £30 had stood unchanged since 1911, when Mr Leask had been appointed deputy to his father. No one had noticed this until now, and Mr Leask had never drawn attention to it.

Mr David T. Rodger came from Dumfries to be Golf Professional and Greenkeeper, and brought in plans to extend and improve the course. This work continued until his death.

The dam at Loch Romach was increased in height from 10 to 11 feet. This gave an increased storage capacity of six million gallons of water.

The attendance at the nomination meeting was even smaller than that of the previous year. There were only 57 people in the hall, and no new candidates, the six retiring members being returned without an election.

The first industrial building for many years was erected at the Greshop by Morayshire Tractors Limited. At a meeting of the Moray Hospital Board in Elgin the Chairman, Mr F. O. Stewart of Dunkinty, described as "absurd and sheer nonsense" a recommendation that eight television sets be bought for the use of the staff, and had the proposal rejected. Sets for Maryhill and Leanchoil were agreed as both patients and staff would use them.

The end of July brought the worst floods for fifty years. Bridges were swept away in both Moray and Nairn, and railway and road traffic halted. For two days rain fell continuously until the rivers overflowed. The foundations of the road bridge at Mundole were threatened, and fifty people had to be rescued at the Broom of Moy. The residents of Tytler Street and Market Street also had to be removed from their homes, the water reaching as far as the Victoria Hotel. A train was halted by flood water between Dava and Dunphail, the 87 passengers arriving in Forres by bus many hours later. A Navy helicopter from Lossiemouth landed five young men at Kildrummy

177

Farm, west of Nairn, to rescue the cattle there and take them to safety across the River Nairn. There were thirty cows, each with a calf. The helicopter was also called in to take away the residents of Kincorth and Moy houses. In 60 hours 4·24 inches of rain had fallen. Much of the soil washed away or irrevocably damaged was of a very high quality; much of it was buried under thousands of tons of gravel and silt. At Househill Farm, near Nairn, it was estimated that one million tons of stone and mud were deposited; in addition, 25 acres planted with potatoes were washed away. The River Nairn had reverted to a course it took some three centuries earlier. Help was asked from the Government in Edinburgh, but the reply was that such disasters had to be faced locally as such things happened in every century.

Within a week there were more serious floods as the river burst its banks at Mundole and took a straight line through to the Pilmuir instead of travelling round the two bends of the river. This time, a special type of army lorry did the rescue work. Invererne Road near the Lee Bridge had to be cut to allow the water to run into the Mosset Burn. Tytler Street and Market Street looked like Venetian canals. The general depression was made worse by the news that a small boy had been swept away when watching the flood waters at Fleurs Place. The Lord Lieutenant this time joined in the appeal for help, which succeeded, and the Government allocated £300,000 for repair work to the banks of the river. The town and people had angry words for the County Council who said they could only spend money on the protection and repair of the roads, all other costs having to be met by the landowners. The Town Council spent £1100 in remedying the damage in the burgh.

A survey of housing showed that there were now 1383 houses in the burgh, 385 owned tby the Council and 100 by the Scottish Special Housing Association, the latter a Government body although the Council collected the rents and acted as factor. The cost of rates worked out at £7 5s per head of population, the actual rate being 13s 6d in the £1. The average rent of Council houses was £27 per annum. The annual cost of public housing (385 houses) was met by 50 per cent from rents, 29 per cent from Government grants and the remaining 21 per cent from the rates.

When the school at Kinloss opened for the autumn term, teaching had to be done in two shifts, so great was the influx of children. In September a final relic of the war came to an end—the subsidy on bread. The Monopolies Act prevented the Master Bakers from fixing prices and a price war broke out which, in the course of time, closed many small bakeries.

The National Farmers' Union issued some figures on the floods of the summer. In Moray and Nairn, 338 acres of cropland had been totally destroyed, 536 acres had been partially damaged, and 23½ miles of fencing had been swept away.

The national change in holiday making was now noticeable, September becoming a busy month for tourists. The Council discussed how they could help this trade, and also make provision of sporting and other facilities for the young. Earlier Councils had considered such things did not concern them, but in most places Councillors had abandoned the idea that the main objective was to spend as little money as possible.

The Remembrance Day ceremonies at the War Memorial now drew no less than nine organisations, accompanied by a pipe band and buglers.

At this time, the Education Committee asked if the burgh would allocate houses for teachers, as difficulty was experienced in attracting them to an area where house prices were almost as high as those in the South-East of England. This was due to the increasing number of Royal Air Force and Naval personnel wanting to purchase their own homes, which they would retain even if posted away, so that they had a house when they retired from the services. Councillor Birnie proposed that ten houses be reserved for teachers, but this was immediately attacked. Because of the heated exchanges no decision was made at this meeting, but later it was disclosed that two had already been retained for teachers, and other applications from the Education Committee would be looked at sympathetically. In the course of time, houses were given on a revolving basis, a teacher getting a house for two years, enabling him to buy his own house.

Equipment for the children's play space at Fleurs was bought at a cost of £342. This included a "Junglegym" which some members thought could be dangerous, but were assured of its complete safety. Unfortunately, within a short time, a boy fractured his skull in a fall from the equipment which was hurriedly dismantled and sold; the boy fully recovered.

Year 1957

The Burgh's most ambitious housing scheme at Castlehill was now under way. This was to be built to the highest standard possible. Although before the war houses in Forres had been built at a lower price than in any other authority in Scotland, they were now among the most expensive. This had been supported by the Secretary of State for Scotland, the constituency member, Captain Stuart. He retired at this time, having been the Member for 34 years.

Castlehill was to have the first block of flats the town had ever built, and the layout was to be as spacious and as attractive as possible. Unfortunately, a mistake in measurements had been made, which was not discovered until the houses were being marked out, so that nothing could be done about it.

There was much anticipation among those on the waiting list, and the houses were allocated to the applicants before the work was started. This was appreciated as they then knew where the house was to be and could, with the help of the plans, prepare their furnishings and furniture.

The committee also had a great deal of work with all the houses. Owners were no longer to pay a share of the rates, the whole burden having to fall on the occupier. Rents had to be adjusted so that, for example, a rent of £60 per annum was reduced to £42, but the increased rate borne by the tenant would bring the total back to what had been paid earlier. Rents had also to be levelled. The lowest rent charged at this time was £9 per annum, the highest £60. There were to be rebates for those unable to bear the whole rent without hardship.

None of the town's 220 pre-war houses had electricity, and tenants were installing a supply at their own cost: many could not face this and appealed to the Council. The Housing Committee, in collaboration with the Hydro-Electricity Board, devised a scheme by which the Council gave a grant to the tenant of an amount equal to the loan charges of the capital cost. This the tenant paid to the electrical contractor—which was the Board—who collected the rest of the cost in quarterly instalments added to the bill for supply over a period of seven years. The Hydro-Electric Board were attracted by this plan which they succeeded in getting through the Houses of Parliament. It is interesting to see how a small distant town could have an effect on national legislation.

180

This happened on another occasion this year. By the Burgh Police Act of 1892, small burghs were not allowed to spread salt on the roads to remove snow or ice, the reason being that it damaged the feet of the horses. This did not apply to roads outside the towns as, when the legislation was passed no one would have thought of putting salt on country roads, as the responsibility for roads lay with the Parish Councils. Now most traffic was by road and all counties salted them at the first sign of snow. This meant that drivers had clean roads until they came to the burghs, where the snow lay until it could be removed by shovel or scraper.

Forres had earlier appealed for this part of the Act to be repealed, as did many other burghs. The reply was always the same, the Government did not have time for such legislation.

At this time medical practitioners were in dispute with the Government and threatened to withdraw their labour in Banff, Moray and Nairn; the matter was solved satisfactorily. Leanchoil Hospital still had a committee of 17 members who raised money for the hospital, for gifts and other activities, but now the North-East of Scotland Regional Hospital Board said this must stop as they could not have non-elected or non-nominated persons involved in the running of their hospitals.

August again saw flooding, the river breaking its banks for about a hundred yards below the railway bridge. This part which had not been repaired was the weakest point. There were many protests as ten thousand tons of rock had been bought from the town's New Forres Quarry at twopence a ton to fill up the gaps made by the previous year's floods. The Department of Agriculture said that it only restored river banks, but did not improve them, this being the duty of the proprietor.

Lord Hailsham, Lord President of the Council in the Conservative Government, said that there were to be great changes in local government; all the powers taken from the smaller authorities earlier in the century would now be returned to them. This gave great pleasure to the small bodies, all of whom chafed at the slowness and the niggardliness of the Counties, especially when dealing with Town matters. But when the legislation was passed fourteen years later, it was found that all small councils were to disappear completely, and be replaced by much larger district and regional councils.

Glenlatterach Reservoir was expected to be filled to capacity in a few years, but the August floods filled it in a day or two. The

181

Laich of Moray Water Board who had built it, felt that an adequate supply of water was now assured, but within a decade there was new concern.

Year 1958

Three weeks after New Year, winter arrived with nine and a half inches of snow, accompanied by thunder and lightning. Within a week further snow fell, this time 17½ inches. A quick thaw followed, the temperature rising from 18° F. to 58° F. in a few hours. River and burn ran very high but there was no flooding.

In February, after a very long debate, the Council agreed that the Golf Club could get a special licence for special events.

There was still a strong feeling that something should be done about the Munro Baths money and Councillor Birnie moved that a paddling pool be built using some of the money. His seconder, Councillor Liddell, changed this to "swimming pool," but this caused the project to be defeated by nine votes to four.

At the annual general meeting of the British Legion the Treasurer, Mr W. A. Taylor, solicitor, reported that the club was running at a loss of £1 10s every week. However, the President, Dr J. C. Adam, assured the members that they had good assets, a club room worth £6000 and were free of debt. The members decided to see where improvements and economies could be made.

The Council had engaged civil engineering consultants to advise on sewage works. The report was received, together with a bill for £391. This was the first major project for at least half a century which would have to be paid for wholly by the ratepayers, there being no Government grant and no bequests. The thought of a bill for many thousands of pounds perturbed some of the members, who would have voted against the proposal if it were not for the constant pressure from the River Purification Board.

The nomination meeting had an attendance of 40, but this was good compared to Nairn with 18 and Grantown with only three. Mr Alastair Sinclair, Principal Art Master at the Academy, came forward to make up the necessary number of candidates to fill the vacancies on the Council.

The hot water system in the Town Hall was now old and inefficient, and was replaced by gas heaters attached to the walls, costing £386. The space taken up by the old boiler and coal stores was cleared.

A very successful professional golf tournament was held, the winner being W. Miller of Crow Wood, going round in 68, 68 and 69. The event, organised by the Golf Convener, Councillor John Falconer and Councillor Sam Anderson, attracted twenty-three entrants.

Caravan sites and camps were now springing up all over the country, and Mr Fraser wanted to have one on his ground at Rosefield. Opposition led to a public inquiry, resulting in a refusal from the County Planning Authority. Permission was given for one at Mundole.

The Slaughterhouse Committee leased the premises to the Fat Stock Marketing Commission, better known as the F.M.C. The combined Lands and Baths Committees approved plans for a paddling pool south of the war memorial and a rustic bridge across the burn at this point. The Council decided to have the pool in the Grant Park, and delay the bridge for the time being.

Loch Romach was visited, the Council inviting a number of guests. There was always a pause at Councillors' Well for a drink, and the Provost of Elgin, W. B. Munro, made a speech of thanks, ending by saying that he had received a most valued document from Forres Town Council in the shape of an invitation to the trip and addressed to the *Lord* Provost of Elgin. This was rather embarrassing as the Council, with most others in the north, had refused to recognise this title as it had no legal foundation, having been adopted by an Elgin Provost after the First World War.

Councillor Falconer, who had now been made a Bailie, presented a cup to be played for by the Council and staff. This was an annual affair until the Council ceased to have enough golfers to make a game worthwhile.

The first diesel passenger train on the Aberdeen-Inverness line stopped at Forres station in July.

The County Health Committee mounted a campaign to wipe out T.B. in the area, and a mobile X-ray Unit spent a week in the town. In all, 2786 people were X-rayed in the week. After a few years this annual service was stopped as so few cases were found.

Treasurer J. W. Thomson resigned unexpectedly. The rates had to be increased by threepence in the £, and his plea for economy was rejected, this being a probable reason for his withdrawal. Later in the month the sum of £13,000 was received for over-payments in the past,

183

of which £7000 went to the Common Good, putting it into a good position.

A new Treasurer had to be elected and three names were proposed, the one receiving the lowest number of votes being eliminated. The two remaining were again voted for, having eight votes each. The Provost declined to give a casting vote, so the names were drawn out of a hat; Councillor John A. Thomson was successful. Later, there was a complaint of an irregularity in the procedure and another election had to be held. The name drawn this time was that of Councillor Pat Mackenzie, ironmonger. Treasurer Thomson must have had the shortest tenure of office of any Treasurer.

In November the Finance Committee accepted a new system by which rates could be paid in instalments. In December the unemployed numbered 108, giving great concern to the members who were too young to remember the conditions two decades earlier.

This was a year notable for successes in sport. First there was the golf tournament mentioned earlier, then the Harriers won the 16-mile road race of the Scottish A.A.A. The St Catherine's Bowling Club celebrated their 75th year, and after an interval of 22 years the Forres Mechanics won the North of Scotland Junior Cup. A team from the Forres Young Farmers' Club were considered the best stock judges of the year, and the Forres Rifle Club won the championship in this sport. Hugh Stuart won the Spence Trophy for Golf, this being considered the unofficial North of Scotland championship. John Shand won the Grant Cup in the Open Amateur Golf Championship; Jack Kemp took the North of Scotland Cricket Cup for bowling; the Findhorn Regatta was revived after a lapse of 21 years; Dunphail held its first Highland Games since 1925; the Forres Harriers won the Braid Cup for the Forres-Alves 6½ mile race; William Black held the District Amateur Boxing award as Heavyweight Champion and Constable W. B. Milne won all three trophies presented by the Scottish North-East Counties Constabulary Sports Club.

Away from sport, a branch of An Comunn Gaidhealach was formed.

Year 1959

The television signals were now much better and television sets more common. This seemed to have its effect on the Hogmanay gatherings at the Cross which were now composed of the younger people, their elders staying at home.

The *Gazette* reprinted a report of 100 years earlier, when the people of Rafford had finally accepted the "new" calendar. Until this year of 1859 they had celebrated the first day of the year and a fortnight later had another one for the old style, on Auld Yule on the 12th January.

A town bus service was started by Simpson's Bus Company which ran the Findhorn and Kinloss buses. The County plan now approved by the Secretary of State, showed the line of the proposed by-pass road. This left the main road at Drumduan, crossing the road from Findhorn at its present junction and continuing behind Rosefield and Park Hotel grounds and stables. Passing south of the football pitch, it went through the old stables in the scrapyard, across Gordon Street, bridging the now filled in mill lade, then another bridge across the Mosset to enter Messrs Christie's nursery ground, and divide the Market Green to debouch where six roads already met. At this meeting, the burgh members immediately protested at this line, pointing out that by going as quickly as possible from the main road to the railway and continuing parallel to that, past the Station Hotel, no buildings would have to be demolished and no good ground used. They maintained this case for almost 15 years until it was finally accepted as the better line, but later, slight modifications were made as the level crossing at Waterford was no longer operated by an attendant.

The nomination meeting was quiet, although there were ten candidates for the seven vacancies.

The railway workshops at Inverness were closed, adding to the number of people looking for jobs in that county. The Elgin Model Lodging House was also closed; it was the last one in the area, having 50 beds costing fourpence a night. There was a small number of regular residents but there were few tramps and vagrants now; they tended to remain in one place in order to obtain social security benefits. Forres Lodging House, in North Road and later in Batchen Street, closed some years before.

At the General Election there were three candidates for the first time: Mackay Mackay (Labour), Donald Macdonald (Liberal) and Mr Gordon Campbell (Conservative), who was elected.

185

Moray County Council started to build 30 houses at Manachie. They had always been against building houses near the burghs, claiming that this helped to relieve the towns from building more houses. Rural dwellers now wanted to be nearer the place of work and where services of all kinds were easily available. Sales vans were also being withdrawn from the more isolated places as depopulation made it uneconomic to operate them.

Roysvale Place sports field was opened and a pavilion built. At Forres station 20 men were made redundant, some transferring elsewhere but others leaving the railway service rather than give up their homes. Flemington Sawmills, beside the football field, built on the site of the old Bobbin Mills, were burned down. They were reopened at Balnageith. The Road Authority wanted to move the war memorial further south so that the Aberdeen-Inverness road could be made straighter. There was so much opposition that they abandoned the idea.

As this was the fiftieth anniversary of the receipt of the bequest of £6000 for baths for the people of Forres from Mr J. Munro, Bailie W. R. Mackenzie moved that the building of a swimming pool should again be considered, but was defeated by ten votes to five. The looming cost of the sewage works had discouraged any thought of more expenditure.

The incumbent of Castlehill Church had left and the proposals for the union of the church with either St Laurence or the High Church were the subject of discussion, but no conclusion was reached and the matter was deferred.

Parking regulations were amended, so that vehicles could be parked on High Street, on one side only. The Provost's lamps had lain in the burgh yard since Provost Fraser demitted office, and were now re-erected outside the Tolbooth door. New panes were bought, embossed with the coat of arms of the burgh, at a cost of £200. The Castlehill Housing Scheme received the Saltire Award for the best of the year in Scotland. The new cemetery at Clovenside was consecrated and Applegrove Primary School was opened.

Year 1960

The New Year brought, for the first time, a three-day closure of all business premises, including hotels and bars. A two-day holiday was now the rule and as the 1st of January was a Friday, nothing was obtainable until Monday. This was not fully realised by many of the public until the last day of the year; shops reported something akin to panic and record trading.

There seems to have been little done in the Council, or at least little made public. There may have been a return to the traditional secrecy, for later in the year when Dean of Guild Mackenzie resigned from the Housing Committee, he gave as the reason that he had had many differences and could tolerate it no longer. There were other signs of internal discord: in a comparatively short period a Bailie had resigned, another had refused re-nomination and the Treasurer had resigned. None of these had given a reason, although this was normally done.

In March it was decided to abandon the old style public nomination meeting and have instead a pre-election one, when the candidates would appear on the platform and give their views or answer questions. This was in some ways an improvement, as the electors would now be able to see and hear those who wished to be members of the Town Council. Previously, many retiring Councillors had never attended a nomination meeting, but waited until the end of the meeting before handing in their nomination papers. New candidates also did this on occasion so that their intentions were not known until the election notices were put up.

In the past councillors who had never appeared in public and whose names had never appeared in the press confined themselves to voting at Council meetings. One fault of the new method was that if seats on the Council were not contested no pre-election meeting would be held. Just before the election, Councillor John A. Thomson asked for more open discussion of the town's affairs, but his proposal was sent to the office-bearers for consideration. The new type of meeting drew a small audience but a good number of questions were asked.

No Gala Week was held this year; these had always been very successful, drawing large crowds and getting good press cover. But expenses were increasing and volunteer helpers were not coming forward in the same numbers as formerly.

187

Auchernack Home was being enlarged; such Homes had lost the Poor Law image and there were long waiting lists of old people seeking places. The change in social attitudes was such that few expected younger members of a family to shelter and maintain their aged parents or relatives. Elderly people who formerly employed domestic help were now unable to do so. However, they were better able to express their needs and chose to live in old people's homes as these improved.

Social services generally were also being expanded and in the town a "Meals on Wheels" service was started. On three days a week meals were delivered to old people living alone; each delivery had meals for two days. This was done by voluntary workers, the Women's Royal Voluntary Service ultimately taking full responsibility. Those who could pay did so at a moderate charge, and later the food was prepared by the School Canteen staff.

Another service, organised by the Medical Officer of Health, was started for those who needed help in their homes with the aid of District Nurses. "Home Helps" came in daily, or as required, to do housework for which the resident was unfit, to prepare meals and to see what other attention was required. Because of the ever-increasing demand for this service financial limitations had to be imposed.

Pony riding and trekking was started by Mr Leslie Clyne, the Council letting the ground at Clovenside for a low figure. Mr Clyne was a lover of both horses and children and made sure that any child who wanted to ride was not deprived of the opportunity. All children were thus able to take part in a sport normally restricted to the more affluent sections of the community.

In July, the Amateur Boxing Association staged a tournament in the open air in Grant Park—a rare event which drew crowds from afar. A water ski-ing club was started at Findhorn by some enthusiasts in the town. This was also very successful, eventually having a club-house and power boats. The Findhorn Yacht Club also expanded. Moray Estates started a new industry at Greshop—a timber preservation plant. New legislation required that all timber used in building had to be treated in this way.

The year ended with disagreement between Town Council and County Council as to who was responsible for the delay in making a pedestrian crossing with "Belisha Beacons" on the High Street, and there was trouble between the Mechanics Football Club and their Supporters' Club.

188

Year 1961

The year entered quietly with only 15 people waiting at the Cross to welcome it. According to an Elgin reporter, only two revellers appeared at the Plainstones, the traditional meeting place in Elgin.

Two items were reported from the January meeting, both complaints. The first was about the size of the Provost's lamps at the Tolbooth door. The speaker compared them to carriage lamps, in no way as impressive as the large lamps they had displaced. The Town's crest was embossed on the glass panes but these were small and the crests could not be seen from ground level. The second complaint was about the size of a quotation for two new hats for the halberdiers. The hats in use were probably more than a century old, and were past their best. They had been sent to Messrs Forsyth of Princes Street, Edinburgh, who suggested that new hats would be required as the wooden frames had perished: the cost would be £25 15s 10d Councillor Miss May Crowe thought the charge exorbitant and that the firm had quoted for the most expensive ones. The Provost jocularly remarked that he had little doubt that some of her striking hats had cost as much, to be angrily rebuffed. However, the hats were ordered and no doubt will last as long as those replaced.

The Morayshire Farmers' Club announced that in future there would be no class at the annual show for Clydesdale Horses as these had now disappeared from farms.

Mrs Edwards of Sanquhar died, and the balance of her husband's estate, of which she had been a life rentrix, was distributed. The major part, Kintail Estate, had been disposed of in 1946 at the time of his death, but from the remainder now realised, Leanchoil Hospital received £15,000 and Spynie Hospital £26,000. The Regional Hospital Board, based in Aberdeen, had stopped surgical operations at Leanchoil, patients having to go either to Elgin or the Royal Infirmary at Aberdeen. Many chose to go to Inverness although it was in the Northern Hospital Board region.

There was considerable concern about the future of Leanchoil Hospital, as it was rumoured that the Board intended to change it to a convalescent or geriatric centre. The Town Clerk, Mr A. H. Macdonald, had been the Forres representative on the Moray Hospital Management Board since its formation, but had now to give up this appointment as he had reached the age limit. The Town Council put forward the name of a former long-serving member, Mr A. H. Forbes,

189

who was duly appointed. He immediately took steps to retain the hospital.

The Regional Board now held, in all, £35,000 of the Edwards legacy for use in Leanchoil, but wanted to use it for other purposes. Mr H. W. Leask was the agent for the Sanquhar Estate and he refused to hand any of the money over until he knew how it was to be spent.

The Seaforth and Cameron Highlanders, both regulars and territorials, had been amalgamated into a new unit—the Queen's Own Highlanders—so that the pipe band of the former local company of Seaforths had been disbanded. A letter was received from the Signals Regiment (Territorials) Aberdeen saying that their pipe band would play in Forres, the charge either £15 or £20; no action was taken.

For many years the residents of Bank Lane had asked for the path to be put in good order, but the reply had been that this was not a public road and the residents would have to meet the cost. The Council now reversed this decision and the lane was tarred. The result was that cars now began to use it, as it gave a shorter approach to High Street from Orchard Road than either Castle Hill Road or South Street. The cars were hidden by the arch before they appeared on the pavement at the point where the bus halt sign was. So many near-accidents happened that the Council took steps to close the lane at this end. This was a long legal process, a decade passing before the Burgh Surveyor could close the archway with steel pillars.

March brought gales, with gusts of 90 m.p.h. The most obvious damage was to the apex of the elaborately carved stone pediment of the façade of the High (St Leonard's) Church which fell making a hole in the roof and broke slates and gutters before reaching the ground. The trade of stone hewer, once a busy one in Forres, had gone and 12 years later the piece still lay on the ground awaiting repair and replacement.

The usual Licensing Court was held in March in the Burgh Courtroom. Mr Horne, a solicitor from Elgin, representing some of the licence holders, protested at the practice of all licence holders having to appear at this Court, and having to stand up and be identified. He claimed that this had been abolished in law, and Forres was the only burgh which persisted with this practice. After some exchanges with the Law Agent, the Chairman, Provost Braid, announced that the practice would continue, which it did for another four years.

As election time approached, some members tried to get back the old style nomination meeting, but the majority adhered to the new way. There was a small attendance with some lively questioning. With seven candidates for seven vacancies there was no election.

There were big increases in property valuations which were now assessed every five years. Farmers were bearing the greatest increases; for instance, Linkwood Farm near Elgin, with the farm house and ten cottages, was increased from £80 to £296. Some distilleries increased fivefold and some of the Town's houses rose from £24 to £50. In October, the Treasurer announced a reduction in the rates of 3s 8d but this was more apparent than real. With the increased valuations most occupiers had to pay a greater amount than in the previous year.

From 1st May this year, if a Council's Finance Committee was formed of all the members of the Council, the Press had to be present. This annoyed many Councillors, who previously had discussed the details of many matters in the Finance Committee and reported the decisions to the Council for formal approval. Thus, no one outside the Finance Committee knew the arguments or how members had voted.

A pavilion was to be built in Roysvale Park for the junior football teams and others. The National Playing Fields Association offered £300 towards the cost, and the Council was to pay the balance of £600. There was talk of some minor changes in design but the proposal was accepted in principle. At the next meeting the Provost moved that the project be abandoned, as he found no one willing to meet the bill. The originator, Councillor Liddell, fought to retain the plan but was defeated by eight votes to six.

Muiryshade Golf Course again saw the Scottish Professional Golf Tournament. It was won by an eighteen-year-old assistant from Down-field, Bobby Walker, his score being 271 (70-64-70-67). John Panton of Glenbervie, who had won this tournament seven times previously, set up a course record of 62.

For a long time the Academy had the use of the Grant Park, adjoining Bronte Place, as a garden. The school had now stopped the gardening class and the Council re-possessed the ground in the Park.

After the summer holidays the Academy could not cope with the influx of pupils and classes were taught in the Town Hall, which was also used as the gymnasium.

During the summer the Fire Brigade reported that there were now only two firemen in Forres. At the end of the month there was a fire at the Park Hotel, but the fire tender required a minimum of four

191

men and could not turn out. The Elgin Brigade was called and came through in 12 minutes. Fortunately the staff, with helpers, had been able to deal with the blaze. The Council helped in recruiting a full Brigade by approaching employers and men, and encouraging some of its own staff to join.

Elaborate preparations were made, a pavilion being built in the Grant Park, for the visit of the Queen and the Duke of Edinburgh. It rained very heavily and the party were late in arriving. Just as they arrived the sun broke through, and everything went as planned. The Councillors and staff were introduced and after some conversation ex-Provost Michie Anderson, Mr A. B. Simpson, ex-Rector of Forres Academy, Mrs A. H. Taylor, a former Matron of Leanchoil Hospital, and Mrs A. H. Forbes were presented to the Queen. The Duke talked of the Park and Forres, which he knew well, having often played cricket in the town when a pupil at Gordonstoun School.

October was the centenary of the cutting of the first turf for the building of the Forres and Perth Railway. The junction of this line with the Inverness and Aberdeen Railway made Forres the most important station in the Highland Railway for 40 years, giving employment to more than 100 railwaymen. The *Gazette* gave some details which are of interest in showing the great changes which have taken place in some aspects of social life since 1861.

There was a great parade including the bands of the 1st Company Forres Volunteers, the Inverness Artillery, the flute band of the Inverness Artillery; 42 members of the Duthil Volunteers; the Nairnshire Artillery Volunteers; the Forres and Nairn Volunteers, marching together; the Inverness-shire Rifle Volunteers; the Inverness Amateur Brass Band; the clergy; 120 Strathspey Highlanders, kilted, and with their pipe band; school children, navvies, sailors, Forres Band of Hope Brass Band, the Forres trades with their banners, aprons and sashes; the Hammermen led, followed by the Bakers, Printers, Carpenters, Tailors, Curriers, Shoemakers and Masons. The report said the kilted pipers were the centre of a curious crowd; it seems the cult of the pipes is a twentieth-century phenomenon. One point can be noted as curious also, the absence of anyone from Elgin.

Returning to 1961, the plans of the new Academy were sent through from Elgin, to enable the Council to examine them. Golf was yearly becoming more popular, the club members now numbering more than 100. The twenty-sixth annual Cage Bird Show attracted 486 entries from all over the country.

The annual accounts showed the improved condition of the Common Good. Farm rents had been increased, timber had reached a size for cutting and other incomes increased. Some members felt that rather more generous attitudes could be taken. At the meeting a request was read from the National Orchestral Society asking that the usual donation of £2 be increased to £3. The Treasurer thought the request impertinent but Councillor Jameson moved that it be granted and was successful in getting a majority of votes.

For many years the Common Good had been mulcted, in many ways not obvious in the accounts, subsidising the burgh expenditure in some years by one third, thus reducing the rates. Consequent depletion of the Common Good was used as an excuse for further economy.

The most prominent and colourful member of the Council at this time was Bailie Sam Anderson. He was much reported in the press and in December, in his capacity of Chairman of the Liberal Party, gained much attention by attacking the action of the proprietor of the grounds at Findhorn. The beach, and much of the dunes, had been fenced and attendants at each entrance charged a fee of one shilling. He had, he said, gone there for 70 years and this charge was "too much." He described it as a "concentration camp" as the money was going into private pockets. As a result of his attack the fences were removed and the charge abolished.

Earlier in the year the Finance Committee had let the Market Green to a car dealer for the display and sale of cars at the week-end. Dean of Guild Mackenzie had protested at this, claiming that the letting of the Market Green was an ancient privilege of his Dean of Guild Court. His objection was over-ridden but the matter did not end there, for a letter appeared in the *Gazette* asking why the dealer got the Green for two days for £4 when circuses and stallholders had to pay £10. The ministers wrote objecting to car sales on a Sunday, and the Finance Committee hurriedly handed the problem back to the Dean of Guild Court.

Year 1962

At the first meeting of the year the Town Clerk reported that the Charter of 1496 gave the Council as a whole the right to let the Market Green and the Dean of Guild gladly gave up his claim. In any case the

193

garage owner withdrew his application as he had not anticipated the opposition to the sale of cars on Sundays.

It was only when accounts for snow clearing were presented that the full severity of the winter was realised. The bill for the County of Moray alone was £7233. The Glenlatterach reservoir had lost four million gallons of water through water pipes being burst by the deep frost. The Laich of Moray Water Board put the blame for this squarely on the shoulders of the R.A.F. personnel at Kinloss, who had gone on leave at Christmas without turning off the water supply as instructed.

Baxters of Fochabers announced that they were to exhibit for the first time at the Food Fair in Cologne as a prelude to the country entering the Common Market. This sales drive must have had its effect on the Council for they decided to advertise the carpet which had been bought for the pavilion erected in the Grant Park for the visit of the Queen. The Provost had opposed this resolutely in the Finance Committee but had been defeated. It later realised the sum of £62 10s.

Costs were rising and the Angling Association had to increase its membership fees. The Council had received a bill for £143 for the erection of concrete posts marking the limits of the town's angling on the river, and councillors objected to this being a charge on the town, but the Town Clerk mollified them by explaining that this would be a charge on the funds of the Murdoch Trust.

The Medical Officer of Health for the county, Dr J. Dewar, introduced a policy of vaccination to immunise the young children against poliomyelitis, which yearly took its toll. The disease soon became quite rare. Provost J. B. S. Braid, who had held office for seven years, being in the first year of his third term, gave notice of his resignation because of the pressure of business. He was unique in being promoted "from the ranks" as he had held no office in the council. His professional knowledge as a civil engineer had been of great benefit to the Council.

The Education Authority had for some years closed down small rural schools when the roll fell to four or five, taking the pupils by bus or car to the nearest school or, where possible, paying the parents an allowance for doing so by their own car. They now decided that this policy must be extended and the secondary departments of all rural schools be transferred to the nearest burgh schools. This meant that only in Elgin, Forres, Nairn, Fochabers and Grantown-on-Spey were there to be secondary schools. As the rolls of these schools would be greatly increased, much building would be necessary. Forres Academy was the most hardly pressed for accommodation and plans were put in hand for a new building to meet the need. Elgin and Nairn were not far behind, and there was much political manoeuvering to decide the priorities.

Nairnshire had been desperately short of water for some years, especially during the tourist season when the population of Nairn increased. Forres still had ample supplies at Loch Romach, although water supplies were allocated to the Laich of Moray Water Board for Kinloss. The Town Council offered to lay a six-inch pipe to the border of Nairn County if the County Council would extend it to Auldearn. Forres did this as a friendly act at no cost to Nairn. The councillors were shocked and angry when they learned that the Laich of Moray Board had sent a bill for the amount of water used to Nairnshire, and insisted that the bill be torn up.

When the water supply of Nairnshire was augmented by the building of the Clunas reservoir this pipe was forgotten. In 1973 after several years of very low rainfall Forres began to be concerned at the possibility of a severe shortage. Water supplies were by that time the responsibility of the North-East of Scotland Water Board, centred in Aberdeen. Fortunately the Provost was now a member of this body and he recalled this pipe was still in existence and could be used to augment the town's supply. The Water Board immediately connected the pipe to the Clunas supply, and by supplying Brodie and Dyke relieved the strain on the resources of Loch Romach.

Three years had passed since an election was held, and during these interest had been so low that the office-bearers had to approach members of the public and persuade them to be enrolled as councillors. This year there was a resurgence of interest and no less than ten candidates were on the voting paper. Interest was centred in Forres only, where the pre-election meeting was very well attended and lasted for more than two hours. In Elgin only 60 people had attended the meeting there and at Rothes only nine.

The new candidates put forward schemes for the improvement of the town and the further building of houses. Two of the members of the previous Council did not succeed in being re-elected which was unusual, indicating the new interest being taken by the electorate. The turnout on voting day was 45 per cent, a high figure for local elections. Treasurer P. J. F. McKenzie was elected Provost and Dean of Guild W. R. Mackenzie was promoted to the Treasurer's post.

195

At the annual general meeting of the Mechanics F.C. the secretary, Burgh Treasurer W. R. Mackenzie, who was also chairman of the North of Scotland Football Association, spoke of the difficulty facing the football teams of the smaller towns. Costs were escalating and the club had ended the year with a deficit of £400.

The amount of rates in arrears was larger than it had ever been, and the Finance Committee recommended that court action be taken against those who failed to pay timeously. Council tenants paid their rents and rates weekly at an office in the Tolbooth Bow and the collector informed the Council that not one Council tenant was in arrears with rent or rates, and that this was the fourteenth consecutive year with this happy state of affairs. Court action was repugnant to many members of the Council, and fortunately the threat alone was sufficient to bring in the money.

Wednesday, 6th June, saw the colourful ceremony of giving the Freedom of the Burgh to the Royal Air Force Kinloss. The R.A.F. Regiment marched through the town exercising their newly-given privileges of doing so with fixed bayonets and colours flying while aircraft flew overhead. The presentation of the casket with burgess ticket took place in the Town Hall, the R.A.F. in return presenting the town with a silver rose bowl. This was followed by a lunch for 100 in the Cluny Hill Hotel.

The Forres Academy Former Pupils' Club had been formed in 1922 by the Rector, Dr J. B. Ritchie, and had organised many literary, musical and dramatic evenings, but television was reducing the attraction of such meetings. As membership had fallen to 15, they met to consider the future and decided that the club be wound up.

As a result of the many economic crises since the end of the war, many building and other projects had been delayed or abandoned so that the building trade took on few apprentices. With increasing activity in the building trade this now resulted in a shortage of men. Every firm had more work than it could handle, and the local authorities with their restrictive budgets felt this first. It was increasingly difficult to get maintenance and repairs done on the council houses, and the tenants became more pressing with their complaints.

The Council had to build a public convenience in Caroline Street by direct labour and the trade unions took exception to this. The workers were paid full union rates although some were not tradesmen and the union accepted the position. The cost of this building was

196

£100. The Burgh Surveyor asked permission to take on more men to overtake the arrears of work as well as the extra work now required. The burgh boundaries had been extended, increasing the area of the town by 50 per cent, with more cleansing, lighting and repairs. A higher standard was now demanded and the newer members were less cautious in spending public money. The older members had been brought up in a tradition of spending as little as possible, and even then being accused of extravagance. The pre-war staff of 11 had grown to 27, and higher wages, shorter hours, holidays and sick pay increased the wages bill at a greater rate.

In July one of the big American broadcasting companies decided to make a film of *Macbeth* in Scotland on the exact locations. They enlisted the services of the Scottish Tourist Board, who suggested that Bailie Forbes would be able to help them when they were filming the part about the witches in Forres. He met them at Brodie one morning and took them to Macbeth's Hillock but they did not think that the place was suitable. In turn, various sites in Darnaway, Altyre and, finally, on the Dava Moor were seen, but none were satisfactory. They left for Cawdor Castle but there, too, they came to the same conclusion and, returning to the U.S.A., they made the film in a studio in New York. It was later shown on B.B.C. television when the witches were seen in what looked like a cave with mist swirling around them.

The British Legion held a meeting to discuss a proposal that the club's licensed premises should be available to the members on Sundays. This was opposed by the executive committee but members voted in favour.

The annual report of the North-East of Scotland Regional Hospital Board stated that Moray Hospitals were not only well run but also were the most economical in the region. Leanchoil costs were 75 per cent of the average, while Ian Charles Hospital at Grantown was even lower at 66 per cent.

A special parade was made when the Battle of Britain was celebrated by the R.A.F. In addition to the airmen, there were units and bands from the Royal Naval Air Service from Lossiemouth, Lovat Scouts of the Territorial Army, the Seaforth Highlanders and the Air Training Corps.

The reduction in working hours and increased costs made necessary some reduction in the cost of the cleansing services and the collection on Saturdays was stopped. The shopkeepers were brought into the discussions as they had made complaints about this, but it was pointed out that they had no statutory right to a free collection, which was a privilege. By the end of the year all staff had a five-day week. Six members of the Council were in council houses and were thus debarred from discussing or voting on housing matters. This put the other members in an awkward position, and an appeal was made to the Secretary of State for Scotland to have this bar removed.

The bad weather which opened the year continued through the spring and summer, the harvest being the most difficult for many years.

Year 1963

The Grantown-on-Spey area had the best winter season since ski-ing was introduced. But a week later there was 19 degrees of frost and snow fell very heavily. Again there were the usual complaints that while the main roads were cleared by spreading salt, the burghs did not do this. This time, by ten votes to six, the Council decided to ignore the law and spread salt. The Burgh Surveyor, Mr McNish, warned the members that they were breaking the law and might be punished. This received considerable publicity in the national press and by next winter the impossible was done—the law was rescinded.

The Post Office said that the posting of parcels and letters had exceeded all previous figures. The Scottish Gas Board reported that the domestic consumption of gas had also increased. Attendances at the Picture House and amateur entertainments had decreased; in some places such organisations had come to an end. These trends showed the increase in prosperity, and the acceptance of television in the home as the main means of entertainment.

Rents of municipal houses were increased in January, the largest rise being £14 for a five-apartment house, making the total rent £52.

Four councillors were appointed to support protests against the closure of the railways. At this time, the Highland District of British Rail, which ran from Dunkeld to Kyle of Lochalsh, Wick and Thurso, employed over 3000 men and in remote parts was the main employer of labour. Already a large number of men in Forres had either to move to other posts or give up their jobs. A number preferred to stay with the railway but retained their homes in the town for their retirement.

198

In January, the last National Service man was discharged at Kinloss. Thus ended a 25-year period of conscription. There had never been conscription in peace time in Scotland before the last two decades.

The continued hard frosts drove the figures on the register of unemployed from around 100 to over 300. Almost the only site of outside activity was at the curling pond, where bonspeils many years in arrears were being played off. There was much skating at Blairs Loch, but further inland the snow still lay 14 feet deep. The Navy had to send a helicopter from Lossiemouth to drop hay for the starving sheep at Tirriemore Farm near Lochindorb as the farmer had been unable to leave his house for more than a week.

About 1860 a native of the town, Major George Dickson of the Bank of Calcutta, died and left the sum of £100 towards the award of a gold medal to the Dux of Forres Academy. At that time a "scholar" was, of course, a scholar of the Classics, and the medal was awarded to the pupil who led in Latin and Greek. After the First World War interest rates fell and the price of gold rose, so that the interest from the legacy was not sufficient to pay for the medal, and the Town Council each year voted to make up the necessary sum of money to get the Dickson Medal. The sum was usually £5 and a wrist watch was now given in place of a medal. It so happened that this year the Academy and the Primary School had both three duxes, all with equal marks, and watches could not be given.

As the winter progressed the weather got worse. A train stuck in the snow in the lee of the Knock of Braemoray, and it took 12 hours to get the 20 passengers to shelter. Two engines with a snowplough had preceded the train to Aviemore and got through; that station reported its arrival to Forres. The train there was sent forward but more snow had fallen. Instead of concentrating on getting the passengers to safety, sandwiches and tea were made in Forres and sent on by an engine, which also stuck. The enginemen, however, scrambled through the snow with the food for the stranded passengers. A bus was then sent, which took everyone back to Forres.

Many farmers returning by road from the Perth sales were unable to get further than Dava, and had to be sheltered in the few cottages there. When the bill was received by the County Council later in the year for the cost of clearing away the snow, it came to £15,000, enough to swallow the year's allocation of money for road works.

In March, the Lighting Committee asked for money for more

199

street lighting, and for a supply of overhead cable. The Council rejected this report and decided by a vote that, in future, all cables would be laid underground, and the existing overhead cables would have to be put underground by the Hydro-Electric Board when any alterations were being made.

When election time came the opponents of fluoridation of the water supply objected strongly and carried on an active correspondence in the press. The Council agreed with them and as it controlled Loch Romach which now supplied most of Western Moray, the County Council could do nothing about it. All the noise and fury on both sides was nullified when the County Council Finance Committee refused to allocate the money necessary to implement the proposal in the rest of the county.

After 33 years of building modern houses, all with baths and hot and cold water, there were still a large number of houses lacking this, many have outside toilets. In earlier days, councillors were almost invariably owners of rented properties and improvement was slow and difficult. But the composition of the Council was now different: no longer did lawyers and factors enter it and many members were tenants of council houses, and wanted everyone to be well housed. It was agreed that grants should be given to improve unsatisfactory houses. If they were not improved they were to be demolished or bought by the Council, who would make the improvements. The difficulty was that not enough new houses could be built quickly, before the next economic crisis came along to slow down all spending.

Glasgow had decided that the only way that it could solve its housing problem was by removing thousands of people from the city to "overspill" areas. Lord Polwarth visited Forres in his search for towns willing to accept people from Glasgow. The Provost and Councillors met Lord Polwarth who urged Forres to take some of the overspill population, offering grants to attract industry to the burgh.

Opinion was divided in the Council, but two members, Treasurer W. R. Mackenzie and Councillor James Flemington—timber merchant and sawmiller—volunteered to go to Glasgow to discuss the matter. This they did and later two representatives visited the town for more talks, but nothing came of them.

When the town's men were repairing roads at the Waterford level crossing, they came upon a forgotten but dangerous relic of the late war. Two barrels of petrol buried at the side of the road were so fitted that they could be exploded if an enemy tank passed the crossing on its way from the feared landing at Findhorn.

As the new school at Kinloss was now ready. Findhorn School was closed as well as the old school at Kinloss. There were, as usual, protests from parents, but rarely from the children. The County Education bill had, for the first time, reached a million pounds, a figure unthinkable only a few years earlier.

Moray and Nairn Education Authority had been leaders in the centralising of schools. This had started as an economy measure, but as the five secondary schools at Elgin, Forres, Nairn, Grantown-on-Spey and Fochabers were now large enough to have departments of specialists, the standard of education improved.

The cleaning of the Mosset became more difficult with the appearance of a new water weed, said to have come from Sanquhar Loch. The dam of this loch had been lowered by several feet as a safety measure, and the weed was released. It grew up to the top of the water and was very thick with leaves, quite unlike the silky, slimy hair-like growth previously seen. It had to be removed at considerable expense. The Loch had held 13 million gallons of water when the dam was at its full height. More than 60 years earlier it had broken, so that the lower part of the town lay under several feet of water and great damage was caused.

Thirteen million gallons was the amount needed to work the water wheels of the mills of Forres—the Waukmill at St Catherine's, the wheel of Brewery Farm and also that of Mill of the Grange, none of which were now in use. The machinery at the laundry and in the weaving rooms had also been operated by these wheels but steam had replaced water power for some time. A few years later, when the town wanted to buy the loch, it was found that under the "servitudes" it would be liable at any time, if asked, to rebuild the dam and provide the water. The loch had so silted up that it was estimated in 1973 that less than a million gallons were held.

The Baths at Forres House, at one time much used, were now running at a considerable loss. During the year the receipts were £38 and the cost £381. Some occupiers who had baths in their houses said that, in the summer especially, they preferred to use the Forres baths, as this was cheaper than lighting a fire and burning coal to get sufficient hot water for a bath. As the capital fund was being eroded by meeting the losses incurred, it was decided to close the Baths; this intention was advertised and, unusually, brought not one protest.

201

It was now Government policy that all secondary schools should have swimming pools attached, although Moray and Nairn had not yet thought of putting this into practice. The Forres member of the Education Committee recalled that a previous representative from the burgh had suggested that Forres would be willing to use the Munro Fund when a new Academy was erected in Forres. The swimming pool was to cost £55,000 and Forres said that they would give £30,000 towards the building. This was naturally very favourably received by the Education Committee but the Scottish Education Department in Edinburgh could not agree to it. There was legislation allowing a large authority to help a smaller authority financially but the opposite had never happened and now, to the Civil Service mind, never could. Most County officials and members agreed with Forres Town Council as to the silliness of the position, and agreement came that it could perhaps be done. But before this was resolved, the contracts for building the new Academy had been accepted, and it was too late. It took until 1972 to get plans and costs for the swimming pool, by which time costs had soared.

For a century and a half, Nelson's Tower had been an attraction for visitors and was kept open from May until September. The attendant got nothing but the tips, and this was not made clear when a vacancy was advertised this year. The successful applicant, who came from Brechin, refused to take up the duties. The committee decided that, in future, a wage of £2 10s would be paid, the attendant to keep the tips also. At one time, the Tower had a very fine telescope on the roof, but after the occupation by the Army and later the Royal Air Force for many years, this had disappeared. A good set of binoculars was provided in its place.

Something happened this year that, but for chance, could have had tragic consequences. On the last day of the season the attendant left for lunch, and as he had had no caller for several days, decided not to return and locked the Tower up for the winter. He had sat all morning in the lowest room and a gentleman on holiday had seen the open door, tiptoed upstairs quietly and was on the roof when the door was locked and the building left. He waited all afternoon, getting more and more distressed, and by evening was almost speechless with shouting. On the ground floor was the Ship's Bell and, on occasion, he rang it. Two members of the R.A.F. from Kinloss arrived to make a routine check of the red warning light on the flagpole; as they approached they heard the slow stroke of a bell and after a minute or two, another. Not

202

having done this duty before they became rather unnerved and retreated, fortunately meeting the Reverend Harold Broom of St John's Church, whose favourite walk this was. The men asked him if the Tower was haunted, which he assured them was not the case, but they were so certain they had heard a bell that he went up to the Tower with them and, as they had a key, rescued the unwilling captive.

Some old properties held by the Cameron Trust for the behoof of one of the town's churches were offered to the Council, as there were insufficient funds to meet the cost of repair and improvement; these were accepted. Properties like this had, in the past, been offered but had always been refused. The argument was that the ratepayers should not relieve the owners of this burden. Following this acceptance, other owners offered such properties and these were gladly accepted as it speeded the process of improvement.

This summer saw the first angling contest at Findhorn; over 70 contestants entered and 290 lbs. of fish were caught.

Forres had long held the lead in the number of people donating blood to the Northern Blood Bank and on a Sunday in September no less than 145 persons attended to give a pint of their blood. A number of donors had already received the highest award for this worthy service.

The Banff, Moray and Nairn River Purification Board were now in full operation, much of their attention being concentrated on the sewage from Forres which flowed untreated into the Findhorn Bay, where the Mosset entered it. This was no offence in law as the waters were tidal. The River Findhorn had the best reputation for purity of all the waters and streams in the Board's area, no pollution ever having been noted in its waters. But the Board had to show that it was active and the Burgh had no representative on the Board which was composed of members from the County Councils of Moray and Nairn County, Banffshire and Inverness, in addition to members appointed by the Secretary of State from industry and agriculture. Distilleries, factories and other works, along with farms, were polluting almost every other stream, silage effluent becoming increasingly prevalent.

Many of the representatives supported the pressure on Forres, thus drawing attention away from other streams. At meetings it was pointed out that in the Forres area alone, R.A.F. Kinloss sewage ran into the Kinloss Burn, and the sewage of the village of Findhorn was collected in a large concrete tank in the centre of the village, near

203

the piers. This emptied its contents in bulk in every 12½ hours, being controlled by a valve which opened at high tide: the meetings were, at times, very acrimonious.

The Council employed a distinguished firm of civil engineering consultants, who drew up plans for a modern sewage purification plant. These were handed to the Board for examination, and the Council were later told by the Board that the design was accepted, but that the plant was to be sited at Kinloss. This meant that the County Council would have to be paid the rates as it would now be in their area. The minimum figure would have been £1500 a year, and this was unacceptable to the town. The Board retaliated by threatening to instigate a "Tidal Water" order, making it illegal for the town to continue as it was doing.

A representative from Forres was appointed to the Board and the attacks almost ceased. But effluent from silage making and the production of whisky was increasing. The distilleries had, in many cases, to carry the noxious liquors by road tankers to the sea and empty them there. On occasion, a driver would surreptitiously dump the contents into a stream, with serious consequences to fish and other life. The villages and burghs on the coast began to object to pollution and the smell of water around them.

Again the Purification Board pressed Forres to build the sewage plant. The town replied that it was willing to do so but, as a burgh with a population of over 3000 was not eligible for Government grants, a great financial burden would be placed upon the ratepayers with very little reduction of the pollution at Findhorn Bay.

The Board applied for a "Tidal Water Order" to apply to the sewage outlet but the officials in Edinburgh drew a line from the point of the Bay, thus including the waters where the Kinloss and Findhorn sewage entered. R.A.F. Kinloss were authorised to erect a plant for themselves, which was done, and Forres also started, after coming to agreement with the distillery companies that the burgh plant would treat the effluent from Dallas Dhu and Ben Romach Distilleries. The work was started in 1971 and the sewage purification works came into action in March 1973. By this time the population, actual and projected was much greater, but the works could meet the demand then and for a long time ahead. Nothing was done about Findhorn village.

The town's case had always been based on a paper presented earlier in the century to the Royal Society's annual conference held at Dundee. This showed that the Forres sewage was not the cause of the obnoxious smell which arose in the area. The smell came from the boggy ground of the Carse, through which "land water" slowly percolated. The smell was caused by the reduction of the sulphates in this slow moving water, into sulphides by bacterial organisms.

The Y.M.C.A. building, a corrugated iron hall in Cumming Street, had to be closed, as few meetings were now held there and the central organisation had to reduce its costs. It was later bought by the Council and demolished to make way for Hainings Road and houses. The tenant of Pilmuir Farm emigrated and gave up his lease of the farm. It was only of 28 acres and was leased to Messrs T. & W. Christie, nurserymen, for £425 per annum. The previous rent, fixed only a few years before, had been £78—a sign of increasing land prices.

In addition to the demand from personnel at Kinloss and Lossiemouth, for a numbers of years there had been a great demand for private housing and the prices paid were on a par with the South-East of England, and far surpassed most of Scotland. To try and hold these prices, the Council developed some of the Common Good land at Councillor's Walk. There they feued 12 sites, ten of them at £11 10s and two at £12 10s per annum. The feu duty was payable until abolished in 1974, but the burgh provided the services and made up the road so that a house could be built much more cheaply than by any other method. So great was the demand that all applications had to be considered and voted upon. The cost was decided by the District Valuer and no profit was made. The houses had to be of a minimum cost of £1500.

For the first time, the burgh workmen were given Christmas Day as a holiday and, for the first time also, Forres Mechanics won the Scottish Qualifying Cup, defeating the Buckie team at Buckie.

The Education Committee now realised that the sports ground was inadequate for the new Academy with a roll of about a thousand pupils. The Committee had assumed that they could take over Roysvale Park as a sports field, but the Town Council had preserved this ground for junior football teams and other games. The Forres Mechanics were now a professional team and thus could not allow amateurs to play on their pitch, and there were no other pitches available.

Year 1964

The work done in the Council during the past two or three years now began to show results.

Regular visitors remarked that the town seemed to be revitalised, with brighter and better stocked shops. Many of the derelict houses, especially those in the closes off High Street had now gone. There were many more flowers, grass plots and shrubs.

Mr W. G. Scott of Whiterow offered to the Council the two rows of houses known as Fraser's Buildings in the Pilmuir. While not very old, they had not been well built and always looked unattractive. The low rents of these properties attracted people moving into the town. Most of them moved into better houses whenever they could, so that there was a constant flow into and out of the buildings.

There was some opposition to accepting gifts of old properties but this was overcome. It was intended to empty all the houses as soon as possible and demolish the buildings, but this was not done as quickly as was hoped. They were frequently used as emergency homes, and it was very difficult to get them cleared.

The Trust of the late William Deas also offered four houses at the corner of Cumming Street and Orchard Road; these were also accepted and cleared quickly to make more ground available for the proposed Hainings housing scheme.

Special mention was made at this time by the organisers of the Blood Bank in Inverness, about the large number of donors in Forres. Among them were the holders of a Gold Award, 18 Silver Awards and 169 Bronze Badges.

A large badger was killed by a train near Brodie Station; as large as a collie dog, it was 40 inches long and weighed 30 lbs. It was the first specimen seen by most of the people in the Brodie area; it was known that some had arrived years before but they were rarely seen.

The Council entered into an agreement with Glasgow Corporation to house "overspill" families and offered to build houses specially for those who would arrive when an industry to employ them along with local people was set up: nothing ever developed from this agreement.

The population of the burgh was now 4700, a considerable increase on the 1921 figure of 4117. But much of this increase was due to the arrival of families who could no longer find work on the farms; often they were elderly people approaching retirement age. Mobile shops

206

which formerly served the rural areas were now being withdrawn as they were unable to compete with supermarkets. This made life more difficult for those who remained in the more remote areas.

Mr Robert Souter, partner in Messrs Mackenzie & Grant, who acted as Town Chamberlain, retired. He had held the post for a considerable time.

Chamberlains now had to be Chartered Accountants or persons with at least five years' experience in municipal accountancy, and as there was nobody in the district thus qualified, Colonel W. D. Johnson of Messrs Johnson & Carmichael, C.A., of Elgin, was appointed, on a part-time basis. As he had no office in Forres, the Council had to alter some of the rooms on the ground floor of the Tolbooth to make a Cashier's Office and employ two cashiers; as the number of houses owned by the town grew, this had to be increased to three.

During the May elections considerable feeling arose about such things as fluoridation, the siting of the proposed new Academy at Burdshaugh, and new housing. The pre-election meeting was a long one, with strong attacks on some of the Council members, and the fireworks came more from the platform than from the hecklers. It was the first time that election literature was distributed, attacking the policy of the Council and especially some of the senior members. The new members were very active revising "standing orders" and bringing forward a number of motions and proposals; this led to a new system of allocating houses.

Inside and outside the Council chambers there was much talk and argument about the new Academy site, with a lively correspondence in the press. It was said the site was too small and liable to flooding and dampness. A Parents' Association was formed to try to change the site to one in the Pilmuir. The Education Authority held to their decision to build at Burdshaugh and, ironically, when the floods did come, the Pilmuir was flooded but the Academy, now in use, was quite dry.

For the first time, teachers could be appointed by the Education Authority, while the School Management Committees were abolished. The members of this Committee were appointed from people interested in education, and did some good work.

In March, the Council's consultants, Messrs Baptie, Shaw & Morton, brought in their report. This advised rejection of the plans for the sewage works—put forward by the Joint County Council—for economic and technical reasons. As a matter of urgency the sewage plant at R.A.F. Kinloss was pushed forward. This had a planned life of only ten years, but was still working satisfactorily after that time, with a greatly increased load.

The Picture House in Cumming Street had to close down and the building was sold to Messrs Fyfes as a furniture store and depot. Architects had been asked to examine the building to see if it could be adapted to a swimming pool, but the report was unfavourable.

The Forres Picture House Company had started before the 1914 war, in the former Baptist Church in Caroline Street; this was known as "the Lyceum." Talking pictures had been introduced in 1927, two years after the new Picture House had opened.

The Council began to make use of the new legislation which made it compulsory for owners of property to carry out necessary improvements. Grants and loans could be arranged. Many took advantage of a scheme whereby grants of £40 were made available to tenants to enlarge their homes.

The Waukmill was taken over by Messrs Black & Sons as workshops, and one part of the former laundry was converted to a funeral parlour. This was one of the first in the area, to be followed later by that erected by Messrs J. Smith & Sons at their premises in Station Lane.

Councillor A. S. Davidson resigned. As principal of the Science Department in the Academy he now had much work in introducing new science courses. Some of the Council pressed for a bye-election, but the majority decided to co-opt, and Mr Graeme W. Fulton was chosen to fill the vacancy.

Dr J. C. Adam retired as Superintendent of Leanchoil Hospital, a post he had held for 40 years. The North-Eastern Regional Hospital Board had pressed for some time for the Edwards legacy of £37,000, but Mr Leask held that it had to be spent on Leanchoil and as the Board's policy was to pool the legacies they held, he refused to hand it over. Finally, the Board agreed to make a modern operating theatre and X-ray unit. This was opened with considerable ceremony by the Chairman of the Board, Lady May Braid. Next day word was received that the theatre was not to be used except in emergencies; this policy was adhered to until 1973.

The Shopkeepers' Association held a meeting to discuss a proposal to have shops open for only five days in the week but this was rejected.

The County Architect reported that the frontage of the Academy, on the south side of High Street was in a dangerous condition; the steeple was likely to fall and the gymnasium could not be used. The badminton teams were transferred to the Town Hall.

The Academy—at that time including the building on the north side of High Street, erected about 90 years earlier—was also in an unsafe state. There were also a number of huts in the playground of this building. While the Academy listed 39 teaching rooms, nine of these were in halls spread over the town. The old Academy on the North side had 13 but this building had been condemned in 1928, while the Jonathan Anderson side had 17. The Education Authority was pressed to make the new Academy a first priority, but this was given to Elgin Academy and then the Elgin Technical College.

Rainfall was well below the average for the year, only 514 mm. (20·58 inches).

Year 1965

At the annual meeting of the Forres Branch of the Aberdeen Savings Bank, Mr T. T. Davidson, Head Master of the Forres Primary School, said that the number of children in his school had fallen by more than 100 in five and a half years. The town were not holding the young married people who had to go elsewhere for work. This had always been the trend, as the town had never had enough industry, for the last 50 years at least, to employ young people.

The Housing Committee published its plans for building 80 houses in the area between Castlehill Road and Cumming Streeet. In this small area there were no less than 27 owners of houses and all had to be involved in the negotiations about title deeds, plans and values. After very many meetings the site was ready for development, but soon difficulties arose. The High Street of Forres runs along the ridge of what had at one time been dunes, with the River Findhorn flowing roughly in what is the bed of the Mosset Burn, except that it had, at one time at least, flowed east past Earnside Farm and into the Loch of Spynie, thence into the sea.

In all this land between Forres and the sea, it was known that there had been rises and falls in the land or sea levels, and that below the six to twelve feet of marine gravel the remains of giant trees were to be found in beds of peat. Peat was also found during excavation for the "Hainings" site but, even worse, there was "quaking bog," 18 feet down. It was a strange sensation to place one's feet on this peat and sway from side to side, and find the peat sway also. A soil engineer had to be flown from England to prescribe treatment. This involved much more digging and the pouring of very large quantities of concrete. Owing to the restricted area, and the need to get the required number of houses built on it, three tower blocks had to be erected. These were of five stories and there was much opposition to the suggestion. But it was necessary to have playing space and also room for parking cars, so it was accepted in the long run. An effort was made to have lifts installed but this was not considered necessary, as the top floor was to have bedrooms only.

The name given to this area, "The Hainings," was a relic of the Royal Burgh's history. The Castlehill had been an original part and this land, extending from the Mosset nearly to the south end of Tolbooth Street, had been the land held in reserve for the King's horses when he and his entourage made the regular visit or "ayre" to the burgh. It had, therefore, never been much built upon and in time of trouble or war the cattle and horses of the burgesses could be gathered there for safety. For the time, these new houses were of a high standard, with central heating, fitted television aerials, tiled floors and stairs and treated hall walls. This made them expensive but maintenance costs were low because of the careful work.

When election time came along the Provost, Mr Pat Mackenzie, announced that he was retiring, along with Bailie Jean Mackintosh and Bailie John Falconer. All had been leading members and their retirement meant that there would be considerable changes in the new Council.

There were seven candidates for the five vacancies and, while there was a good attendance at the pre-election meeting, there were few questions. The new candidates were young men and showed a sparkle and fire almost like party politicians, some offering frank criticisms of the sitting members, and promising a lively time.

Just before the election the Railway Board announced that they proposed to close the railway line between Forres and Aviemore. This meant the closing of five stations—Dunphail, Dava (both housing district post offices), Grantown-on-Spey, Broomhill and Boat of Garten. As the closures would bring about a loss of jobs in an area where there was no alternative work, a special committee was set up to fight the proposals and many meetings were held in Forres and in the district.

Many councils had made protests, but Forres was in rather a different position. Elsewhere it was proposed to close small and uneconomic stations whereas here, a whole line was to close; furthermore this line had been part of the original Perth to Inverness railway. So important was this that the Council took, for them, the unprecedented step of making an appeal to the Queen. This was of no avail although all that was sought was an impartial inquiry into the actions of the Consultative Committee at Grantown-on-Spey. Provost Forbes represented the town there but was not allowed to give any evidence, as the Chairman ruled that Forres station was not being closed.

The Council tried to purchase 11½ acres of ground at Greshop Farm, to be developed as industrial sites. There was strong opposition to this by the Highland Agricultural Executive Committee. At a meeting with this committee, the Provost stated that as long as he was in office, no agricultural land would be used for council housing, as the policy had been adopted of using cleared ground within the burgh itself. In the end, the town was successful and the land was made available although it was some years before any development took place. The first of the buildings to be built there was a centre for the Moray Estates Development Company, who sold the ground to the town in the first instance.

The Council had no clear plan or organisation. When something new came before the Council—such as to make a sports field—a committee would be appointed, and long after decisions had been made the committee would be in existence. There were now 17 committees, some of them rarely meeting, composed of from three to eleven members. The Provost put forward a plan to reduce the committes to eight in number, the number of members to be eight in each, and no person to hold more than one convenership. Previously it was possible for a member to serve on as many as six committees. If there were nine members on a committee this meant that more than half the Council were on that committee, and if the members were unanimous about a proposal the Council could not alter it. A member, if a fairly new one, might be on two committees; one of these could be the first to meet, *e.g.* Finance, of which every-

211

one was a member, and a small committee which might meet at the end of the series of meetings. This could mean waiting for three hours or more between meetings. The report was rejected as there was not sufficient notice. Longer notice could not be given as the Provost was elected on the Friday and the Council met on the following Monday.

Council meetings, church attendances and all formal occasions had a rather Victorian air. Members had to dress in striped trousers, black swallow-tailed coat and top hat. This was no longer accepted by the younger generation, and those who did not have the dress avoided occasions when formal dress was mandatory: the rule requiring formal attire was therefore relaxed.

The Dean of Guild, Miss Mary A. Crowe, died in office.

The Senior Town Clerk, Mr Alastair Macdonald, also died, at the age of 74. He had served throughout the First World War as a Captain in the Seaforth Highlanders and had a distinguished career, being awarded the M.C. and two bars. He had been in command of the Home Guard during the Second War, and had taken an active part in all activities concerning the burgh. His elder brother, Colonel Archibald Macdonald, had been a member of the Council for many years, and their father had also been a member of Council and a Bailie.

The Council supported the movement to retain the Territorial Army, but this was ineffective. In December, at the annual show of the Forres Bird Cage Society—which usually received exhibits from far afield, especially the North of England—there was a big fall in the entries because of the cessation of the direct railway line from the south. The increased rail charges because of the longer distance the packages had to travel also affected the entries.

The dispute over the closing of the railway lasted a long time and there was a row between the local Member of Parliament, Mr Gordon Campbell, and the Minister of Transport, Mr Tom Fraser.

Some years afterwards the Provost and Town Clerk were at a function where they met Mr Fraser, then Chairman of the North of Scotland Hydro Board. On learning that they were from Forres, he said that when he was in the Ministry of Transport, the town of Forres had given him more trouble than any other place. He was somewhat abashed to learn that he was speaking to the men concerned.

Year 1966

Forres was now a development area and grants were available to any firm or person willing to set up a new industry and give employment. The Planning Committee went to work on this problem. The town was moderately prosperous but its fortunes had always depended upon the prosperity of the agricultural community, which was now low. For many farmers, seed potatoes had been the main crop and, because of their freedom from disease, Scots potatoes had always received a good price in England. The arrival of pesticides and preventative chemicals allowed English farmers to use potatoes, which they had grown themselves, as seed. Local farmers were then left with seed potatoes and the Potato Marketing Board had to buy and find a use for them. Most of these potatoes had to be destroyed or left to rot as the normal price for potatoes could not be obtained for small seed potatoes.

Another source of employment was to go. The gas pipe being laid from Inverness to Aberdeenshire was now complete, and a conversion plant opened up at the Longman in Inverness to adapt the liquefied gas brought from the refinery at Fawley by sea, to burn in domestic and other burners. The Forres Gas Works had to close and the staff was made redundant. At one time, a walk round the gas works was thought to be the remedy for whooping cough, but this ailment had also gone with immunisation.

The closure of the gas works caused other changes. Bakers had always used coke for their ovens, at least the old Scotch ovens which were almost universal in the North. Coke was not now obtainable cheaply and conveniently from the local gas works, and the freight charges from the nearest supply at Perth were high. In any case, all coal gas plants were to be phased out.

A General Election was held in March; a Labour Government was returned but there was no change in this constituency.

An estimate to bring the slaughterhouse up to the required standard came to £40,000 and there were some moves to close it down altogether.

A memorandum on the railway line over the Dava was now printed, a copy being sent to every M.P. and to 160 different bodies. This was a most competent paper, the joint work of Councillors Lewis Grant

213

and John Mackenzie: senior pupils at the Academy had helped with charts and graphs. This memorandum greatly influenced the Parliamentary Committee dealing with railway matters, and they asked that a deputation visit them in London. The Provost, Councillor Mackenzie and the Town Clerk met the Committee, who promised the town full support in its efforts to reopen the railway. But the Railway Board would not be diverted, and the rails were lifted as soon as the legal waiting period had expired. Most of the rails and iron chairs were shipped from Burghead to be melted down in Germany; the wooden sleepers were sold locally.

Councillor Mackenzie put forward a motion that all local recreational clubs should be able to look for financial assistance from the Council. At his election, the Provost said that he hoped the Council would look beyond what they had to do by law, and act in the social field. The proposal was hotly debated but the majority were not ready for this new concept although, within a year or so, they were disbursing thousands of pounds in this area.

A contract had been arranged with Messrs Wimpey to build the houses in the Hainings and at Claremont and Tailwell. There was considerable delay in obtaining official approval and in the interim a new tax, the Selective Employment Tax, was introduced, adding greatly to the cost.

The Tailwell site was a difficult one. Fifteen years earlier the Council had decided to build there, but the Scottish Office had declared that because of the gradient, houses of a modern design could not be erected. The Housing Committee had always pressed this site, and the design and layout of the new contractors was accepted. When completed, they were the most popular of the new houses because of the excellent view of the sea.

Difficulties were encountered, as the foundations had to go down much deeper than anticipated. This had been one of the earliest places of settlement in Forres, and the old cellars of the merchants, where they had stored the wine imported from France, were uncovered. It it said that in the sixteenth century, Findhorn imported more claret that Leith. Certainly, much of this wine was drunk in the north, the Government at one time restricting the amount that the gentlemen could buy; for instance, two Chiefs—Duart and MacLeod—could not buy more than 5760 bottles a year in 1616. The Laird of Culloden—known as "Bumper" John Forbes—always had a cask of claret in a corner of the hall, with a large wooden measure, for anyone who wished to have a drink. The cellars had been floored with pebbles set in a lime made from crushed seashells.

There was opposition to the Post Office's notice of earlier closing, now to be 5.30 p.m. Some time was also taken by a petition of 15 residents in Tytler Street against a proposal to change a furniture store to a funeral parlour. After several inconclusive meetings, the Planning Officer was asked to attend. He reported that the street was of mixed character, part residential and part commercial, with some crafts, so that the petitioners had no case.

No election was necessary in May, the candidates equalling the vacancies. Bailie Sam Anderson (one of the most colourful of members) retired, and the Dean of Guild, Charles Sutherland, did not accept renomination. There were few elections this year in Scotland, as though the recent General Election had drained away any interest.

A Scottish Week was held in July, as visitors during the Glasgow Fair complained that there was little entertainment. A profit of £250 was made instead of the loss expected. The Committee gave £100 towards the revival of a pipe band, the money to be used for the purchase of drums.

A branch of the Scottish National Party was formed, and opened a clubroom. Two Clubs were formed, the Forres Motor Club and the Ecurie Forres; the latter was for racing model cars, equipment being set up in the former office of the Leabridge Sawmills, now defunct.

Before the Gas Works closed down, a defect occurred which filled the pipes with a gas so evil smelling that people had to leave their houses. More than 60,000 cubic feet of gas had to be released from the gasholders, and it was some time before the fumes dissipated; it seemed a final gesture.

More young business and professional men were being attracted to Council work and would have liked to take part in the work outside Forres—in the County Council, Police, Fire, Water and Hospital Boards, etc., which drew much of their membership from town councils. These held their meetings during the day and Bailie Sinclair put forward a motion that they be asked to hold their meetings in the evening so that members could be present. This none of the bodies would agree to do, thus restricting, as before, active participation to people with ample leisure, in most cases retired people who had time to attend meetings in Elgin, Aberdeen and elsewhere. This meant that the most energetic and progressive members had little say in local government in areas such as Moray.

215

Each year saw an erosion of the powers and actions of town and county councils, and the Government set up the Wheatley Commission to go around the country and investigate the problem, and make recommendations for reorganisation. The Provost gave evidence to the Commission on behalf of the burghs when it visited Elgin.

When the railway to the south was closed, a promise was given that adequate buses would be run, and that the roads would be improved to allow the buses to travel safely. One of the most dangerous points on the road was the bridge over the Divie at Edenkillie Church. The first, and most suitable, design would have gone between the Church and the Manse but the minister refused to agree to this. As this was Church ground, compulsory purchase was not possible.

It was again necessary to extend the burgh boundaries, as there was not sufficient ground available within the burgh for any further industrial development. The Inquiry was again held by Sheriff Principal Douglas M. Campbell, and the necessary land at the west and north was annexed.

As a result of the Planning Committee's efforts, a party of industrialists visited the town from the Midlands. A brochure had been produced by the Council and distributed. All expressed interest but only one set up a factory in the north—in Aberdeen.

The first political debate within living memory of the councillors took place. This was on a motion by Councillor John Mackenzie protesting against the imposition of the Selective Employment Tax, which hurt the tourist trade and farming, the main industries in the north and west, very much. Before the debate took place the Government announced that farming would be exempt. The motion was carried but the tax continued until replaced by Value Added Tax in April 1973.

On 1st June the Provost and Town Clerk visited the town's only centenarian, Miss Mathieson, Invermay, and presented her with a glass goblet engraved by Mr Harry Gordon. The last centenarian, William Green, had celebrated the occasion during the war years, when little attention was paid to such things.

This June had the worst rainstorm remembered, 2·38 inches falling in 24 hours In Elgin about 20 families had to be rescued from their homes, but in Forres only the industrial premises of Messrs Reid and Plasmon Ltd. were affected. But much damage had been done at Loch Romach, banks being washed away and water mains exposed

216

FORRES 1973   *Aerofilms Ltd.*

THE TOWN CENTRE (c. 1960)

FORRES 1973 *Aerofilms Ltd.*
Showing the Academy (*foreground*), Applegrove Primary
School (*centre*) and the river and Findhorn Bay

and broken. Emergency measures had to be made to ensure a supply of drinking water, and considerable expense was incurred in repairing the damage.

At the Highland Games in August the 26-mile marathon from Inverness was won by a well-known Aberdeen man, Alastair Wood, in 2 hours 13 minues 43 seconds. This was the fastest time recorded in Scotland. The organisers received an offer of £200, and later, other sums, to send the winner to the Commonwealth Games in Jamaica.

The National 18 foot Yacht Championship was held at Findhorn, with 31 yachts competing.

The large malting plant at Burghead started work, giving new life to the burgh. STD telephoning was introduced; the Post Office had difficulty in finding a suitable site but finally extended the Post Office building.

Christmas was white, the first time for many years.

The *Gazette* repeated some items from the issue of 1866, which showed the great changes taking place at that time, just after the railways had arrived:

A meeting of the farm servants in the area had been called to form the "Ploughman's Protection and Benefit Society for Forres, Rafford and Kinloss." The Treasurer and Secretary had to be recruited from the town—a tailor and a shoemaker. This must have been the first trade union in the area.

Religious services were held on a weekday to pray for protection from the cattle plague which was rampant. All the churches held services, starting at twelve noon.

The Forres and Findhorn Railway ran a special train to see the launching of the largest ship ever built at Findhorn, the *Minnie of Mayfield*. She was 112 feet long, 25 feet in beam, with a 15 foot deep hold, carrying 650 tons—a considerable size. She slid down the ways smoothly with the decks crowded with passengers, but began to sway as she touched the water until she toppled over, and would have turned turtle had the masts not struck bottom, thus preventing her from sinking. All aboard were saved within five minutes. This was the last ship to be built there and her first voyage took her to South America with a cargo of rails. The writer's father was present and frequently spoke of the launching.

217

Year 1967

The newly formed pipe band appeared at the Cross on Hogmanay but the celebrations were restricted by the icy condition of the streets and roads. The previous year had been very wet, with 824 mm. (32·98 inches) of rain.

The first party of 45 secondary pupils from Forres Academy visited the ski slopes at Aviemore on 14th January. In all, 300 pupils took part in the course, which covered ten Saturdays. All the equipment was provided by the Moray & Nairn Education Committee.

The farmer tenant of New Forres farm signed a trust deed and the Council had a bad debt of three years' rent on their books amounting to £600. When a survey was made of the other farms, another was found to be in arrears and steps were taken to recover these.

The provision of new holes on the Golf Course required the clearing of five acres of trees, and as these had been dedicated under the schemes of the Forestry Commission, the Council had to repay £246 18s, the amount which they had received in annual grants. Councillor William Coutts resigned on being appointed bank manager in Huntly. He had been Secretary for the Forres Sports for some time and carried on the duties from his new home for a while.

At last, after fifty years, the swimming pool became a certainty. The Council and the Education Committee had had many negotiations and a meeting was held with the Forres District Council (the landward part of the parish) who agreed to pay one-eighth of the cost of the pool—£5000. The Education Committee had to pay £27,000 and Forres Council £35,750—£20,000 of this from the Munro funds. The pool was to be part of the new Academy but Government restrictions on spending delayed a start until 1972, by which time costs had escalated.

On the last Sunday in January, very high seas at Findhorn had inundated two acres of ground at the back shore, a number of cars being stranded in three feet of water. There had been considerable erosion at this part, and council workmen had been trying to repair this. The final cost of restoration along the coast came to £20,000.

The Council agreed to build a new clubhouse at the Golf Course. The existing one had originally been part of the farm building. The plans for the sewage plant at the King's Meadows were ready but a start could not be made as no permission could be granted for borrowing the necessary money.

Forres was still hopeful that the railway might be opened but this was dampened by an announcement that all lines in the north-east, except that from Inverness to Aberdeen via Mulben, were to be closed and the rails removed.

It was decided to purchase the ground at Waterford Mills so that it could be cleared for industrial sites. Agreement was soon reached with Messrs Jones & Sons, sawmillers, but the negotiations with the owners of the mills dragged on for six years. The cost of the proposed bridge at Edinkillie was too high to be accepted and despite the earlier promises the project was postponed indefinitely.

The houses at Claremont were now ready but the contractors reported that the retaining wall at Bogton Road, between 100 and 150 years old, was unsafe and would require to be replaced by a new wall at a cost of £3260, a figure which shocked the Council.

At the pre-election meeting only 20 electors were present and there were not enough candidates to fill the vacancies. Mr Ian Ross, Kendal, was co-opted to make up the necessary number.

This year's Scottish Week was an even greater success than the first, the great attraction being a parade of nine massed pipe bands.

The railway manager for the Highland Area, Mr Allison, made a visit to the Provost to discuss the request that Forres Station be moved back to the site at the east signal cabin or, better still, at the Waterford level crossing in the event of the Dava line closure. This would be more convenient when the by-pass road was made, and would eliminate the existing acute curve with its speed limit of 25 m.p.h. The trains could then run straight through on the original lines, formerly used as shunting yards. Mr Allison said that the Railway Board would agree to this if the Roads Department would pay the cost of re-laying this track, which had been untouched for over a century. The Government would not agree to this, saying that Forres would always be a stopping station so that the speed limit did not matter.

During the summer a party from Aberdeen University had been excavating at the headland of Burghead and had sent samples of the timber found to Japan for carbon 14 dating. The analysis gave its date as second or third century A.D. This confirmed the tradition that there had been a fort here in Roman times but gave no clue as to the builders. It was too early for the Vikings but may have been Pictish. Earlier historians had identified Burghead with the "Alata Castra" or "Winged Fortress" of the Romans. The monk, Richard, now considered to be a mythical person, had said that it was the "Ptoroton of Ptolemy."

The Council gave £50 towards the cost of adapting one of the coaches on the diesel service to Aberdeen, to carry stretchers for patients going to hospital. This was finally done at considerable cost but was never fully used except in winter, when the roads were blocked or dangerous. The Loch Romach water supply was taken over by the North-East of Scotland Water Board, with an area office at Elgin. Following the erection of the £10,000 golf clubhouse, the Council built a shop and house for the professional and made a large car park there.

The Council refused to accept the design of the swimming pool as the maximum depth was to be about seven feet, too shallow for diving. As the County Council said that it could not be made deeper, the Town Council called in consultants who submitted new drawings, showing a depth of ten feet. This was afterwards accepted by the Education Committee, although it raised the cost.

In October, the Provost was asked to cut the first sod for the new Academy. Plastic sacks were introduced for garbage collection. These were successful and it was agreed that in time all collections would be by this method.

Nine lives were lost when a Shackleton aircraft from Kinloss dived into the sea not far from its base, and in the week before Christmas another crashed into a mountain near Fort William, with the loss of 13 lives. One member was the husband of a Forres girl but contact was now so close between the two communities that the feeling of sorrow was general.

Moray County Council now abandoned its policy of building houses only in the landward areas. Communications and services had been so much reduced that many gave up the tenancy of such houses and moved into the towns and villages. The County Council found itself with empty houses, and long lists of applicants for houses nearer work and schools. They decided to build a large number in Forres and the Town Council made land available for this and provided the services.

The line of the by-pass road was now definitely fixed, being moved to the south, thus requiring the demolition of houses in Mosset Terrace, but no starting date could be given.

The condition of the slaughterhouse was now a cause for concern. It had been leased to Messrs F.M.C. who wanted it brought up to the standard which would allow meat produced to be exported to the Continent when Britain entered the Common Market. In this they were supported by the farmers, who looked for better prices from this trade.

After protracted discussions with the lessees, farmers and the Government, a completely new building was accepted as the only way the necessary standard could be reached. A specialist contractor offered to design and erect it for £27,500. Just as this offer was accepted by the Council the Government announced another cut in spending, thus postponing the project. Mr Gordon Campbell, M.P., was approached and he succeeded in getting permission to proceed with the work. Ground was bought from Altyre Estate—in Waterford Road—part of it for the slaughterhouse, the rest being taken up by Messrs Jones & Sons for a new sawmill, and by Mr Stewart for a car body repair workshop, his premises at the Lea Bridge being now too small.

Buying old properties was now a continuous but slow process. The Scottish Co-operative Wholesale Society owned a cottage, "Woodbine," in Cumming Street which was beyond repair and offered it to the Council for 1s. This avoided lengthy conveyancing and allowed the site to be cleared for new quarters for the Forres Cycling Club.

The deficit in the accounts of the Cemetery Board was increasing annually. There were now three cemeteries to be maintained; St Laurence, Cluny Hill and Clovenside. A high standard of maintenance was aimed at so that burial and other charges had to be increased. This, also, was a long and slow legal process. The charges had to be approved by the Sheriff, advertised for a statutory period, and so on. It had been many years since the charges were last fixed. Bank Lane was finally closed at its High Street end with bollards—another long legal process being necessary.

In May, by Government decree, all municipal house rents were raised but as the Housing Account was in good shape, the rise was restricted to 4s per week.

The angling season had been a good one, catches of 185 salmon, 184 grilse, 537 sea trout and 3603 finnock being reported. The association had its first lady member, Mrs Harold Duncan, who attended the annual meeting.

The Scottish Development Department had changed its mind again about house buildings at Tailwell, reverting to the old argument that the site was too difficult. The Secretary of State was persuaded to send three of his officials to examine the site, and they in turn were persuaded that building was feasible.

When the candidates mounted the platform of the Town Hall at the pre-election meeting they outnumbered the audience, which was composed of a councillor, the wife of a candidate and one elector. The meeting was abandoned. Dean of Guild William Guthrie died suddenly on his way home from committee meetings and was succeeded in this office by Councillor Fulton. A member had to be co-opted and Mr Alex Walker, a native of the town, recently retired from his post as Commissioner of the Metropolitan Police, agreed to accept office.

During a cricket match in the Grant Park there was a sudden thunderstorm and the spectators hurried for shelter. A party of seven boys moved under one of the trees which was struck by lightning, killing eighteen-year-old Colin Dingwall from Kinloss. Three others were struck but not seriously burned.

Mr Ron Ross, joiner, died and his premises in Cumming Street, formerly the Free Church, were bought by the Council for use as a housing repairs store. The executors now offered the machinery and tools to the Council at a very low figure and this was ultimately accepted.

Most Councillors were, or had been, businessmen and it was natural that they should want as much work as possible to be done by local firms. But the building trades were running down, only one joinery firm being left, and it was difficult to get repairs done expeditiously. All branches of building were busy, and men with the necessary skills were scarce. The Council had always had a nucleus of tradesmen as they did most of the repairs on the town's farms, using timber from the town woods. As a result, the work was usually done quickly and cheaply, with a good credit balance in the Housing Repairs Fund, a most unusual condition elsewhere. Within two years, more than £20,000 of work was done by an augmented work force of 16 joiners, masons, painters, plumbers and electricians. These could draw on 20 labourers and, in addition to repairs, many houses which would otherwise have been demolished were rebuilt, adding quickly to the stock of houses needed. Every now and again the Council insisted that offers be taken from contractors as a check on the costs.

The New Forres Quarry, a part of the Common Good, had for long been leased to Moray County Council. This was the fifth quarry the town had opened at New Forres in its long history. The stone, whinstone, was very hard and was now rarely used by masons but it made excellent road metal. The royalty paid by the County Council was very small, and all stones used for road repairs within three miles of the burgh had to be given free. The equipment was worn out and £80,000 of new plant was to be installed. When the Town Council sought an increase in the royalty the County Council refused. The council then withdrew the lease and the County Council was obliged to buy the quarry. The Council engaged a mineral valuer from England who valued it at £27,000. The Government would not agree to this as the purchaser was not a private business but a local authority who must get the lowest possible figure; this was agreed at £13,000.

This was the first capital asset of the Common Good sold and made some turn their thoughts to selling off more, before the Council was absorbed by a large and remote body.

Of the two railway bridges, on the Nairn Road and at the junction of Manachie Road with the Grantown Road, the latter was very dangerous with a blind junction and a steep slope. Each winter cars skidded, endangering the newly-erected houses at Thornhill Crescent. The Roads Department was asked to demolish the two bridges; the Road Surveyor said the arches would be filled in but there would be no demolition. The Provost and Bailie Fulton had visited Mr Gordon Campbell, M.P., although his party was out of power, and he promised his support for any action to remove the bridges. When he became Secretary of State for Scotland in 1970 Mr Campbell was again approached. Money allocated for "reflation of the economy" was made available and Moray's share was spent on removal of the bridges. The removal was a major job, the roads being reinstated to a very high standard.

Mr Tom Fraser, Chairman of the Hydro Electric Board, and the Board's Commercial Manager, Mr J. C. M. Baillie, visited the town with a party of 13 industrialists. These were met and entertained but, again, none decided to set up work in Forres.

The golf clubhouse was not entered on the Valuation Roll as it did not show a profit, so that the members did not have to pay rates.

Unemployment figures began to rise.

The Army offered to demolish Fraser's Buildings, which were at last vacant, and the ground was earmarked for the Moray County Council houses. The Council agreed but, after examination, the Army decided that it would be dangerous to use explosives as there were occupied houses nearby. The burgh workmen took the clearance in hand.

Year 1969

The older residents said that the numbers attending the arrival of the New Year at the Cross began to have the appearance of the crowds seen there in the days before films, radio or television. Two things helped this. The clock tower was now floodlit and this, as well as the lights in the clock faces, was switched off a few minutes before midnight, until the bell chimed. The Pipe Band, now fully accoutred and trained, was also an attraction. The full moon and the mild weather kept the people on the streets for much longer than usual.

The County Council now realised that they were not going to have the sole use of the Roysvale Park and purchased ground beyond Sanquhar House for football pitches for pupils of the Academy.

Almost all council houses now had an electricity supply, but many found that the wiring system could not cope with the demands of all the appliances used. The Council offered to rewire such houses as soon as possible, at an increased rent of £4 or £5. Because of the shortage of electricians and the pressure of work, this was a slow process.

On North Road the school canteen was no longer required after the new Academy was occupied, and it was demolished to provide sites for the Tailwell houses. The buildings had been designed a century earlier as an infant school, and had been used for many years as the Academy science room, until the new Academy was opened in 1926. For a number of years it was the hall for the Salvation Army but when that organisation built their new hall in Urquhart Street it lay empty until used as the school canteen.

Many of the feus of the town's land within the burgh were for small amounts, some as low as threepence a year. Their collection cost more than the amount received, so they were terminated by agreement. They were redeemed at 10 years' purchase, that is to say, at ten times the annual charge.

224

An examination of the housing list showed that, despite a continuous programme of house building, the list still held the names of 250 applicants, and about 50 new names were added every year. The first houses built by the town, the Cicely Place scheme, were now 50 years old, and even later houses at Burdshaugh, Roysvale and Castle Street were now out of date. In all, 88 of these houses had the bathroom opening off the kitchen, which was now illegal. Many thousands of houses all over Britain were like this, and plans were being made to alter them to conform to modern standards.

For a number of years the Council had tried to buy the property at the south-west corner of Gordon Street, so that this street could be widened through its whole length. The proprietor was unwilling to accept the price fixed by the District Valuer. The Provost and the Town Clerk approached the owner and agreed with him that a slightly higher price should be paid. This was rejected by the District Valuer and the planning authority decided to enforce a compulsory purchase. A Public Inquiry had to be held, with a "Reporter" from Edinburgh. After some weeks it was decided that the property should be taken over. This was done and the price given was much higher than the owner had been willing to accept some months earlier. Added to the legal and other costs, this made the total about five times the figure originally asked. Much of this was due to the rapid rise in the price of property.

Gordon Street was to be the main entrance to the town when the bypass road was constructed, but this plan was later abandoned when road design alterations were finally accepted by the Secretary of State.

The County Council were now looking for a site for a Community Centre and decided that the Market Green was the most suitable. The Town Council did not quibble about this, and offered to buy the site of the old Academy on the north side of High Street. This, it was hoped, would be developed as a town square, with some houses at the north end on North Road. The County Council had agreed to sell it but now changed its mind and decided to erect the Community Centre there.

The Government decided that 250 houses for R.A.F. personnel would be built in Forres, west of the County of Moray houses. This decision was welcomed by the Education Authority as there was no room in Kinloss school for the children of the families who would occupy these houses. It was difficult to find transport to take the children to schools in Forres as all available buses were already engaged in school transport. The Traffic Commissioners were unwilling to grant more licences for buses, as they claimed that most of the buses already in Forres, being used only for school transport, were idle most of the day. This, they considered, was both uneconomic and inefficient. However, the decision to build the houses was cancelled. It was thought that housing used by Naval families at Lossiemouth would become available for the R.A.F. when the Navy left the area. This was a disappointment to the town which had spent many thousands of pounds laying drains and roads in preparation for new housing.

A year or two later the R.A.F. found that they required Lossiemouth Air Station in addition to Kinloss and that more houses would be required at Forres.

There were eleven candidates at the annual election. None had ever stood for election before, although one or two had been co-opted a few months earlier to fill vacancies. There was a good attendance of electors and a number of questions were asked. As no one had enough experience to answer, the chairman had to deal with all questions asked.

The burgh boundaries had again to be extended to include 82 acres of land at the Greshop, mostly for housing. The Brewery Bridge was demolished and rebuilt; as it had a hump back and was also narrow, the Traffic Commissioners were unwilling to allow buses to use it because of the danger. The old stone bridge of two arches was replaced by a level and wide bridge. The old one was often referred to as th "Star Bridge" because of the stars carved in some of the stones. These were built into the new structure.

The County Council put up for auction the 1926 Academy building, incorporating the Jonathan Anderson Institution of 1828, but reversed their decision. It was later decided to modernise the building as a Primary School to take the children from Kinloss who could not be accepted there.

The Golf Professional, Mr Rodgers, died and Mr John Taylor from Dunfermline was appointed. Mr Rodgers had extended the course and taken in land planted with trees. These had been "dedicated" to the Forestry Commission and the town was faced, as it had been once before, with paying back a considerable sum of money to the Forestry Commission. Mr Hamish White of Cassieford, who was now owner of Lochyhill Farm, kindly agreed to sell ten acres of this farm so that the destroyed plantation could be replaced by a new one.

The Wheatley Report was issued. This proposed the disappearance

226

of all burghs in Scotland, except the four cities. They were to be absorbed with landward areas to form 47 districts, which would be combined for some services, such as education and planning, into seven regions. This was later increased to nine regions, when the Bill was being dealt with in Parliament. Forres was to be in the Moray District in the Grampian Region. Nairnshire was to revert to the Highland Region, with which it had always had an affinity; that County had never been happy in the forced union with Moray in 1929.

After much local effort to attract industry to Forres a firm had at last decided to set up in the burgh. This was Tamworth Industrial Fabrics, who wanted to start up as soon as possible. It would take at least a year to build a factory, but the technical classrooms of the old Academy were now available, and the Education Committee agreed to sell them to the burgh. The Planning Committee agreed to allow them to be used as a factory and demolish them as soon as the new premises were ready. The technical rooms had been built to a very high standard and were eminently suitable for the work done in them, so that the firm was most unwilling to vacate them. But it had to be done and the buildings were eventually demolished. The space was used for houses which were built in 1973.

The Falconer Museum, now about a century old, was in financial straits. The endowment at the time of its erection had seemed ample, but with increased costs and wages it could not meet its debts. The Provost and the Parish Ministers were the Trustees. The Council took over the responsibility for doing the necessary work, such as installing electricity and interior decoration. When the caretaker died it was found that his house was sub-standard and again the Council had to do much work. Several committees were formed—a Finance Committee of Councillors and a Management Committee of persons interested and knowledgeable in museums. This was headed by Mr A. Kean, a partner of R. & R. Urquhart, Solicitors, who had earlier, when in Elgin, been a leading figure in the modernisation of the Elgin Museum. He was ably assisted in this by Mr Kenneth Ross, Principal Teacher of Biology in Forres, and Mr Ian Suttie, who held a similar position in Elgin Academy.

The Museum Committee approached the staff of the Scottish National Science Museum, who were interested in the Altyre collection of Red Sandstone Fossils, which they considered of national rather than local importance.

At the end of the year the Provost wrote, for the *Gazette,* a review of the decade ended, which had probably seen more changes than had taken place in any previous ten years.

In the New Year's Honours List the Town Clerk, Mr Archibald Macdonald, was awarded the M.B.E. for his work in connection with the R.A.F. Kinloss. For many years he had been a member of a panel which advised R.A.F. personnel on social and legal problems.

Year 1970

The last hour of the year saw more than 300 people gathered at the Cross to welcome the New Year to the skirl of the bagpipes. There was 20 minutes of spontaneous dancing before the revellers started on the traditional first footing.

The year started coldly and within a few days more than three inches of snow covered the ground and 13 degrees of frost was registered, resulting in icy roads with a consequent increase in car accidents.

As the Forres Curling Club had played on the indoor ice rinks at both Inverness and the new centre, Aviemore, the secretary had booked 13 consecutive Saturdays at Inverness. Play on the Thornhill Pond was now given up, and it soon became neglected.

An outbreak of flu in the district was classified as "quite serious," and so great was the number of doctors' prescriptions that the chemists appealed for the return of empty medicine bottles to enable them to meet their needs. The future prospect for farming looked bleak, and a party of eight farmers called on the Provost with a petition for government aid, and asked for the support of the Council. It was presented to the Council who fully endorsed it.

The Wheatley Report said that burghs such as Forres would no longer have police courts, so that the courtroom would not be required. It had been fully rebuilt inside, and when completed was so attractive and comfortable that the Council decided to use it for their chamber, and use the old room as the waiting room for members. The original courtroom had been a bleak and desolate place, with brown painted walls, wooden seats, and dock. The magistrates' bench was raised very high, a relic of the days when the office was a majestic and remote one, so that the bailie, unless he was a firm and clear speaker, was often unheard by the accused or officials. Much work was also done on the Town Hall; the sum of £500 was spent on kitchen equipment, while the interior of the hall was painted at a cost of £2246. It was hoped that this would encourage the use of the hall but the tendency was now to hold functions on licensed premises, with more than one bar.

A new club, the Varis, was formed, catering for retired business men, with regular meetings and speakers, and a series of visits and excursions during the summer. The number was restricted to 40, the first president was Mr Alex Walker, Cluny View.

Charges for the golf course were increased and a councillor expressed concern that this would cause a fall in the membership and also in revenue. The opposite, in fact, occurred and in a short time players were suggesting that some limit be placed on the number of visitors as the greens were now suffering from excessive use.

Again as a result of the Wheatley Report it was agreed that some of the Common Good be sold, and the money used to provide a tangible and permanent memorial of the ancient burgh. Under the terms of the Report the burgh would no longer be a centre of administration, but would be absorbed into the new Moray District. The town's legal adviser, Mr Peter Maxwell, Q.C., was asked to advise. His opinion was that the lands and properties could be sold if (a) they were not dedicated to the free use of the burgesses, and (b) no buildings connected with the dignity of the town were standing on these lands. This meant that six farms, 200 acres of forested land and the quarry could be safely disposed of, as could many of the feu-duties. It had long been held that royal burghs could not alienate Common Good lands, which in the case of Forres had been granted to the burgh by King David I in May 1150 and theoretically were still in the hands of the sovereign.

The farms were sold to Mr Frank Davidson, Baldorny, Nairn, for £37,500. The tenants had been asked to offer for their farms, but at prices equal to or higher than that made by other bidders. None purchased their farms, but all continued as tenants. Mrs Mackie Campbell of Troon paid £51,000 for the woodlands, and Moray County Council bought the quarry at New Forres for £13,600. Moray County Council had estimated that new plant would cost £80,000, but during the period of long negotiations costs increased to £170,000, and they decided to leave the quarry unworked. The Secretary of State informed them that they had a statutory duty to provide suitable stone for road works within the county, so the new plant was installed. After some initial difficulties output was greatly increased to provide for the growing demand.

The Registrar-General reported that the population of the burgh at 1st June 1969 was 4711. This was still 100 below the peak of 1911.

New flashing columns were erected at the pedestrian crossing at the Tolbooth, the first in Scotland outside Edinburgh, although 17 English towns had them. With the approach of decimalisation of the currency, the Shopkeepers' Association was revived and held a number of well-attended meetings to discuss that problem, but also took the opportunity to raise various other matters, such as the condition of High Street, and put them before the Town Council.

Workmen started to demolish the former primary school on the north side of High Street. Erected in 1877 following the Act of 1872, which made education compulsory, it accommodated all the children of the town. By the end of the 1914-18 War it was greatly overcrowded, until additions were made to the Anderson Institution on the other side of the High Street, to transform it into the new Academy. The Institute erected in 1828 had two classrooms only, with the Rector's flat above. When Applegrove Primary School was opened it was intended to demolish the old primary school but again, after the 1939-45 War, the Academy was overcrowded, and the building was kept until the third Academy at Burdshaugh was opened. The two carved heads from the old entrance were incorporated into the structure at Burdshaugh.

All countries were experiencing increasing mis-use of drugs, and a drug "pusher" was arrested in the town while offering drugs for sale to two Forres youths. The offender was a girl.

Some heat was engendered when a request was received from the Joint County Council for the purchase of two acres of land at the Califer to be used as a site for a scenic viewpoint. Grants from the state were now available for such projects through the Countryside Commission. The objection was not to the principle but to the actual location required. However, the site was sold, although no work had been done on it at the time of writing.

A century had now passed since the Findhorn Railway closed, and its history, as well as that of its proposed successor, appeared in the *Gazette* in the editions of April and May, to which the interested reader is referred. The Mosset Park had its first international football match, when the Youth team of Norway played that of Turkey in the

International Tournament. Only local teams seemed to be of interest, for there were few spectators.

Prize Day was no longer held at the Academy, and only the Dickson Medal for the Dux of the Academy, and the Pirie Memorial Prize for the intermediate dux were retained. Both were endowed and had to continue. The Dux had to be the winner in Latin, but this subject had almost disappeared from the curriculum. Many primary schools in the Forres Area had earlier ceased to award prizes.

In anticipation of Local Government Reorganisation the Town Council considered how the balance of funds in the Murdoch Fishing Trust might be spent. Arthur Stuart Murdoch was the son of a farmer at Cassieford, near Forres. He had emigrated to Australia at the age of twenty-three to continue his career in banking. He had been a member of the St Laurence cricket team during the 1880s along with C. M. Fraser and Sir Alexander Grant. On his visits to Forres in later years, he spent much of his spare time fishing on the Findhorn. He died in Melbourne in 1936. Mr Murdoch had bequeathed the residue of his estate to the Town Council to purchase fishing rights in the River Findhorn. He had, however, also directed in his will that if within twenty-one years, following the death of his brother John, the Trust Funds had not been used to acquire fishing rights the Town Council should purchase lands in or near the town for a public park.

John Smith Murdoch had died on 21st May 1945 and so by this time, more than twenty-one years later, the Town Council felt free to purchase ground adjoining the Burgh boundary including the Sanquhar Loch.

However in 1962 the Town Council had purchased fishing rights on the Findhorn for £15,000 from the Trust Fund and the Angling Association now contested the Council's right to spend the remaining sum of £13,000 for a public park. The town decided to accept the advice of their Counsel to petition the Court of Session. Subsequently, however, the Burgh representatives and the Anglers' Association agreed to accept the ruling of two judges in chambers. The matter was not resolved until 1973.

A General Election was held in June when Mr Gordon Campbell was again successful with an increased majority. The Scottish National Party had been very active, and a door-to-door survey showed that the Party's candidate would be successful. There was considerable disappointment among the members when the result was declared.

The new abattoir opened on 24th September, but soon more work had to be done to bring it up to the standard necessary for Common Market exports. The Forres Highland Games was now one of the leading meetings in Scotland, with more than 100 visiting competitors.

For some time Forres House in Grant Park had been a source of contention between two groups in the council. One thought that it should be demolished because of its increasing decay, and the increasing cost of repairs. The opposition held that it was a useful and necessary building, and the costs were less than any possible alternative. A new caretaker had been appointed, and his flat was completely modernised. On the first weekend of occupancy, while the tenants were away for the weekend, the building went on fire and was damaged beyond repair.

The Dublin poetaster, St John Gogarty, translated a Greek aphorism thus: "Everything changes . . . Time deranges, Men and women and mountain ranges." Nowhere was this more easily observed than in the coastline on either side of Findhorn Bay, which could alter almost day by day. For unknown centuries the sand deposited by the tide westwards was carried by the winds eastwards until it was returned to the sea where the strong scouring current carried it back to its starting place. Lying outside the entrance of the bay was a low skerry which had in the last century grown into a barrier that prevented all vessels except the smallest of yachts from crossing it except at high tide. Yet a century earlier at least four steamers called at fixed times weekly until the arrival of the railway put them out of business. The river had changed course in the 1829 floods, moving eastwards into the bay, a movement of some miles.

Many fishing vessels used the bay, and when war broke out on 4th August 1914 the sailing ships were laid up on the Binsness shore for the duration of the war. Time and storm removed the woodwork, leaving only the cast iron boilers which had been carried to boil out the oil from the livers of the cod which they caught on their great lines, or "gratlins" as they were called by the fisherfolk. The boilers have now gone, either buried in sand or taken for scrap metal.

Mussel scaups were laid in the bay and these extended out to join up with the skerry, forming a mass as strong as concrete. This meant that the sand, shingle and stones brought down by the river could no longer reach the sea. The pressure of the sea water, with a greater density than that of the river, held the stones and sand back, so that at the present time, an adventurous visitor can cross by foot at low tide from the village to Binsness. As the years passed the stones built upstream, so that in 1970 the river bed 200 yards downstream of Waterford Farm was six feet higher than in 1920, when it was the favourite swimming place for the townspeople, and known as the "Ten feet piles," that being the depth there.

About 1920 afforestation farther upstream necessitated draining the land before planting the young trees. Before this the rain falling on the rough ground and peatlands had been released slowly to the streams and finally to the river and the sea. With the introduction of drains the run off was quick, and as the forest area spread year by year floods became common. When the council asked the Scottish Secretary for help to repair the damage done in the burgh after the flood of 1957 the reply was that a flood of this size was to be expected once a century, and the cost should thus be borne by those affected. In the following year another flood occurred as great as that of the previous year.

In the 24 hours before dawn on 16th August, 3·34 inches of rain had fallen in the Glenferness area, and on that morning some of the worried residents in the danger area visited the river beside the Nairn road. Since the work which had been done in the banks was above the river level and the rain had stopped, the residents returned home relieved. At 6.45 a.m. the burgh officials were told that water was flowing fast and deep towards the town by Tytler Street and the railway track, reaching the Mosset Burn at Ben Romach Distillery. It was some time before the breach was discovered behind Greshop House which had been flooded to a depth of six feet in a few minutes. The residents from the houses there had to be rescued by helicopter, one being transferred to an ambulance to be taken to hospital. R.A.F. Kinloss provided men and drying machines. The graph at the recording station at Greshop showed that the river had risen gradually to four feet above normal. Suddenly a ten foot wall of water swept down under the railway bridge, bursting the flood banks and flowing into Greshop. No work had been done there for many years, as the breaks had always been further upstream.

The proprietor of the ground, Brigadier Grant Peterkin of Grange Hall, had the breach filled at once with stones, on which earth was laid and held by netting wire pinned down. This was fortunate for within two days the river had risen again, but the repairs held. Elgin was not so lucky with the Lossie, the second flood being as harmful as the first.

The government spent £300,000 on repairing the banks of the Findhorn, Lossie and Spey after these floods, and Moray County Council and the burghs of Forres and Elgin set up a flood warning and rescue service, with wardens and automatic warning signals to deal with future floods. In course of time it is possible that the banks will have to be continually raised as the river bed fills up and the position could be reached when the river will flow above the surrounding ground.

The new premises and improved golf course increased the revenue greatly and the club decided to extend the premises of the clubhouse at a cost of £5600.

The Common Good money was now in hand, and more staff were engaged to carry out extra work. The Museum and Cross were cleaned, bringing the stonework back to its original honey colour. The museum square was to have trees, a fountain, seats, flower beds, and granite and marble checkerboards where draughts could be played. The council took over the responsibility of maintaining the museum, which now had little money to spend as a consequence of inflation which reduced the value of its endowment income.

A contract was made for the erection of sewage works. At £360,000 this was the town's most expensive project so far, but the two distilleries agreed to share part of the costs. Moray County Council bought land at Pilmuir as a site for 187 County houses. It was unusual for one authority to build within the boundaries of another, as thus they lost the rates payable, but the people from the rural areas wanted to live in the town. High costs and falling population meant that services such as travelling shops and buses were withdrawn. Forres was also becoming an attractive place to live in, the result of the Council's work over the last decade.

The ground at Pilmuir had two streams or "strypes" now covered, but extra drainage was required, and the burgh undertook this work although it was not expected to cost as much as it did, £82,000.

The burgh built a centre at Greshop for Moray Estates Company, who centralised the handling of their farm products there. The area was laid out for any future developments, the government intimating that they meant to build an "advance" factory in the near future, and find an occupier for it.

Talks were held about the acquisition of the Sanquhar grounds, but the proprietor asked for a price many times larger than that fixed by the District Valuer, and the deal fell through.

Two notable former councillors had died: former Provost Michie Anderson and former Bailie Sam Anderson.

The year had been the busiest in the Town Council's history, about 200 meetings being held

Year 1971

While most of the country was covered by snow, none fell on Forres at Hogmanay and over 300 assembled at the Cross to welcome the New Year. The pipe band was present, its numbers augmented by some former players who paraded in civilian clothes.

The Provost, in a New Year message in the *Gazette,* compared the work done by the Council in 1970 compared to that of 1870. In that year 17 meetings sufficed to deal with all the matters coming before the members. A century later over 200 meetings had to be held, while four delegates from the Council travelled to 80 meetings as far apart as Inverness and Edinburgh.

Whitaker's Almanac recorded that Forres had the lowest rates, at 70p, of any Scottish burgh with a population over 3000. The valuation of the town was also low, at £25 per head of population. This was due to the absence of any highly rated industrial buildings, the greatest part of the town's income from rates being assessed on domestic buildings. The first council houses were built in 1919 and there were now 693 with an average rent of £54·70 per annum while 20 tenants qualified for a rent rebate.

The houses built by the Moray County Council at Pilmuir were near completion and a meeting was held with that body to name the new streets. The new names were Stuart and Moray Streets, and Randolph and Nursery Lanes.

At the year's first statutory meeting the Cemetery Committee put forward proposals for beautifying the Kirkyard at St Laurence Church. This had been the only cemetery in the town from time immemorial until Clunyhill Cemetery was opened last century. It appears that tombstones were uncommon until the latter part of the eighteenth century, for none were found with earlier dates. Those who had died by plague were always buried outside church lands, and for centuries this was the commonest cause of death. The earlier tombstones were made from sandstone, and time and weather had removed all inscriptions from this friable material. When the present church was built in 1906 it was much larger than any of its predecessors, and to make room for the builders many stones had to be uprooted and laid aside. When the church was completed these stones were replaced haphazardly, many of them being placed so close together that only by sickle or scythe could the grass be cut. The use of the sickle was unknown and scything was a rare skill. All this ground belonged to the council who were responsible for its care and maintenance, but not for the gravestones which were the property of the owners of the lairs.

The proposal was to remove all the broken, fallen and illegible stones, and to place the remainder in orderly rows with sufficient space to allow grass cutting machines to operate. It was discovered also that many of the old type "tables" had sunk and were buried at varying distances under the grass and earth, as well as broken pieces of stones.

When this was done the area would be re-seeded, shrubs, trees and flowers planted, and new paths made. The high wall at the High Street did not allow passers-by a view of the church, and this wall would be lowered as well as the entrance.

The Fine Arts Council, to whom the plans had been sent, approved the proposed alterations. None of the committee expected any opposition to the proposals, and were shocked at the resulting uproar.

Very rarely in the past did committees initiate anything new, as most matters arose in the statutory meetings, and if agreed were then remitted to the appropriate committee for report and action when necessary. This had changed with new types of committee, the Planning Committee in particular putting forward a stream of ideas. The members realised that time was getting short, and any plans had to be put into execution while the Council still existed. Other less active members felt they were being pressed to action without having much say in the decisions apart from accepting or rejecting them.

Several members of the public made an appeal to the County Planning Committee, who were aggrieved that they had not heard of the proposed changes in the churchyard until now. They visited the churchyard and had to be informed that they were there on sufferance, and were chagrined to be told that they had no powers over church buildings or lands in law, but that their views were welcome and would be taken into consideration.

The decision that civil authorities had no jurisdiction over church affairs evolved from centuries of strife between Church and State in Scotland, and this solution of three hundred years ago had kept Scotland free of the religious strife still existing in many countries. The principle was summed up in "The Kirk cares for the souls; the Council cares for the bodies, dead or alive." Each had a monopoly.

236

The Kirk Session had been brought into discussions early, and three members of the Cemetery Committee were also members of the Session; they were placed in a difficult and embarrassing position, from which they disengaged themselves with skill and tact. Although the church was in agreement, opposition still continued. The workmen were taken from the cemetery squad, who had been trained to act with respect and decorum in an area that is sensitive. They, however, threatened to strike as they objected to being watched and photographed at their work.

Approaches were also made to the Secretary of State who refused to take any action. A humorous incident took place as a result of this. Two persons, determined to get the work stopped, collected a bag of what they thought were pieces broken from tombstones, and set out for the residence of the Secretary of State who was on holiday in the north. His home was guarded by the police because of the troubles in Ireland, and they stopped the car to question the passengers. Opening the boot they saw the bag and, retreating to a safe distance, asked the driver to open it, fearing it might be a bomb. He did so, disclosing the stones, which were pieces of kerbing which had been broken during the war when all iron railings were taken away for scrap metal to help with arms manufacture. They did not continue the journey. Eventually the work was completed to the full satisfaction of those who had family gravestones.

The reorganisation of local government was to take place in May 1975. The new councils were to be elected in 1974, and both old and new were to work in "tandem" until the change took place. This put a definite time limit on the work the council could do and the Provost proposed that the number of committees be reduced to make them more efficient, each member serving on an equal number of committees. Since the Local Government Act of 1929 there had been many changes in the functions of burgh councils, county councils, joint boards and other bodies. In the past in Forres when new council business arose, a small *ad hoc* committee was appointed which continued in being after its original remit had been dealt with. At this time there were 14 such committees, some having as many as ten members, which was a majority of the council. Others had as few as four. The office-bearers predominated in these committees, and newly-elected members might be on only one or two until vacancies arose in the course of their terms of office. This meant that power lay in the hands of the longest serving members. Considerable discussion took place before the number of committees was reduced to eight, each member serving on four committees, the committees having eight members. The Provost had to be on every committee, and the senior bailie was on five. This was still a large number of committees, but the council would not agree to reduce them although five would have been sufficient. Frequently in the past, two and sometimes three committees would have to join together to get a final decision on some matter affecting them. This held up decisions and wasted time.

In February Councillor Fyfe asked to be removed from the Golf Committee as he found himself always at variance with the other members. This was a most unusual request and he was asked to remain until the new council was formed in May, the observation being made that a clash of opinions was a necessary process in the democratic system. He accepted this view.

Following the floods of 1970 a flood warning system had been set up jointly with Moray County Council and the Burgh of Elgin. This was put to the test in January when the rivers rose with great speed. The organisation stood the test well, and the work done in strengthening the river banks contained the waters, which fell as quickly as they had risen.

January brought an unusual occurrence for the town—a strike. This was in the Post Office and lasted for three weeks. Forres was one of the militant areas, but volunteers returned to pay out old age pensions.

Mr A. A. Logie, chairman of the British Legion, announced at the annual general meeting that "one-armed bandits were losing their grip." The club, like most licensed premises, drew a considerable income from these gambling machines, and the club was concerned at this reduction when they were contemplating expanding their premises. Despite this the club had a good year and disbursed £1000 to local charities.

The Golf Course committee recommended that the club premises should be improved at a cost of £6500. The committee chairman, Councillor R. F. McIntosh, did not wish to put this proposal forward as was his prerogative, as he did not agree with the decision of the committee. Bailie Fulton, a former opponent of any expenditure on the golf course now supported the motion, explaining that only £4000 of the sum would be provided by the Council, and interest at 4 per cent would be paid on this, equal to a rent increase of £320 a year.

Messrs Taylor & Sons' Mills and Laundry had lain empty for some

238

time, and Messrs Wm. Black, joiners, had bought part of the mills, converting it into a workshop and funeral parlour. The council bought the remainder as well as the former Lemonade Works opposite, which had closed fifty years earlier. The buildings were demolished. The Burn Green was part of the deal, and it was agreed that this be returned to public use, with ponds to be developed as a wildfowl sanctuary. Advice was asked from various bodies, including the Slimbridge Trust, and a grant was given by the Countryside Commission. To allow the Rose Garden to be included in the new layout, part of the garden at Auchernack was bought from the County Council.

The laundry buildings cost £3950; the house, which was divided into two houses, cost £1800 and the Lemonade Works £1100.

The site of the works was later sold to Messrs Archibald Macdonald, painters, who had to remove from their store in South Street to make way for Leys Road.

Kinloss School could not find space for the increased number of pupils, and no site suitable could be found for a second school. The former (1926) Academy building was lying empty, and the Education Authority decided to convert it to a primary school. The work had to be done hurriedly at a cost of around £80,000, and the school was renamed "Anderson's Primary School" while the existing primary school was named "Applegrove Primary."

This meant that Forres children would have to go to Anderson's School also, and the town had to be divided into two zones. This task was given to a committee formed of Mr T. T. Davidson, Headmaster of Anderson's, the Reverend Donald Fraser, who was the churches' representative on the Education Committee, and Provost Forbes who was the town's elected representative.

The best form of division would be by a line north and south, but both schools were in the eastern part of the town, and as the town was to have over 100 R.A.F. families living in the Pilmuir area, it was thought that these parents would like their children to be with the children from Kinloss. Finally the dividing line was drawn along the centre of Pilmuir road, through High Street and turning down Tolbooth Street, and continuing eastwards to High Street. This brought forth strong protests from parents, whose children would have to go to Anderson's School, although Applegrove would be a little nearer. The parents at Kinloss whose children had to travel by bus to Forres were equally vocal. Some wrote to the Member of Parliament for their home constituencies, and the Minister of Education must have at first been at a loss to receive letters from Welsh and English M.P.s asking questions about schools in the North of Scotland. Some councillors were affected by the transfer of their children. The *Gazette* could scarcely cope with the letters sent in and the national press also printed a number. The Provost was naturally the chief target of the protests. A special meeting of the Council was requested by these members, and there was much plain speaking. But the plans went through and when the renovation of the school was finished it was considered to be the most modern primary school in the north. With a careful choice of headmaster and staff the school soon won as high appreciation as had Applegrove in the past. It was the standard of Applegrove which had motivated the local protests.

In May two of the parents were up for re-election, both ladies, and neither was successful. There was a good attendance at the pre-election meeting but only 28 per cent of the electorate voted. Three new councillors were returned: Mr A. A. Logie; Mr David Vallance, a retired schoolmaster from Perthshire; and Mr Kenneth McLennan, a well-known businessman. Provost Forbes was re-elected and was also re-elected Provost for a third term.

Work was started on the Museum Square, and here again there was a clash. Two plans had been put forward, one by Mr Harold Gordon of Greywalls Studio, and the other by the County Planning Officer. The result was a compromise between the two, which did not fully please them. Dwarf walls at the entrance had to be removed. Criticism was muted as the cost did not fall on the ratepayer, as a legacy to the town of £3000 was used.

This legacy is of interest as an example of the old Scots pride and desire for independence, and dread of the "poor law." Mrs Gregor, a widow, and her sister, Miss Janet Watt, had long resided at 8 Cumming Street, where they practised as dressmakers. Mrs Gregor had a daughter, Constance, a girl of great promise and a brilliant pupil of Forres Academy. While studying at Aberdeen University she had a mental breakdown which progressively worsened. At this time grants for education were unknown. Constance was kept at home until such time as her mother and aunt were physically unable to attend her or cope with her violent behaviour, and she had to be placed in Bilbohall Hospital. While there she had to be maintained as far as possible by her mother, as the Poor Law assistance financed by the Town Council was meagre and grudgingly given. To economise, the two old ladies would walk to Elgin, returning by train, and wore their

240

clothes almost to rags. In 1947 when Constance had been in confinement for 20 years, her mother was 85 and her aunt 87. Both made wills putting the house in trust with Mr H. W. Leask, solicitor. Both died in the following year just when the new Health Act came into force, removing all cases in hospital from charitable help. Forres had in any case lost its Poor Law Office in 1928, which was superseded by Public Assistance.

Annually Mr Leask sent a cheque to the hospital board in Elgin to pay for any luxuries or necessities, which were few. When confinement was abolished and all door locks removed, Constance had to be sent to a secure hospital, and after several changes, the Board in Elgin lost all trace of her. Since she had no relatives, the resident psychiatrist in each of the hospitals where she was treated became her legal guardian, and when she died in Aberdeenshire in 1969 there was no next-of-kin to inform. The hospitals did not know of the Trust, and presumed that the annual cheque was from some charity. The balance of the money in hand was passed backwards until it finally reached Mr Leask; it was some time before he could find out what had happened.

The trust was now closed. The house which had been put in trust had been sold in 1948 and the money invested. The Council decided to place a plaque in the Museum Square to commemorate the two devoted women.

A local body had to be appointed which would consider applications for planning development which might affect the physical appearance of the town and the Council asked the Amenities Association to take on this duty, as it would continue after the Council had disappeared.

The possibility of union with the High Church was under consideration when Castlehill Church celebrated its centenary, but the union did not take place. Next year when the Reverend Leslie Scott of Castlehill and Reverend Mr Fairlie of the High Church retired, Castlehill was joined with St Laurence, the High Church taking the title of "St Leonard's."

The Common Good lands and woods had been sold, and the Treasurer, Norman Redman, appealed to the public for suggestions as to how it should be used.

Any project had to be of benefit or available to all residents. It could not be something chargeable to the rates, nor could it be used to reduce the rate burden. About 60 letters were received and

241

all were carefully studied and discussed, and the reasons for the rejection made public. The three projects put before the Council all came from members of the Council.

More than forty suggestions for the use of Common Good money were received. After much discussion it was thought that the best use was to build a community centre and a swimming pool, both in partnership with the County Education Authority. These projects could be of a higher standard than if they were left wholly to the Education Authority. Conditions were made by the council; the centre had to have a library, a registrar's office, a squash court and a large sports hall. The swimming pool had to be of a standard to allow training competitions.

Bailie W. R. Mackenzie, the second longest-serving member, had devoted much of his life to the advancement of sport with special interest in young people. He was secretary of the Forres Mechanics Football Club, which held its ground at a low rent from the town. This ground would have to be vacated at some time in the future when the trunk road was diverted to the north of the town, and a new playing ground would have to be found. The Council had offered ground east of the pitch, and had promised to give the club money received from the Ministry of Transport when the land was taken over.

The bailie wanted the Common Good money to develop a complete sports complex including a clubhouse, which would be licensed, as the club hoped to get most of its future income from the social club. The proposal was rejected, as the football team was a professional one, and could not qualify for subsidy from public funds.

Bailie Fulton wanted a new town hall, about the same size as the existing hall, but more modern and comfortable. This also was rejected on the grounds that there were ample facilities, not only in the town hall but in all three schools, and elsewhere.

Provost Forbes had urged the Education Authority to enlarge the proposed teaching pool at Forres Academy to facilitate training to international competition standards. He was certain that Forres Town Council would give the money from the Munro legacy towards this. When a youth and community centre was mooted for Forres he asked that this be enlarged, Forres contributing to the extra costs from the Common Good funds.

He now put both projects forward to the Council, outlining the additional facilities that this would provide; such as a squash court, television, a library, and a very large games hall. If the County Council put the office for the registrar there, he said that everyone would be involved in the use of the centre "from the cradle to the grave."

Bailie R. F. McIntosh summed up the arguments, drawing the conclusion that the swimming pool and the community centre seemed to be the best, and the matter was left to a later meeting, where the two proposals were adopted.

While Mrs Eleanor Brodie of Brodie was searching a loft in the Castle she came upon an old document, which was found to be a thousand-year-old "Latin Pontifical." It was finely written in a large and legible Carolingian miniscule, a style introduced in the last half of the tenth century. The large initial letters were decorated in red, blue and green. The black, red and green inks retained their freshness and colour but the blue was somewhat faded.

There was a glossary of the unusual Latin words, a practice common in Scotland, and one which was of the greatest help to palaeographers and linguistic scholars, adding greatly to our knowledge of the Anglo-Saxon spoken in Scotland at the time. The manuscript was purchased by the British Museum for £14,000. It is possible that it was in use in the first church in Forres. On its flyleaf was the signature of the minister of Drainie of 1700, but there is no record of how it came to be in the possession of the Brodie family. After the Reformation the Brodies obtained some of the Kinloss Abbey lands, such as Milton Brodie and Brodieshill.

The burned out shell of Forres house was removed, and work started on a sunken garden to a design of Bailie Alistair Sinclair.

The Royal Naval Air Service was leaving Lossiemouth to make way for the R.A.F., and gave a farewell display in Grant Park. One of the events was a flight of aerobatics by Captain Clemente Fezzini of the Italian Air Force in an Aer Macchi aircraft.

The County Health Committee mounted a campaign against the use of addictive drugs by young people in the area.

For the fifth year in succession a Horse Jumping Show was held at the Mechanics playing field, organised by Mr Hamish Philip of Mundole Farm. This event was growing in importance because of the excellence of the site, and national competitions were now included in the programme.

The Findhorn Residents' Association appealed for funds for the re-erection of the Market Cross of Findhorn, £500 being needed. Findhorn had been a Burgh of Barony for a short period, raised by the

243

Laird of Muirton, but like so many others it did not flourish. More than 300 burghs of barony had been made, but few had survived. Moray County Council combined two of their houses in Culbin Road to form a children's home. Large institutionalised orphanages were now a thing of the past.

When the railway between Forres and Aviemore was closed, it had been replaced by a bus service. Towards the end of the year the bus company decided to cease running these buses, and on a Friday evening placed a small type-written notice inside the bus saying that from Saturday the buses would be stopped. In the dark no one read it, and on Monday morning about 20 people waited patiently until the truth came out. Mr A. Laing of Logie drove them back for some days until a taxi service was organised.

This year the Forres Friendly Society paid out £7000 to 600 members, and as much had been paid out in May. This society was started in 1787 and was one of the few still surviving in Scotland. In 1871 it had paid out £215 2s 8d to 60 members, each of whom received a dividend of 5s 10d.

The Mechanics F.C. thought of buying the laundry house as club premises but found it was unsuitable. The British Legion looked at Alves Close in Orchard Road for the same purpose, but found it too small.

Pilmuir Road was extended westwards to service the many houses to be built there. New pavements were made, but the house-owners were not asked to pay for this. The R.A.F. re-affirmed their intention to build 188 houses for personnel. They had decided on this earlier, but had changed to building at Kinloss. They now found that no suitable site could be found there.

Year 1972

The first issue of the year of the *Gazette* said: "The New Year was ushered in at the Market Cross with a revival of all the traditional welcome associated with the occasion in earlier years. . . . The crowd of about 500 did not disperse for some time, and the event was a very happy one." Unfortunately a new trend appeared, no less than four breakages of shop and house windows being reported.

The spirit of cheerfulness manifested was a reflection of the improving state of the town. Unemployment was much reduced, and

244

business was good. No longer did shops lie empty waiting for buyers, for they now rapidly changed hands, with much modernising and redecorating. For some years now it had been the policy of the Town Council to improve the amenities and services, and especially housing and the provision of parking space for cars. Any site was used, even if only for a short period. Parking charges had been abolished, encouraging shoppers from a distance. Elgin had complained that people from the Buckie area by-passed Elgin for Forres.

There were many enquiries for houses and sites for houses. The Council had earlier made sites available at Councillor's Walk, planning and providing the services of roads, water, drains and lighting, the sites being sold at cost price as fixed by the Government District Valuer. This policy was continued at Pilmuir and the first steps were taken to do this also at Little Crook, once the town yard was removed.

The possibilities of oil in the near waters brought the first big firm to Moray Firth. A Texan firm, McDermott's, started work at Ardersier, and announced they would eventually need 1700 employees. The Tamworth Industrial Fabrics Company occupied the factory at Lea Road built to their requirements by the Town Council, and a large building was erected at Greshop for the Moray Estates Development Company. The school rooms vacated by Tamworth Fabrics at North Road were demolished to become the site of Seaforth Place houses. The burgh had bought six acres of land from Moray Estates at Greshop, and later when that company expanded they bought back one of these acres. So rapid had been the increase in the value of land that they had to pay more for one acre than they received for six sold to the burgh.

The sites of the former railway bridges were made up, greatly improving the approaches to the town from the south and west, also making more building sites available.

Some time previously a demonstration was given in Elgin of a road-sweeping machine, which was seen by a few members from Forres. Later a machine was demonstrated in the Grant Park for sweeping up leaves. The Roads Committee recommended that the machine costing £2850 be bought, but when it was delivered there was a dispute. Unfortunately the two machines had not been seen by the same members, and it took some time to clear the matter up, the road sweeper being bought.

For some time the Council had tried to obtain the Burdshaugh farmhouse and buildings. The farm no longer had any land and the buildings were now very dilapidated. At long last a price fixed by the District Valuer had been accepted by the owner of Sanquhar Estate and plans were made for clearance and laying out the area as a public space with a road from the Medical Centre which was under construction.

At this stage a developer, who had been encouraged by a Planning Officer in Elgin, offered a higher price than that of the town, which was accepted by the owner. There was uproar when this was learned by the council because of the upset to their plans, and by residents in the neighbourhood who did not view with any pleasure such a development. The development at the bridge of a motel had gone through without much protest, but since the farm site was also to be developed for licensed premises there were strong objections.

Approval was asked from the Council and given by a majority of one. A special meeting of the Council was called in an attempt to upset this approval but again the majority in favour was one. The County Council discovered that the Planning Officer had not put this before the Planning Committee and they met in Forres and refused planning approval. But in the interim the Provost and Town Clerk had a meeting with the estate trustees, and had persuaded them to be bound by the previous agreement, and in addition to sell to the town part of Sanquhar estate, including the Loch to be made a public domain.

The government was now offering grants for the reclamation of derelict land, and the town applied for grants in respect of Sanquhar and the Waterford Mills.

The Provost and Town Clerk had privately approached the Hanover Trust, a foundation for building houses for retired people, and the Trust agreed to build in Forres. The Council gave the site between North Street and Gordon Street, and were the first burgh in Scotland to enter into such an arrangement, Elgin following immediately afterwards.

The low rainfall of the previous year (21·69 inches of rain, with 1350 hours of sunshine) had put the water supply in jeopardy, and rationing was feared. The installation of pumps at Kellas to boost the supply from Glenlatterach to the Forres reservoir in the Cluny Hills removed this threat, although restrictions were placed on the use of water in gardens and for washing cars.

During the preliminary excavations for the construction of the

246

sunken garden on the site of the old Forres House a forty-foot well was found and this was included as a feature.

Despite the low rainfall the Angling Association reported an excellent year's sport, no less than 96 salmon, 141 grilse and 3056 sea trout being caught. It was a good year for all sports, but the Golf Club decided not to buy the course offered to the Club for £35,000. The Council had suggested the Club might wish to buy as they might not be able to retain any control or keep any privileges when the course would be administered by a new authority after 1975.

The Forres Cycling Club opened their new rooms in Cumming Street. These had cost £4000, the club raising one half and the Council giving the other. This was done with a number of sports clubs, the money coming from the funds realised by the sale of the Common Good lands.

The Amenities Association ceased producing a tourist guide for the burgh, as the new regional tourist association being set up would have a guide for the whole area.

Moray County Council planned an "adventure playground" at the 100 houses built in the Pilmuir, and this raised a dispute in the County Council more bitter than any seen in Forres. The County Council asked if the burgh would meet some of the cost, to mute the criticisms. The town offered £5000, but the project was cancelled. The town began to sell its feus, as legislation to abolish the feu duty was promised. Many of the local feus were for a few pennies, and these had been cancelled earlier because the cost of collection surpassed the amount brought in.

Tenants of the council could now buy their houses at prices fixed by the District Valuer and a large number expressed their intentions to do so. But the prices announced were higher than anticipated and only a few confirmed their applications. The prices ranged from £4250 for a five-apartment in Anderson Crescent to £2900 for a three-apartment in Roysvale Place. The Council then announced that if buyers would sign an agreement to offer their house to the Council if selling within five years, a reduction of 20 per cent would be made. Although the Council would have no obligation to purchase these houses, a number of tenants accepted these terms.

At election time Councillors Dean, Fyfe and Walker did not return, and Miss Martha Morrison and Mr Gordon Smith joined the Council.

Towards the end of the year the ruler of Uganda, General Dada Amin, expelled 40,000 Asians who had not taken Ugandan nationality.

247

Most of these came to Britain and an appeal was made to local authorities to offer houses for these refugees. Forres provided a house, furnished by the Women's Royal Voluntary Service, for an Asian family. The boys fitted in well at the Academy and at Applegrove, both schools expressing admiration at the high standard of education they had received in Uganda. Mr Ladha got employment, but as his wife spoke little English she became depressed, her doctor suggesting that she should rejoin her compatriots. The family later left for the Manchester area where they had relatives.

The burgh received the award for the northern region in the "Britain in Bloom" competition.

In September the R.A.F. Kinloss celebrated the tenth anniversary of the receipt of the "Freedom of the Burgh" by "beating the retreat" with pipe and brass bands and armed escort in the High Street, A minibus, adapted for the use of invalids, hospital patients and old and infirm people was presented to the town by R.A.F. personnel. This was greatly appreciated. An "Osprey Trust" was set up to operate, maintain and finance this vehicle. The presentation was made by Group Captain Charles Chesworth, the station commander.

Year 1973

The year started on a Monday but a crowd of about 500 assembled at the Cross at midnight on Saturday and a larger number appeared on Sunday night. The advent of television had for two decades kept most people indoors at night, but habits were again changing. Increasing employment and prosperity meant more wining and dining out. At one time it was difficult to buy a meal after seven o'clock but now evening meals and snacks were available to a late hour in most licensed premises.

Britain entered the European Common Market on New Year's Day and the Post Office closed on Saturday afternoons. The latter change aroused more feeling than the E.E.C. although there was little enthusiasm for this either.

The previous year had been the driest recorded, with only 16·79 inches of rain, which was half of what had fallen exactly one century earlier. In 1873 the rainfall was 32·67 inches. In many places in the North-East Water Board's region, water had to be carried in by

248

tanker but Forres only had a restriction on the use of hoses. A heavy fall of snow in February, when more than four inches fell in less than four hours, removed any anxiety about water shortage.

August brought a severe frost, the temperature falling to 4° C. below freezing point and in Grantown-on-Spey it fell to 10° below.

The Council had a large programme of work in hand, but it was difficult to make progress for the arca was now experiencing a boom. The discovery of even more oil wells in the North Sea brought about expansion and building all over the north. On one occasion, the *Gazette* had an advertisement for a labourer, and this in an area where previously there were always large numbers of unskilled workers on the list of unemployed. Private houses were getting priority and the community centre, swimming pool, sewage works and housing were all suffering delays.

The sewage works were the first to be completed, but a considerable amount of work remained to be done before it could be operated in a satisfactory manner. The chief trouble was the very large quantity of fresh water which found its way into thc sewers. This ran at half a million gallons a day more than anticipated; as much of it as possible was diverted to flow directly into the Mosset Burn and the river.

Work was started on the Burn Green and the pond. In the early stages of planning this work, the Lands Committee thought that a better view would be obtained of this now attractive site, if the walls of the Castle Bridge could be removed and replaced by railings. An attractive tubular aluminium railing was designed and a price obtained. Unfortunately, through an administrative error, this estimate was entered in the Roads Committee's schedules and passed through the Town Council.

Messrs Briggs were the successful contractors and, to the consternation of the members of the Roads Committee, they started work on the removal of the wall. Work was stopped as soon as possible but not before the removal was completed, and the gap had to be filled with wooden protective shutters. The resulting discussions in the Council were more acrimonious than usual and the wall had to be reinstated at a higher cost than carrying out the contract. The specially-designed railings had to be paid for and relegated to the stores.

The extra work on the Council's programme meant more meetings and more expenditure, and some of the Councillors felt that they were being put under unnecessary pressure leading to frequent clashes.

The site of the old Gas Works was redeveloped, as well as

the site of the Waterford Mills. The Waterford Mills had been in an increasingly dilapidated state since production ceased in 1919. They had been built about 1860 to give employment at a time of destitution and hardship and were now used only as stores.

The Mills had used the sulphuric acid produced at the Forres Chemical Works further down the road to make fertiliser from bones imported from the continent through Findhorn and Burghead. The work had been welcomed and had undoubtedly slowed down the emigration common to all Scotland. Unfortunately, the sulphuric fumes tore out the lungs of the workers, bringing death at an early age.

Forres had always been a centre for the building trades and that of hewer was another dangerous occupation, many dying at an early age with "Mason's Disease." At one time there were as many as sixty hewers engaged.

The Town Council had approved its final housing scheme, incorporating "sheltered housing" in Leys, and other houses in gap sites around the town. The plans had been lodged for some months with the Joint County Planning Committee but no permission had been received. At a meeting of the County Council the Provost complained about the delay, adding that unless permission was granted within twenty-four hours the costs would be greatly increased. The Forres representatives were told that the plans had only been lodged a few days earlier.

Despite firm statements from the Provost and Bailie Fulton that the plans had been put in many months before, and that the Provost had discussed them with the Planning Officer, they were not believed and a motion was carried to silence their protests. The following day the Planning Officer came to Forres and admitted that the plans had been put in timeously and permission would be granted, but the dateline had been reached and the contract was increased by £34,659.

Towards the end of the year the community centre, including a County branch library and the swimming pool at the Academy were opened. The library had formerly been housed in a prefabricated building in the car park, built in 1964. The new building was named "Forres House."

The Council purchased buildings in South Street, to be demolished to allow the new Leys Road to join South Street. These premises had been built last century by Messrs Robertson as the Forres Steam Joinery Works, but latterly had been used for garages and stores. The steam was used for moulding pieces of timber into the required shapes.

The town adopted the conservation plan for High Street, drawn up by the planning officers, and plans were made for the development of the Market Green. From August this Green was closed to the travelling carnivals which had used it for half a century. Few of these spent more than a few days on their way to the annual Nairn Games.

The Manor House at Thornhill was demolished as the ground had been bought for housing development, and Councillor John F. Mackenzie pressed for a sub-police station in the centre of the town which was rejected by the Police Board.

The Registrar-General reported an increase of thirty births in Forres, as well as increases in the deaths and marriages. The increase in births was contrary to the general trend of the country as a whole, and was due to the number of young couples taking up residence in the town whereas, previously, most new residents had been retired people. There was ample employment for all and the town was fortunate in having space for new housing projects.

Sport took a lot of space in the press. An attempt was made to form a boys' football club, which most northern towns had, but the emphasis in the Academy was on other sports, especially ski-ing, and while a large number of boys came to the meeting most were under 14, the minimum age.

The Mechanics Football Club were concerned at the certain loss of their playing field, and pressed for an early start to be made on the replacement. The Council said that it would hand over to the club all the compensation money received for the ground required for the new road but that the club must undertake the development. Until a definite date was given for the start of the work on the road nothing positive could be done.

The Harriers Club celebrated its silver jubilee and the Secretary, Mike Scott, reported that the year had been the most successful in its history, the club having won every individual track event in northern sports, with the exception of the 400 metre race, in which they were second. More than a dozen silver cups had been won.

Football lost one of its leading figures through the death of Bailie William R. Mackenzie, and the Council lost the second-longest serving member, Bailie Mackenzie having joined the Council 29 years earlier. He had served in various offices in football for longer.

With the many projects in hand, the Council members had been gloomily forecasting a large increase in the annual rates but the Treasurer, Dr D. J. Murray, had a more cheerful story. The domestic rate was fixed at 51p and the water rate at 11p. Government grants had been increased by £87,000.

Councillors John Mackenzie and Ian Ross did not desire to stand again and with the death of Bailie Mackenzie there were three vacancies, which were filled without an election by Councillors Ian Campbell, Hugo Kennedy and William S. Wallace, the latter being a former member.

A children's home was opened by the County Social Works Department for children in care. It was formed from two newly-built houses belonging to Moray County Council, at 5-6 Culbin Road. This type of home was considered preferable to institutions like Aberlour Orphanage which were unable to provide an intimate family atmosphere.

Like other sporting associations the Small Bore Rifle Club found its membership increasing and added pistol shooting to the facilities, adding the word "Pistol" to the name. The Highland Games in Grant Park had over 3000 spectators and were now the leading Highland Games in the north.

The Angling Association had to restrict its membership to 180 as the river was being overfished. The Curling Club celebrated its centenary with a dinner. The pond at Thornhill was no longer used, members travelling to the indoor rinks at Aviemore and Inverness.

St Laurence Church had been given two silver chalices in 1643 by John Nicholson, a solicitor in Edinburgh, to be used as communion cups. The General Assembly of the Church of Scotland gave permission for them to be offered for sale and they realised £7000. The church had also sold the Bank Lane Hall and were to convert Castlehill Church into a Church Hall. The Reverend J. C. Porter was inducted to what was now St Leonard's Church, formerly the High Church.

Mr Kenneth McLennan, a member of the Town Council, leased ground at the riverside at Waterford for a caravan site. Such a project had long been desired as the town's traders felt that they were missing a considerable amount of business for the lack of one.

At Findhorn, the Royal Engineers announced their intention of blowing up two pill boxes, relics of the war, but succeeded in destroying one only. In the village John Cameron, known as "Shake," died at the age of 89. He had been the last pilot employed at the harbour. The last cargo had arrived about 1920, when the skipper of a small motor fishing vessel had taken a load of coal from a Fife port in the hope of making some money to meet the expenses of his boat. It was beached north of the pier and as it took so long to sell the cargo it never went to sea again. The fishing industry at that time was in dire straits.

Dr John C. Adam retired after having been in practice in the town for 50 years. He was unique inasmuch as he had followed his father who had served the community for 30 years. The Council later named a road in Chapelton after Dr Adam, and one for Dr J. M. Brewster, who had also retired but continued in the Council as Dean of Guild.

At the January meeting of the Council it was decided that action be instituted in the Court of Session concerning the disposition of the Murdoch Trust Funds. The Angling Association had engaged Counsel who had advised them that the Town Council was obliged to spend the remaining funds in the acquisition of further fishing rights. The Court's decision was reported to the Burgh Council in November when the Town Clerk reported that the remaining funds, which now amounted to almost £15,000, could be used to purchase land for a public park, but the court observed that the interest accruing since 1956, when the first fishings were bought, should have been paid to the heirs of the donor. This sum, together with the expenses of the Council and the Angling Association, came to £7000, leaving only £8000.

Forres as a Royal Burgh had been a member of the Convention of Royal Burghs which met annually in Edinburgh. In 1833 the Convention had been abolished but at the request of some burghs had been re-established to provide a convenient way for the Government to consult with the burghs. But since that time modern communications had superseded this slow method; it was now little more than a formal meeting. Provost Forbes and Mr Archd. Macdonald, Town Clerk, had attended for a year or two only. The annual dues were now £137 and the Provost suggested that it would be a waste of money to pay this and it was not remitted. The Convention decided to sue in Nairn Sheriff Court which had no jurisdiction outside that county, a wry reflection of the Convention's knowledge of, and interest in, some of the more distant burghs. Proof was not brought forward and it would appear that the 207 burghs in Scotland had paid considerable sums annually, under the impression that this was a compulsory levy, for 140 years.

The "energy" crisis caused by the with-holding of oil by the Arab States at the time of the Israeli-Egyptian war came suddenly. The town hall was prepared as a shelter but was not required, the town arranging for supplies of firewood to those unable to get a supply.

With the expansion in the demand for telephones the exchange had to be enlarged.

Year 1974

The burgh's independence began to be eroded when the new District Council of Moray was formed on 16th May. Elections had been held to choose members of the new District and Regional Councils in Scotland, which would fully take over on the same date in 1975. In Forres Provost Forbes had been returned unopposed to the District Council, and Brigadier Grant Peterkin of Grange had been successful in a three-cornered contest for the regional electoral division which included Forres burgh and the parishes of Edinkillie, Dyke and Moy, Rafford, Forres and Kinloss.

The existing burghs and counties did not hold any elections this year, all members continuing until 1975. Only those elected by the various councils and who had completed the statutory three-year term had to be replaced. No change was made in the Town Council as the two members concerned were re-elected to their positions; these were the Provost and Junior Bailie Richard F. McIntosh.

But these events were overshadowed by the "fuel crisis" which followed the Israeli-Arab War and the resulting shortage of oil, which also increased in price fourfold. A strike in the coal mines of Britain exacerbated the shortage of fuel, and work in the more essential factories was restricted to three days a week, while others had to close down completely. The resulting shortages in materials and manufactured goods had repercussions all over the country.

The burgh was engaged in its final housing scheme, at Leys and at various gap sites in the town, and work almost stopped here. Completion of the houses was expected in the spring, but as late as December delivery of items such as electric switches was still awaited. The tenants had been allowed to move in as soon as they were habitable, so great was the demand for houses. Work on the many private houses being built at Forbes Hill, Thornhill, West Pilmuir and Chapelton were affected to the same extent.

A General Election was held in February and Moray and Nairn produced a shock for the Government party with the defeat

254

of the sitting member, Mr Gordon Campbell, who was Secretary of State for Scotland. He had been the member for 20 years, and the Conservative Party had held the seat without difficulty since 1922. The Scottish National Party candidate, Mrs Winifred Ewing, was successful, while the Labour candidate was at the bottom of the poll.

Reorganisation of the National Health Service took effect from 1st April. One of the first proposals of the local Health Board was to reduce the 38 general practitioner beds in Leanchoil Hospital to 12, the remaining 26 beds to be reserved for geriatric patients. Dr Harry Morgan, superintendent at Leanchoil, and Provost Forbes, members of the former Board of Management for Moray Hospitals, protested strongly against this decision, and appealed for the number of general practitioner beds to be increased so that each doctor in the area would at least have two beds available for his cases. No response came from the Health Board and at the next meeting of Forres Town Council, Provost Forbes raised the matter and received the full support of the members. It was agreed that a public petition be arranged, but so quick was the reaction of the general public that almost 4000 signatures were received within a few days without any machinery being set up. The petition was duly despatched to the new Board in Aberdeen.

The decision of the hospital authorities was based on the premise that the population would continue to decline as it had done since 1911; this was apparently confirmed by the 1971 Census. The Council knew that the population was now increasing. The great increase in the number of houses in the process of construction demonstrated this suggesting that the population figure should be 50 per cent higher.

The Sheriff presided at a meeting of the Fiars Court in Elgin where the price of grain was fixed. Even at this time the archaic practice of quoting the salaries of some ministers, school teachers and other functionaries continued. The salaries were given in "chalders of bere" and the Fiars Court converted this into money terms by fixing the price of barley and other grains. This Court fixed wheat at £12·24 for each quarter of wheat, the quarter being 280 lbs. Barley was £11·93 per quarter, but oats was measured by 112 lbs. and valued at £6·25. In future years the measures would be in metric weights, and it was hoped that the whole system would be abandoned at an early date.

The long drawn out negotiations for the purchase of part of the Sanquhar estate seemed almost completed when a further difficulty

255

arose. Downstream of the Mosset Burn the landowners had a "right of servitude" to the waters for driving the water wheels of their mills. These included the Mills of Forres (Plasmon Ltd.), Messrs Reid, Engineers, the Tweed Mills and Laundry on the Burn Green, and the Mill of Grange. All had long ceased to use water power, and some of the lades had been blocked. The laird of Grange, Brigadier Grant Peterkin, refused to give up his "bond of servitude," which entitled him to draw on 13½ million gallons of water from Sanquhar Loch if ever needed.

About thirty years earlier experts had declared the dam at Sanquhar unsafe and it had been lowered by several feet, so that the loch now held only one million gallons. To replace the dam the Town Council would have to spend many thousands of pounds, probably to no purpose, and therefore resiled from the agreement. Following the publicity given to this action, the objector withdrew, and the negotiations were completed.

The fall in employment following the scarcity and fourfold increase in the price of oil and other fuels did not occur in Moray and Nairn or in Ross-shire. At Alness and Ardersier giant oil rigs to draw the oil from the North Sea were being built, offering hundreds of highly paid jobs. The Council lost about a third of its manual work force because of this, making the task of finishing all the work planned before the hand-over to the new District Council very difficult.

The remaining workers concentrated on such things as preparing the industrial sites at Greshop, Waterford and the former gas works. The government started work on an "advance" factory at Greshop, and various firms took up the Waterford sites, although the sole active one, Rank-Hovis MacDougall, closed abruptly at the end of October. It dealt mostly in cattle food and fertilisers, and both were now in short supply.

Mr Colin Wilson, the only blacksmith in the area, acquired a site at the gas works since his Caroline Street premises were too small, but he was delayed from moving there when an objection was made to the line of the new by-pass road. While it was unlikely that anything would follow from the remaining objection, which was from someone outside the town, nothing could be done until it was resolved or withdrawn. Apparently the objector claimed that the road should come round by the road which passed Lingieston, and refused to withdraw. Mr David Anderson, firewood merchant, Bogton Road, had also to remove from his premises which were to be demolished to make way for an altered line of Bogton Road and intended to move next to Mr Wilson. This also was held up. Mr Anderson, using the only work-horse in Moray, was fortunate in being unaffected by the shortage of fuel.

At the beginning of the year the Reverend W. M. Reid came from Hurlford to become Minister at St Laurence Church. The difficulties in clearing the churchyard at this church were not yet resolved, and Mr Reid brought the whole wretched dispute to a close by asking that all stones be removed.

The Medical Health centre was in operation at Castlehill, and because of the amount of motor traffic engendered, Strathcona Road was continued at the west end to open on to Orchard Road. It was intended to have the former farm laid out as a public area, but this was also held up by the shortage of staff.

The increasing air traffic at Dalcross resulting from the growth of construction work at Ardersier brought about a temporary closure of the airport to allow the runways to be strengthened. Part of the Royal Air Force station at Kinloss was used for civil airlines until December, and much congestion took place on the High Street.

Traffic wardens were to be employed in August to implement new traffic regulations. Because the Government printing works had been closed by strikes for many weeks, the necessary legal forms were not available; for a time the regulations could only be enforced in the presence of a policeman.

Another General Election was held in October, when the sitting member, Mrs Ewing, was again returned. The result of this election was described as a revolution, the five per cent vote in favour of some form of devolution for Scotland in the spring election now becoming an eighty-five per cent vote. On the whole it was an orderly election, "a revolution with good manners."

The Joint County Council Planning Committee suggested that Forres High Street be entered as part of the "European Architectural Heritage" international competition in 1975. A public meeting was called to discuss this and the Council was authorised to appoint an architect who would advise the High Street residents. Grants were offered of 50 per cent towards the cost of work to bring out the characteristics of the buildings.

Like so many other things, the results would not be seen until after the Town Council had gone.

The problem of the sewage purification plant at Bogton came to a climax in October when the Treasurer presented the budget. A large increase in the rates was necessary and the largest item within the Council's control was the rapidly escalating costs of these works.

It was known that Forres was built above a continually flowing underground water supply and while the civil engineering consultant firm who acted for the Council had made provision for this, the calculation had been too low. This underground or "vadose" water was flowing into the sewers as well as the storm water pipes. The latter carried this clear water to the Mosset Burn or to the sea without passing through the sewage works. But hundreds of thousands of gallons of such water did reach the reception tanks and completely upset the biological processes there. Some hundred thousands of gallons were traced and diverted but the problem still continued, and experts had to return to the town to try to find a solution.

The County Council requisition had increased by more than a third, much of it due to the extra costs of education and water supplies.

The burgh yard at Robertson Place was now transferred to Waterford Road; the abandoned yard was to be cleared and, with the adjoining ground at Little Crook, was to be developed for private housing. As in earlier cases the Council would lay the roads and other services and sell the plots of land at a price fixed by the District Valuer. As such plots were much cheaper than those from private developers, there was much competition for them and stringent rules were drawn. The applicant for instance had to be on the town's housing application list and qualify by need for a house.

The new Moray District Council had recruited all its officials by the 16th of December and there was little work of importance for the Council. Burghs elsewhere were having difficulty in getting a quorum for their meetings, as most members were frustrated at their loss of power in local affairs. The changes were the greatest in the ancient burghs since the days of their foundation, and there were attempts to get the whole new scheme delayed.

This frustration and anger began to show in the chambers, where very minor matters could start very bitter disputes.

Reports of the work of the Council in its final weeks may be found in the *Forres Gazette*. The town was fortunate in having its own paper which faithfully reported the smallest item before the Council. For half a century the *Forres News* had also reported the work of the Council.

In December 1974 the Council was composed of 17 members as it

258

had been for most of its existence, made up of: Provost A. H. Forbes; Bailies Alistair Sinclair, Graeme W. Fulton and Richard F. McIntosh; Treasurer Dr Douglas J. Murray; Dean of Guild Dr John K. Brewster; Councillors Ian A. Campbell, Joseph Davies, Hugo J. Kennedy, Alexander L. Logie, Kenneth Maclennan, Martha B. Morrison, Norman C. Redman and Charles K. White.

The officials were: Archibald Macdonald, M.B.E., Town Clerk; William D. Johnston, Chamberlain; George Forbes, Burgh Surveyor; and Henry W. Leask, Burgh Prosecutor.

Mr Macdonald had succeeded his father, and his firm of solicitors, Messrs R. & R. Urquhart, had provided the Town Clerks since 1834. Mr Leask had also succeeded his father, joining him as assistant in 1911, and had held this office for 63. These records are unlikely to have been equalled or surpassed in Scotland.

*　　*　　*

May 1975 was the end of 825 years of the burgh's history. What had been described in 1833 as ". . . the longest lived political and economic system ever invented," had survived for another 142 years. Many involved in local government believed that it could have been retained in a modified form for it was able to adapt in the past to the great changes that these last eight centuries had seen.

With it went the ceremony and ritual that had meant so much in the days before colour printing, radio, films and television. No public occasion was complete without the appearance of the Provost and Councillors in the appropriate regalia and dress, accompanied by their men-at-arms and the notabilities of the district. The Provost was always noticeable in his red robes trimmed with fur, gold chain and cocked hat. The ermine on the robes of Forres were in heraldry retained for the sole use of those of the rank of earl, and regularly aroused the anger of the Lord Lyon King of Arms. The holder of this office just after the Second World War threatened to throw the Provost into a dungeon if he did not desist from flaunting the ermine, and the Town Clerk travelled to Edinburgh to face him in his iron-doored office to tell him that his threat would be ignored.

259

When royalty visited the town the Provost had seniority after the Royal Family and the Lord Chamberlain. The Council also showed that it was the civil authority, and when the army or the Royal Air Force paraded with band and weapons, the Council followed at a discreet distance and determinedly refrained from marching in step to emphasise this independence.

On the second Monday of every month except August the Council sprang to attention as the Provost, followed by the Town Clerk, entered the chamber, wearing the chain of office and carrying the brass snuff box modelled on the death mask of Nelson. No business could be done until the snuff had been sent round each member and returned to the chair. In the earlier days of the writer, most members took a pinch of snuff, placing a small pinch on the back of the left hand, and sniffing it then. Gradually this ceased and the last ounce of snuff lasted more than eight years, only an occasional visitor trying it.

But there were many other changes, for councillors were no longer expected to give their time and energy for the sole reward of the satisfaction given by service to the community. No member had ever received payment for any time or action within the burgh boundaries. The cost of travel on the town's affairs beyond three miles could be claimed, as could "subsistence" for food or lodgings of more than four hours. The necessity for such trips rarely arose, apart from the annual attendance at the Convention of Royal Burghs in Edinburgh, and this was also discontinued by Forres.

In the future the cost of postages, telephones and travel would all be a charge on the authority, and secretarial help was to be provided also. In the lifetime of the burgh wreaths for funerals of deceased members of Council or the War Memorial were, until recently, paid for by a levy on each member.

Within the burgh the Provost and Town Clerk had the duty of meeting and entertaining visitors on behalf of the town, but the small sum allocated for this purpose was never claimed. The Council of seventeen members was a large one for such a small town, and all residents knew at least one member. The members also knew many of the residents very well and in committee it was often difficult to maintain impersonal discussions.

During its eight centuries at least two thousand men and five women served as councillors. None have their names emblazoned on the scrolls of fame, and none have become prominent or well-known outside the confines of the town. In each generation some were more active than others, but soon their names joined the others in obscurity. There was never a lack of willing candidates for office, and the annual elections were one of the years' main events in the past before modern communications brought the world to everyone's door. The large Common Good of Forres with its farms, fishings, shootings, forests and quarries gave an interest to councillors lacking in councils where the affairs were purely those relating to the burgh.

The system whereby one-third of the council retired in rotation had great advantages. It meant that someone seeking office did not have to wait three or four years, but only at the most less than a year. It meant also that there was always a council in being, and when some new principle or action was in dispute the Council could be changed within a year and a day, by the two elections held in that period.

Politics played no official part, and on the one occasion when candidates appeared under party labels, all were unsuccessful. Later the chairmen of the three local political parties worked together in harmony in the Council, and in the following year, with the arrival of a member of the resurgent Scottish National Party, the calm apolitical atmosphere was continued.

But our tale is ended and perhaps a suitable *envoi* would be from Shakespeare's *The Tempest*:

Our revels now are ended. These, our actors, as I foretold you, were spirits, and are melted into air . . . thin air. And like the baseless fabric of this vision . . . shall dissolve and . . . leave not a rack behind. . . .

261

APPENDIX

In 1935 the Council consisted of Provost C. M. Fraser; Bailies Caldwell, Macdonald and Michie Anderson; Dean of Guild Merchant; Treasurer J. B. Taylor; Councillors Auld, Bruce, Cameron, Duncan Campbell, Cormack, Hutchison, A. D. Macdonald, John Mackenzie, Morrison, Robertson and William Ross.

Date of first election:

1935 George A. Anderson, Alfred H. Forbes.

1936 Frederick Macbeth.

1937 John Cowie, William Taylor

1938 James S. Paterson.
No elections were held in the war years, 1939-1945.

1944 Co-opted:
Peter Garrow, Pat J. F. Mackenzie, William Mackenzie, John W. Mustard, James W. Thomson, John F. Thomson, William Watters, James M. Younie.

1945 Jean Mackintosh, William R. Mackenzie, Stirling Kirkland, Ian Stewart.

1946 Edward Jameson.

1948 John Falconer, Robert A. Ferguson, George W. Rutherford, John A. Thomson.

1950 Robert Gordon, William J. Young, Robert B. S. Braid.

1952 Mary A. Crowe, William Liddell.

1955 James Birnie, Peter Mitchell, Farquhar A. Anderson.

1958 W. Harold Broome, Alistair Sinclair, Alexander Fraser.

1959 Alistair S. Davidson, Charles W. Sutherland.

1960 William Budge.

1961 John W. Fraser, George Walker.

1962 Joseph W. Wood, Jean Jenkins, James L. Flemington.

1963 William J. Guthrie, Margaret Mackenzie.

1964 Alexander Dow, John F. Mackenzie, Lewis Grant, Graeme W. Fulton.

1965 John M. Brewster, William Coutts, Norman C. Redman, Charles K. White, Richard F. McIntosh.

1966	Kenneth Brunton, Alistair Gollan.
1967	Ian M. Ross.
1968	William S. Wallace.
1969	William F. S. Fyfe, Alexander Walker, Margaret Main, Douglas J. Murray.
1971	David R. Vallance, Alexander A. Logie, Kenneth McLennan.
1972	Martha Morrison, Gordon Smith, Joseph Davies.
1973	Hugo Kennedy, Ian Campbell.

PROVOSTS

C. M. Fraser	1926-40	Robert B. S. Braid	1955-62
John Bruce	1940-46	Pat. J. F. McKenzie	1962-65
A. Michie M. Anderson	1946-55	Alfred H. Forbes	1965-75

BAILIES

William Caldwell	1934	John Falconer	1958
Alexander Macdonald	1934	John F. Thomson	1959
A. M. M. Anderson	1934	Jean Mackintosh	1959
John Bruce	1938	William R. Mackenzie	1959
Alexander M. W. Cormack	1940	Farquhar A. Anderson	1960
James Auld	1940	George W. Rutherford	1960
Duncan Campbell	1940	Alexander Dow	1965
Stirling Kirkland	1948	Graeme W. Fulton	1969
Alfred H. Forbes	1950	Alistair Sinclair	1970
Robert A. Ferguson	1952	Richard McIntosh	1971
Ian Stewart	1945		

DEANS OF GUILD

Alexander Merchant	1936	Charles W. Sutherland	1962
Dr John Bruce	1936	Mary A. Crowe	1962
James Auld	1937	William Guthrie	1967
Duncan Campbell	1940	Graeme W. Fulton	1968
Peter Garrow	1945	Dr J. M. Brewster	1969
William R. Mackenzie	1958		

TREASURERS

James B. Taylor	1934	William R. Mackenzie	1962
Richard J. F. Cameron	1944	Lewis N. Grant	1966
James W. Thomson	1948	Norman C. Redman	1968
John A. Thomson	1958	Dr D. J. Murray	1972
Pat. J. F. McKenzie	1958		

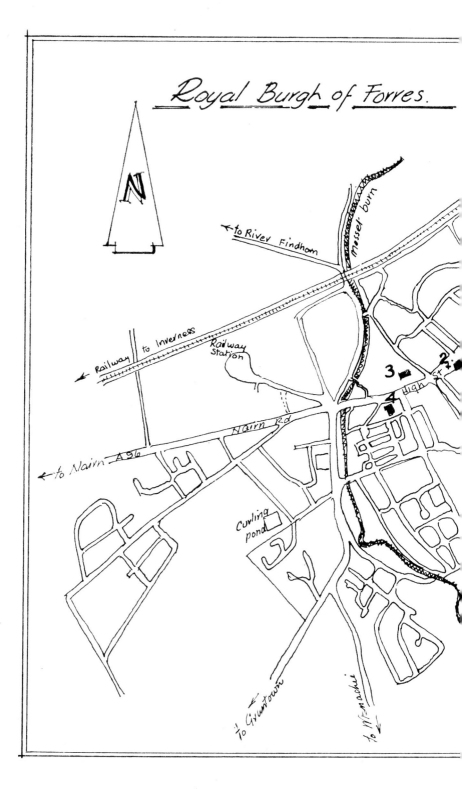